CLIMATE CHANGE, DISASTER RISK, AND THE URBAN POOR

Cities Building Resilience for a Changing World

Judy L. Baker, Editor

THE WORLD BANK
Washington, D.C.

ISBN: 978-0-8213-8845-7
eISBN: 978-0-8213-8960-7
DOI: 10.1596/978-0-8213-8845-7

Cover design: Naylor Design, Inc.
Cover photo: iStockphoto.com

Library of Congress Cataloging-in-Publication Data has been requested

Contents

Boxes

Color Section

Tables

Foreword

The number of people living in slums is on the rise all over the developing world. Increasingly, as cities grow, marginal land is consumed by residents who cannot afford to live elsewhere. This land is often on steep hillsides, flood plains, coastal zones, or situated near hazardous waste, putting residents at high risk from the impacts of climate change and natural hazards.

Slum dwellers typically live in poor quality and overcrowded housing, and have limited access to water, energy, sanitation, and solid waste services. A heavy rain can quickly turn to a disastrous flood. Such flooding can destroy the assets of the poor, halt economic activity, destroy their productivity, and interrupt their income. It can contaminate the water supply, lead to disease, and displace populations.

This study calls on cities to take a lead role in proactively addressing the risks of climate change and natural hazards at the local level, with a focus on populations at highest risk. It suggests a number of actions that cities can take to build resilience, beginning with mainstreaming pro-poor risk reduction policies into urban planning and management. Such policies—including those dealing with land use, relocation, or new development—come with difficult tradeoffs that must be carefully balanced in consultation with stakeholders at the local level. They also come with substantial financing needs that must be met through public and private resources, and will require new financing opportunities.

The cities of the Mayor's Task Force on Climate Change, Disaster Risk, and the Urban Poor—Dar es Salaam, Jakarta, Mexico City, and São Paulo—provide examples of good practice at the local level to address risk, through slum upgrading programs, early warning systems, safety net programs, and adaptation planning. Such examples demonstrate what is possible when local governments work across boundaries—both administrative and institutional, and in collaboration with communities—to develop and implement sustainable solutions.

We invite other cities to share successful examples of programs and policies that have built resilience for the urban poor so that this knowledge can be broadly disseminated. We also call upon the development community to work with cities to identify financing solutions for the pressing needs that are faced by the urban poor in today's changing environment. The World Bank is committed to supporting such efforts through both our financing and our global knowledge products and services.

Rachel Kyte
Vice President
Sustainable Development Network
The World Bank

Sanjay Pradhan
Vice President
World Bank Institute
The World Bank

Acknowledgments

This study was prepared by a team led by Judy L. Baker, lead economist, the World Bank. Key contributions to the overall study and case studies were provided by Christa Anderson and Maria Catalina Ochoa. Background papers were prepared by Anthony Bigio and Stephane Hallegatte (*Planning, Policy, Synergies and Tradeoffs for Urban Risk Management, Climate Change Adaptation and Poverty Reduction*); JoAnne Carmin, Sabrina McCormick, Sai Balakrishnan, and Eric Chu (*Institutions and Governance in a Changing Climate: Implications for Service Provision for the Urban Poor*); Soumya Dharmavaram (*Courting Hazards: Where the Urban Poor Live*); Ari Huhtala, Daniel Hoornweg, and Marcus Lee (*Climate Finance for Cities*); Kristina Katich (*Beyond Assessment: A Review of Global Best Practices Addressing Climate Change and Disaster Risk Management for the Urban Poor*, and *The Impacts of Climate Change and Disasters on Urban Services*); and David Satterthwaite (*How Local Governments Can Work with Communities in the Delivery of Basic Services*). Background research was conducted by Aafrin Kidwai and Austin Kilroy.

The study was part of the work program of the Mayor's Task Force on Climate Change, Disaster Risk, and the Urban Poor, comprising the mayors of Dar es Salaam, Jakarta, Mexico City, and São Paulo. David Miller, mayor of Toronto (2003–10) and Chair of C–40 (the Large Cities Climate Change Group) (2008–10) was an adviser to the Task Force.

The preparation of city-level case studies for Dar es Salaam, Jakarta, Mexico City, and São Paulo were carried out as part of the work program, with teams led by each city government. From the World Bank, these studies were led by Eric Dickson (Mexico City), with Gisela Campillo, Marcus Lee, and Peter Ellis (Jakarta), and Federica Ranghieri and Andre Herzog (São Paulo and Dar es Salaam). Each of the case studies has resulted in an individual report that acknowledges the extensive teams involved in the report's preparation. The work benefitted from the financial support and insight provided by Cities Alliance, the Global Facility for Disaster Risk Reduction, and the World Bank Institute Climate Change Practice (WBICC).

Peer reviewers included Margaret Arnold, Uwe Deichmann, and Abhas Jha. Helpful comments were also received from David Miller, Glen Pearce-Oroz, Apurva Sanghi, and the team members listed above.

The work is a joint effort by the Finance, Economics, and Urban Department and the World Bank Institute. The study was carried out under the overall guidance of Zoubida Allaoua, Marianne Fay, Abha Joshi-Ghani, Christine Kessides, and Konrad von Ritter.

Abbreviations

ACCRN	Asian Cities Climate Change Resilience Network
ADB	Asian Development Bank
ASCCUE	Adaptation Strategies for Climate Change in the Urban Environment
AURAN	African Urban Risk Analysis Network
BAPPEDA	Badan Perencanaan Pembangunan Daerah (Jakarta)
B/C	benefit/cost ratio
BEHD	buildings expected to be heavily damaged
BMA	Bangkok Metropolitan Administration
BPBD	Badan Penanggulangan Bencana Daerah (Jakarta)
BPLHD	Badan Pengelola Linkungan Hidup Daerah (Jakarta)
CAT DDO	Catastrophe Risk Deferred Drawdown Option
CCRIF	Caribbean Catastrophe Risk Insurance Facility
CDCF	Community Development Carbon Fund
CDM	Clean Development Mechanism
CER	certified emission reduction
CGE	Emergency Management Center (São Paulo)
CIUP	Community Infrastructure Upgrading Program
CLACC	Capacity Strengthening of Least Developing Countries for Adaptation to Climate Change
CODEL	local emergency committee
COMDEC	City Emergency Management Agency (São Paulo)
COP	Conference of the Parties
CRC	climate resilient cities
CRED	Centre for Research on the Epidemiology of Disasters
CTF	Clean Technology Fund
CVCCCM	Virtual Center on Climate Change for Mexico City

DANIDA	Danish International Development Agency
DAWASA	Dar es Salaam Water Supply and Sewerage Agency
DCC	Dar es Salaam City Council
DKI	Special Capital District of Jakarta
DRR	disaster risk reduction
ETS	emissions trading system
FAR	Floor-area ratio
FIP	Forest Investment Program
FONDEN	Fondo de Desastres Naturales (Mexico)
GDP	gross domestic product
GEF	Global Environment Facility
GEO-CAN	Global Watch Observation Catastrophe Assessment Network
GFDRR	Global Facility for Disaster Reduction and Recovery
GHG	greenhouse gas
GPOBA	Global Partnership on Output-Based Aid
Ha	hectare
HABISP	Sistema de informações para habitação social (São Paulo)
HRM	Halifax Region Municipality
IBGE	Instituto Brasileiro de Geografi a e Estatística
IBRD	International Bank for Reconstruction and Development
ICLEI	Local Governments for Sustainability
IDA	International Development Association
IFRC	International Federation of Red Cross and Red Crescent Societies
IIED	International Institute for Environment and Development
INPE	Instituto Nacional de Pesquisas Espaciais (São Paulo)
IPCC	Inter-Governmental Panel on Climate Change
IPT	Instituto de Pesquisas Tecnológicas do Estado de São Paulo
IPVS	Index of social vulnerability (São Paulo)
ISDR	United Nations International Strategy for Disaster Reduction
JMP	Joint Monitoring Programme
KICAMP	Kinondoni Integrated Coastal Area Management Project (Tanzania)
LDCF	Least Developed Countries Fund
LECZ	Low Elevation Coastal Zones
LRAP	Local Resilience Action Plan
MAMUCA	Mancomunidad de los Municipios del Centro de Atlantida (Honduras)
MCCAP	Mexico City's Climate Action Program
MCMA	Mexico City Metropolitan Area
NAPA	national adaptation program of action

NAP-DRR   National Action Plan for Disaster Risk Reduction
NGO   nongovernmental organization
NYCPCC   New York City Panel on Climate Change
OBA   output-based aid
OECD   Organisation for Economic Co-operation and Development
OFDA   Office of Foreign Disaster Assistance
OPP-RTI   Orangi Pilot Project Research and Training Institute (Pakistan)
PCG   partial credit guarantee
Pemprov   Provincial Government of the Special Capital District of Jakarta
PHPF   Philippines Homeless People's Federation
PNPM   Program Nasional Pemberdayaan Masyarakat (Indonesia)
PPIAF   World Bank Public-Private Infrastructure Advisory Facility
PPP   public-private partnership
RBF   results-based financing
REDD   Reduced Emissions from Deforestation and Forest Degradation
SATKORLAK   Satuan Tugas Koordinasi dan Pelaksana (Indonesia)
SEHAB   Secretaria da Habitação e Desenvolvimento Urbano (São Paulo)
SLD   Shared Learning Dialogue
SMART   Sustainable Mitigation and Adaptation Risk Toolkit
SPDMI   Strategic Plan for Disaster Mitigation in Istanbul
SVMA   Green and Environment Secretariat (São Paulo)
TCIP   Turkish Catastrophic Insurance Pool
UNEP   United Nations Environmental Programme
UNFCCC   United Nations Framework Convention on Climate Change
URA   Urban Risk Assessment
VTC   Volunteer Technology Community
VUUP   Vietnam National Urban Upgrading Program
WDR   *World Development Report*
WHO   World Health Organization
WWF   World Wildlife Fund

Overview

Poor people living in slums are at particularly high risk from the impacts of climate change and natural hazards. They live on the most vulnerable land within cities, typically areas deemed undesirable by others and thus affordable. Residents are exposed to the impacts of landslides, sea-level rise, flooding, and other hazards.

Exposure to risk is exacerbated by overcrowded living conditions, lack of adequate infrastructure and services, unsafe housing, inadequate nutrition, and poor health. These conditions can swiftly turn a natural hazard or change in climate into a disaster, and result in the loss of basic services, damage or destruction to homes, loss of livelihoods, malnutrition, disease, disability, and loss of life.

This study analyzes the key challenges facing the urban poor, given the risks associated with climate change and disasters, particularly with regard to the delivery of basic services, and identifies strategies and financing opportunities for addressing these risks. The main audience for this study includes mayors and other city managers, national governments, donors, and practitioners in the fields of climate change, disaster-risk management, and urban development.

The work is part of a broader program under the Mayor's Task Force on Climate Change, Disaster Risk and the Urban Poor. This task force was launched at the Mayor's Summit in Copenhagen in 2009 with the aim to better understand these issues, identify examples of good practices, and propose policy and investment programs to improve the resilience of the urban poor. The task force comprises the mayors of Dar es Salaam, Jakarta, Mexico City, and São Paulo, who have recognized the importance of these issues in their cities and have demonstrated strong support for taking action. In each of the four cities, urban risk assessments have been carried out that provide the basis for much of the knowledge in the study. Summaries of those cases are included in annexes 5–7 of this report.

The study is organized in four chapters covering (1) a broad look at climate change and disaster risk in cities of the developing world, with particular implications for the urban poor; (2) analysis of the vulnerability of the urban poor; (3) discussion of recommended approaches for building resilience for the urban poor; and (4) review of the financing opportunities for covering investments in basic services and other needs associated with climate and disaster risk.

Several key findings emerge from the study and provide guidance for addressing risk:

- **The urban poor are on the front line.** The poor are particularly vulnerable to climate change and natural hazards because of where they live within cities, and the lack of reliable basic services there.
- **City governments are the drivers for addressing risks.** Local governments play a vital role in providing basic services that are critical to improving the resilience of the urban poor.
- **City officials build resilience by mainstreaming risk reduction into urban management.** Adapting to climate change and reducing disaster risk can be best addressed and sustained over time through integration with existing urban planning and management practices.
- **Significant financial support is needed.** Local governments need to leverage existing and new resources to meet shortfalls in service delivery and basic infrastructure adaptation.

Recommended Actions to Build Resilience of the Urban Poor

There are a number of actions that can help build resilience for those at greatest risk in cities. Implementing these actions will involve a strong commitment by local governments working with communities, as well as national and international institutions.

Assessing risk at the city and community levels to inform decision making and action planning. City-level case studies carried out in Dar es Salaam, Jakarta, Mexico City, and São Paulo as part of the Mayor's Task Force program have demonstrated the importance of understanding environmental, socioeconomic, and institutional risks as an important first step to developing plans for adaptation and disaster risk reduction. A risk assessment can define the nature of risks, answer questions about the characteristics of potential hazards, and identify community vulnerabilities and potential exposure to given hazards. Such information helps in prioritizing risk measures, giving due consideration to the probability and impact of potential events, the cost effectiveness of the measures, and resource availability. Experiences from the four task force cities and elsewhere also demonstrate that, through the process of assessing risk, it is imperative to get multiple agencies and community residents involved to exchange ideas, collaborate, and communicate with the aim of establishing effective adaptation and disaster risk reduction plans.

Integrating policies for climate change and disaster risk reduction for the poor into urban planning and management. Policies to address climate risks and natural hazards have links to many sectors and therefore come with important synergies that are best captured through systemwide approaches. Comprehensive urban planning is thus critical to integrating approaches to addressing such risks but can often be challenging, given the many institutions involved in managing cities. Cities such as London, New York, Quito, and Toronto demonstrate comprehensive planning approaches that address risk. At a minimum, cities can identify risk-prone areas and through urban planning discourage new construction in these areas.

Balancing policy tradeoffs among risk reduction, urban development, and poverty reduction in decision making. Policy decisions typically involve difficult decisions with outcomes that will have both positive and negative consequences that local decision makers and stakeholders must carefully weigh. Decisions and investments in public service provision, disaster risk reduction, and climate change adaptation will have consequences for many decades to come, given the longevity of many infrastructure investments. Yet these decisions are particularly sensitive to changes in climate conditions, where there is much uncertainty. This makes decision making particularly complex and has invoked some new approaches for policy makers to consider. From an operational perspective, policy makers must also consider the context of broader priorities that involve tradeoffs to be balanced.

Better policies for land use planning and management will have the biggest impact. As cities grow, they expand into marginal areas such as flood plains, water catchments, and steep hillsides, requiring land-use planning to consider flood, seismic, and other hazard zones when determining where new development should be permitted. Efficient transport systems can make land available in new areas by enabling access and mobility, thereby reducing incentives to develop in vulnerable locations. Preventing building and settlements in high-risk areas can save lives and prevent destruction. At the building scale, retrofitting of existing building stock may be necessary, in addition to more robust design standards for new construction. A framework for the regularization of land tenure, including partial or incremental solutions, can spur investments and encourage improvements in infrastructure. Proactive policies can assist in making safe and affordable sites available for low-income residents, reducing risk for the poor.

Strengthening institutional capacity to deliver basic services and reduce vulnerability to climate and disaster risk. In many cities, weak institutional capacity is a major constraint to delivering services. Local governments often do not have adequate staffing, technical skills, or financial capacity. Climate change and disaster risk only exacerbate the challenges of urban management and service delivery. Informal institutions, such as nongovernmental organizations and community-based organizations, have emerged to respond to the needs of the urban poor in the absence of formal institutions. They contribute to adaptive capacity by addressing gaps in service delivery and, at times, facilitating coordinated action in both ongoing and emergency contexts. These institutions play an important role; however, they are not a substitute for formal institutions and the associated provision of basic and infrastructure services. Investments in building capacity for better urban planning and management have the potential to strengthen the resilience of cities. There are several approaches to capacity development at the city level, with many successes in city networks at the country, regional, and international levels; training programs; and knowledge exchange through twinning and other programs that allow cities to learn from each other. Emerging examples include Boston, Cape Town, Ho Chi Minh City, London, New York City, Quito, Rotterdam, and Toronto.

Bridging communities and local governments to work together on local solutions. At the household and community levels, much is already happening that governments can draw upon. There are also examples of successful partnerships between community organizations and local governments around basic services. For example, initiatives in Ilolo, Philippines, and Quelimane City, Mozambique, demonstrate effective community mapping and the creation of partnerships for effective service delivery. Such partnerships show that cooperation can be facilitated through mutual recognition of the role that each group plays, improving the dialogue to dispel misunderstandings, understanding and recognizing what is happening at the local level, and forming partnerships with local organizations. For the poor, understanding what the city can and cannot provide and what its constraints are is a first step. This also can mean communities proactively demonstrating what resources and capacity they have rather than making demands and opposing government policies or practices that go against their needs. For local governments, this means recognizing the contribution that the urban poor make to a city's economy and society and involving them in discussions about needs and priorities. Local participation is crucial to ensure that the approach taken suits the needs of residents and meets quality standards. Many of the examples of partnerships between local governments and community organizations in Africa and Asia have been initiated by federations of slum dwellers who are engaged in initiatives to upgrade slums, secure land tenure, develop new housing that low-income households can afford, and improve provision for infrastructure and services.

Opening new finance opportunities for cities to address pro-poor adaptation and risk reduction. Cities need financing for urban infrastructure, basic services for the urban poor, capacity building, risk assessments, and tools for integrating climate change and disaster risk management into urban planning. Cities currently rely on national and local tax revenues, the private sector, public-private partnerships, and loans and concessional sources through multilateral development banks and donors. Existing programs also provide smaller-scale grants or technical assistance for projects and programs at the city level. Most international funds, however, are channeled through national implementing entities. Given the enormous need, it is recommended that international donors consider a new Program for Climate Finance and Assistance for Cities that would bring together existing resources and draw on new and innovative instruments. This program would facilitate access to resources through a more unified "window" that would reduce overhead and administrative complexity. To encourage cities to achieve specified targets, such a program could consider a more standardized approach to benchmarking and monitoring through metrics commonly agreed upon by the international community, such as a city-level greenhouse gas index, urban risk assessments, or Local Resilience Action Plans. By meeting specified targets, cities would then be eligible for accessing such financing through a designated window.

1

Vulnerable Cities: Assessing Climate Change and Disaster Risk in Urban Centers of the Developing World

Key Messages

- Exposure to the impacts of climate change and natural hazards is on the rise in cities.
- The urban poor disproportionately bear the brunt of changing weather patterns and natural hazards.
- The scope and intensity of disaster risks vary considerably across cities, with differential impacts on the urban poor.
- The increased exposure of the urban poor to extensive risks can transform frequent everyday hazards into disasters.

Introduction and Objective of the Study

Cities are concentrated centers of people, assets, and economic activity. This concentration increases exposure to the impacts of climate change and natural hazards, making urban residents particularly vulnerable to rising sea levels, storm surges, earthquakes, and floods. Climate change also poses risks of drought and extreme heat.

The risks for the urban poor are often even greater, exacerbated by their limited access to basic infrastructure and services, and by where they live within cities.

With rapid urbanization, cities throughout the developing world struggle to meet the basic needs of their growing populations. Today, some 1 billion urban residents live in slums, which lack basic infrastructure and services. More than half the urban population in Sub-Saharan Africa and 40 percent in South Asia lack access to basic sanitation (Joint Monitoring Programme (JMP) 2010). In Sub-Saharan Africa, close to 20 percent of urban residents do not have access to safe water (JMP 2010). Many more live without access to proper drainage or wastewater removal.

The poor typically settle in areas undesirable to others and thus affordable. This includes informal settlements on precarious land, at high risk from landslides, sea-level rise, and flooding. These neighborhoods are made even more vulnerable by overcrowded living conditions, unsafe housing, inadequate nutrition, poor health, and lack of safety nets. When a disaster hits, impacts can include the loss of basic services, damage or destruction to homes, reduction or loss of livelihoods, threats to food security, and the rapid spread of malnutrition and water- and vector-borne diseases.

One has to look back only to the past few years to get a sense of the destruction natural hazards can cause in cities, particularly for low-income residents. In the past two years alone, major disasters—such as earthquakes in Japan (2011), Haiti (2010), Chile (2010), and China, (2010); and flooding in China (2010), Pakistan (2010), and Brazil (2010, 2011)—have killed many. Annually, almost 70,000 people are killed by natural hazards, with the majority of related mortality and economic losses being concentrated in low- and middle-income countries.[1]

The objective of this study is to analyze the key challenges facing the urban poor, given the risks associated with climate change and disasters, particularly regarding the delivery of basic services, and to identify strategies and financing opportunities for addressing these risks. The study is aimed at mayors and other city managers, national governments, donors, and practitioners in the fields of climate change, disaster risk management, and urban development. It is organized into four main chapters. Chapter 1 introduces the study and presents an overview of risk in cities of the developing world and the implications of those risks for the urban poor. Chapter 2 analyzes the vulnerability of the urban poor based on location and other characteristics, particularly those related to access to basic services and infrastructure. Chapter 3 is more forward looking, focusing on recommended approaches to building resilience for the urban poor and discussing the key policy issues and tradeoffs that must be considered. Chapter 4 concludes with a practical discussion of existing financing tools for climate change, disaster risk, and urban development and how they could be further oriented for growing needs. Throughout the study are examples from the four city-level case studies undertaken as part of this work, as well as good practices from other cities. Annexes include a literature review, good practice cases, and summaries of the four city-level case studies.

This study is part of a larger program under the Mayor's Task Force on Climate Change, Disaster Risk and the Urban Poor. This task force was created in December 2009 at the Climate Summit for Mayors in Copenhagen, with strong support by key members: the mayors of Mexico City (lead convener), Jakarta, Dar es Salaam, and São Paulo. The task force's work program has three main objectives and is supported by the World Bank Group. These objectives are to (1) take stock of our understanding of the linkages between urban poverty and climate change; (2) identify examples of good practices where shelter and services for the urban poor have been improved and have resulted in reduced vulnerability; and (3) propose policy and investment programs and municipal management practices that benefit the urban poor. Each of the four cities has carried out in-depth studies to assess risk in their cities with a particular focus on the urban poor that provides an important contribution to the overall study.

Background, Analytical Framework, and Approach

The existing literature on climate change, disaster risk management, urbanization, and urban poverty is expanding rapidly with important contributions emerging in recent years. Some of the key documents include the Inter Governmental Panel on Climate Change (IPCC) Assessment Reports; the World Bank's 2010 *World Development Report on Climate Change*; the World Bank and UN study, *Natural Hazards, UnNatural Disasters, 2010*; the World Watch Institute's State of the World Report, *Our Urban Future* (2007); the *Global Assessment Report on Disaster Risk Reduction* (ISDR 2009); and the *World Disasters Report: Focus on Urban Risk* (IFPC 2010). These studies, reviewed in annex 1, have brought to the fore many of the risks that cities face, and in a few cases, some coverage of the particular challenges in low-income areas.

There is consensus that the poor disproportionately bear the brunt of changing weather patterns and natural hazards, and have limited adaptive capacity to cope with climate change. There is much reference regarding vulnerabilities to flooding, land subsidence, heat waves, and increased health risks. One of the frequently cited works is Moser et al. (2008), which refers to pro-poor adaptation in cities. It examines the role of assets—"natural, physical, social, financial, and human capital"—in increasing the adaptive capacity of the urban poor. These assets are particularly important because city authorities may not have adequate financial resources to provide services, and may be reluctant to work with the poor, particularly in informal settlements, where formalizing the assets of the poor could increase the likelihood of holding local governments accountable for provision of services.

There is relatively less published research available on the relationship between the impacts of climate change and natural hazards on access to basic services, and vice versa. Of all basic services, water, sanitation, and drainage have received more attention because of their direct impact on human health. Other gaps in the literature include limited empirical evidence on the impacts of climate change and disasters on the urban poor, and little documentation of how risks for the urban poor have been addressed and how cities can integrate policies for improving resiliency among the urban poor into urban planning. While this study does not purport to fully fill this void, it attempts to contribute to improving our understanding of the issues.

Analytical Framework

The analytical framework used in the study is based on the approach developed by the IPCC, which looks at the risks posed by natural hazards and defines vulnerability as a function of a system's exposure, sensitivity, and adaptive capacity. This framework was introduced in the 2001 IPCC Third Assessment Report and has been adapted somewhat over time. Various studies analyzing the impact of climate change have used different adaptations of this framework. As discussed in the IPCC Fourth Assessment Report (2007, Section 19.1.2), "Key impacts that may be associated with key vulnerabilities are found in many social, economic, biological, and geophysical systems, and various tabulations of risks, impacts and vulnerabilities have been provided in the literature."

The application of the analytical framework will focus on a core function of cities—the provision of basic protection and services for its residents. For the purposes of the study, these basic services will include housing, water and sanitation, drainage, solid-waste treatment, transport, roads, and public and environmental health. Table 1.1 presents the analytical framework, with definitions used most commonly by the IPCC working groups.

A further distinction useful for the analysis of risk is the concept of intensive and extensive risks found in the disaster risk literature. Intensive risk refers to areas where major concentrations of vulnerable people and economic assets are exposed to very severe hazards (for example, major earthquakes, tropical cyclones, severe flooding, or tsunamis). In contrast, extensive risks refer to wide regions exposed to more frequently occurring low- or moderate-intensity losses (for example, localized flooding, fires, and landslides in informal settlements). The frequency and intensity of such everyday hazards is increasing with the very gradual rise in variability and extremes in temperature and rainfall induced by climate change. These widespread low-intensity losses are associated with other

TABLE 1.1
Analytical Framework for Assessing Risk

Sector	Natural hazard	Vulnerability		Adaptive capacity
		Exposure	Sensitivity	
The study will cover the subsectors related to the basic provision of shelter and services for the urban poor: housing, water and sanitation, drainage, solid-waste treatment, energy, transport services, roads, and public and environmental health.	Hazards (risks in economics literature) are potentially damaging physical events or phenomena that may cause the loss of life or injury, property damage, social and economic disruption, or environmental degradation.[1]	The nature and degree to which a system is exposed to significant climatic variations (IPCC 2001)	Sensitivity is the degree to which a system is affected, either adversely or beneficially, by climate variability or change. The effect may be direct or indirect.	The ability of a system to adjust to climate change (including climate variability and extremes), to moderate potential damages, to take advantage of opportunities, or to cope with the consequences

Source: Glossary, IPCC (2007); ISDR (2009).
1. A distinction made in the disaster literature is the definition of a disaster as the hazard's effect on society as a result of the combination of exposure and vulnerability. Disasters, not hazards, cause deaths and damage. (World Bank and United Nations 2010).

risk impacts, such as a large number of affected people and damage to housing and local infrastructure, particularly affecting the urban poor. Such events are typically not associated with major mortality or destruction of large economic assets (ISDR 2009). Yet frequent everyday hazards can turn into disasters for the urban poor, who lack basic infrastructure and services.

Approach

The approach for carrying out this study is based on several efforts. Background papers were prepared on topics that were not well covered in the literature and were considered key to understanding risks to the delivery of basic services for the urban poor, given climate change and disaster risk. Four city-level case studies, in Dar es Salaam, Jakarta, Mexico City, and São Paulo, have also been carried out to gather new empirical evidence on the risks of climate change and disasters for the urban poor, particularly with regard to the delivery of basic services. Key findings from those studies are integrated throughout this report, and case study summaries for each city are included in annexes 5–7.[2] The case studies follow a methodology for assessing urban risk that is based on three pillars: institutional assessment, hazard assessment, and social assessment.[3] Because the amount of data available for the different cities varies, the depth of the information on each case study varies. The key findings are summarized in tables 1.2 and 1.3.

Climate Change, Disaster Risk, and Urban Areas: Assessing Hazard Risk

The unprecedented rate of urban growth in the developing world is increasingly exposing the population and economic assets to the potential impacts of climate change and natural hazards. The world's urban population is currently estimated at 3.3 billion. Most of the urban population resides in the developing world, where nearly all future urban growth will take place. During the next 20 years, it is projected that over 95 percent of the population growth in developing countries will take place in urban areas, with the urban populations of Africa and South Asia increasing by an average of 62 million people each year.[4] In East Asia

TABLE 1.2
Hazards Impacting the Urban Poor in Case Study Cities

Hazard	Dar es Salaam	Jakarta	São Paulo	Mexico City
Earthquake	○	●	○	●
Wind storm	○	○	○	●
River flow	○	●	●	○
Floods, inundations, and waterlogs	●	●	●	●
Drought	●	○	○	●
Volcano	○	○	○	○
Landslide	●	○	●	●
Storm surge	○	●	●	○
Extreme temperature	●	●	NA	●

Source: Author.

● High risk
◐ Medium risk
○ Low risk

TABLE 1.3
Summary Findings of Risk Assessments for Dar es Salaam, Jakarta, Mexico City, and São Paulo

	Dar es Salaam	Jakarta	Mexico City	São Paulo
Overview — Pop.	• 2.5 million in 1,590 km² • Between 4% and 8% annual population growth	• 9.6 million in the metro area (650 km²); 28 million in greater Jakarta • 250,000 immigrate to Jakarta yearly	• 21.2 million in the metro area (4,250 km²) • 3% annual population growth rate	• 19.7 million in the metro area (2,140 km²) • Increasing low-income population in the periphery
Vulnerability of the urban poor — Hazards, vulnerability, and basic services	• Main hazards — heavy rainfall, flooding, droughts • 70% of Dar es Salaam's population lives in poor, unplanned settlements; human development indicators very low. • Basic infrastructure is very low; access to clean water and sanitation is a major problem; less than 60% of the road network is paved. • Drainage channels are regularly blocked, causing houses to be flooded by sewage-based waste-water, causing water-borne diseases.	• Main hazards — water management and flood control. About 40% of the city is below sea level. • Regular flooding affects city throughout the year with impacts on traffic, damage to homes, and economic losses. • There is currently no citywide solid waste-management plan for Jakarta. • Poorest people live close to river banks, canals, drainage areas.	• Main hazards — high seismic risk, no natural drainage for runoff from the surrounding mountains, and vulnerability to flooding. Regularly affected by severe storms, heat waves, and droughts • Projections estimate rise in mean temperature by 2–3 °C by end of this century; extreme precipitation episodes expected to increase. • By 2015, water consumption rates will increase by 20% compared with 2000 levels. • Infrastructure and public services are stretched thin. • City's generation of garbage is increasing at a rate of 5% a year. • 15% of the population is ranked with high level of housing and population vulnerability.	• Main hazards — heavy rains, flooding, landslides, and washouts. • 13% of the population is considered as having high or very high social vulnerability. • More than 85% of high-risk households (890,000) are located in slums across the city. • More than 5% of slum areas are highly likely to be affected by destructive events. • 52% of households in slums are without access to sanitation facilities and 33% of households in slums have no access to paved roads close to their homes. • 20% of sewage lacks proper treatment.

(continued next page)

TABLE 1.3 *continued*

		Dar es Salaam	Jakarta	Mexico City	São Paulo
Building resilience for the urban poor	Achievements	• Government is identifying all properties in informal settlements in Dar es Salaam and issuing land/property licenses or right of occupancy to improve security of tenure, which could be used as collateral for economic empowerment. • Significant slum upgrading program is also under way.	• Large-scale adaptation infrastructure projects being developed include Jakarta Coastal Defense to protect from tidal surges, and Jakarta Urgent Flood Mitigation Plan. • Innovative early-warning systems via SMS at the urban ward level inform people of upcoming floods.	• First city in Latin America to introduce a local climate action strategy to reduce emissions by 7 million MT between 2008 and 2012. • Strategy is part of a 15-year plan in which the city is investing US$1 billion a year (9% of the yearly budget) in land conservation, public spaces, air pollution, waste management and recycling, water supply and sanitation, transportation, and mobility.	• The São Paulo Agenda 2012 and the Municipal Climate Law set out targets by sector to be reached by the municipality, private actors, and other public bodies. • Risky areas for landslides are already identified and geo-referenced by the municipality, allowing the prioritization of adaptation actions. • Major slum upgrading efforts based on social vulnerability index and incidence of areas subject to landslides.
	Challenges	• Disaster risk management has largely been ignored and needs to be integrated in all aspects of urban planning in Dar es Salaam. • Limited capacity in city planning departments to assess the long-term sectoral impacts of climate change for the city.	• Adaptation plans to cope with extreme weather and sea level rise are not coordinated across multiple agencies. • Lack of comprehensive disaster risk management program or disaster response plan for Jakarta.	• Disaster risk in Mexico City is primarily handled in a reactive manner and limited preventative measures have been implemented. • Evident need to improve the sharing of information among the relevant government agencies.	• Additional efforts are needed to increase coverage of sewage system and avoid illegal disposal of sewage into water courses. • Mitigate risks in flood- and landslide-prone areas and consider relocating families where mitigation proves ineffective.

Source: Author.

alone, 500 million people will become urban residents over the next 25 years, joining the current 750 million people living in cities.

Likewise the geographic location where the bulk of the urban growth is happening also increases population exposure to climate change and natural hazards. Urban centers are often located in naturally hazardous zones, prone to floods and cyclones—Low Elevation Coastal Zones (LECZ); earthquake, volcanic, and landslide zones; and drought zones (figure 1.1 in color section). Nearly two-thirds of the urban settlements with more than 5 million people are located partly in a low-elevation coastal zone (Mc Granahan, Balk, and Anderson 2007). Indeed, 70 percent of the countries with population in the low-elevation coastal zone have their largest urban area extending into that zone (Mc Granahan, Balk, and Anderson 2007). Climate change poses a risk of more extreme weather and can cause devastating urban flooding and coastal storms, as well as longer-term changes such as sea-level rise and increased ambient temperatures. Risks are especially high in low- and middle-income countries, where a third to a half of the population in cities lives in slums (Kinyanjui 2010).

Urban exposure of population and economic assets to natural hazards and to the impacts of climate change is therefore increasing significantly, with a high degree of vulnerability for a large share of cities, especially those located along the coastal areas. At the same time, the frequency and intensity of natural hazards are becoming more significant, compounded by the early manifestations of climate change, which are likely to result in more severe impacts in the decades to come. Table 1.4 shows the impacts of the major disaster events that affected cities over the past decade.

The risks for each hazard—floods and cyclones, earthquakes, volcanoes and landslides, drought, and heat waves—vary considerably, with different impacts on the population. Notably, many cities are affected by multiple hazards. The Mexico City metropolitan area, for example, is affected by seismic risk, severe storms, heat waves, and droughts. Also, with no natural drainage for runoff from the surrounding mountains, the area is vulnerable to flooding, particularly to the west. Main risks for cities, with particular implications for the urban poor, are discussed below, followed by a summary (tables 1.5 and 1.6).

Floods and Cyclones

Close to 2 billion people, or 38 percent of the world's populations, live in highly flood-prone areas. Low Elevation Coastal Zones (LECZ) that are often exposed to cyclones and storm surges cover 2 percent of the world's land area, but contain 13 percent of the world's urban population (McGranahan, Balk, and Anderson 2007). Tropical storms and cyclones affect 1.4 billion people, or 24 percent of the world's population that live in densely populated coastal areas. Areas most prone

TABLE 1.4
Large Disasters with Major Impacts on Cities, 2000–2010

Disaster	Main countries affected	Year	Main cities affected	Total number of deaths	Total number affected	Total damages (US$)
Floods	Pakistan	2010	Peshawar, Sukkur, Thatta, Mingora, Multan, Chilas	1,985	18,102,327	9.5 billion
Floods	China	2010	Fujian, Guangxi, Fuzhou, Nanping	1,691	134,000,000	18 billion
Earthquake	Chile	2010	Concepción	562	2,671,556	30 billion
Earthquake	Haiti	2010	Port-au-Prince	222,570	3,700,000	8 billion
Sichuan earthquake	China	2008	Beichuan, Dujiangyan, Shifang, Mianzhu, Juyuan, Jiangyou, Mianyang, Chengdu, Qionglai, Deyang	87,476	45,976,596	85 billion
Cyclone Nargis	Myanmar	2008	Yangon	138,366	2,420,000	4 billion
Java earthquake	Indonesia	2006	Yogyakarta	5,778	3,177,923	3.1 billion
Kashmir earthquake	Pakistan	2005	Muzaffarabad	73,338	5,128,000	5.2 billion
Hurricane Katrina	United States	2005	New Orleans	1,833	500,000	125 billion
Floods	India	2005	Mumbai	1,200	20,000,055	3.3 billion
South Asian tsunami	Indonesia, Sri Lanka, India, Thailand, Malaysia, Maldives, Myanmar	2004	Banda Aceh, Chennai (some damages)	226,408	2,321,700	9.2 billion
Earthquake	Iran	2003	Bam	26,796	267,628	500 million
European heat wave	Italy, France, Spain, Germany, Portugal, Switzerland	2003	Various	72,210	Not reported	Not reported
Floods	Germany	2002	Dresden	27	330,108	11.6 billion
Gujurat earthquake	India	2001	Bhuj, Ahmedabad	20,005	6,321,812	2.6 billion

Source: EM-DAT: The OFDA/CRED International Disaster Database, Université catholique de Louvain-Brussels — Belgium and IFRC (2010).

Note: Technological and biological disasters are not included. OFDA: Office of Foreign Disaster Assistance; CRED: Centre for Research on the Epidemiology of Disasters; IFRC: International Federation of Red Cross and Red Crescent Societies.

TABLE 1.5
Global Frequency and Risk of Natural Hazards

	Natural hazard	Number of events (2002–2010)[a]	Mortality risk[b]	Vulnerable urban areas
Geophysical	Earthquake	228	High	Cities on or near fault lines
	Volcano	53	Low	Cities near volcanoes
Geophysical and hydrological	Tsunami	19	High	Coastal cities
	Mass movement (landslide, rockfall, avalanche, subsidence)	167	Low	—
Hydrological	Flood	1,501	Medium	Coastal cities
	Storm surge	25	Low	Coastal cities
Meteorological	Storm and cyclone	899	High	Coastal cities; tropical cities
Climatological	Drought	133	Low	Cities in or near desserts and dry areas
	Extreme temps (heat and cold)	173	Medium–high	Inland cities
	Wildfire	101	Low	—

Source: EMDAT, OFDA/CRED International Disaster Database 2011.

Note: In addition to the standard classification of natural hazards represented in the above chart, this study also examines additional incipient natural hazards linked to climate change. Climate change will impact the frequency and severity of many of the hazards listed in the chart, but will also have slow-onset impacts, which are not represented above, most notably (1) water scarcity and (2) sea level rise. As emerging hazards, water scarcity and sea level rise are not included in the chart, but are included throughout this study.
a. Events included if (a) more than 9 fatalities, (b) 100 people reported affected, (c) a call for international assistance is issued, or (d) a state of emergency is declared.
b. Mortality risk is classified as follows for 2002–2010 data: Low, deaths < 10,000; medium, deaths < 100,000; high, deaths > 100,000.

are Central America, the Caribbean, Bay of Bengal, China, and the Philippines (see figure 1.1 in the color section). The population in large cities exposed to cyclones is projected to increase from 310 to 680 million during 2000–2050. South Asia is expected to see most of this increase, where 246 million residents of large cities will be exposed to severe storms by 2050 (Lall and Deichmann 2009).

Coastal cities are exposed to a rise in sea level and face the impacts of flooding, increased storm damage, coastal erosion, changes in sedimentation patterns, and salt intrusion. The IPCC estimates that global sea levels rose by about 2 mm per year during the 20th century. Flooding and water logging can render large

Table 1.6
Incremental Impacts of Climate Change and Natural Hazards on Urban Systems and Residents

Incremental impacts on urban systems	Impacts on urban residents
Built environment • Stress on building foundations • Road washouts • Changing disease vectors • Stress on storm-water and sewage systems • Stress on water treatment systems • Disruption to shipping and ports • Increased energy demand • Increased road surface damage • Increased demand for water **Natural environment** • Coastal erosion, altered ecosystems and wetlands • Salinization of water sources • Slope instability • Groundwater depletion • Reduction in green space and growing conditions, including urban agriculture • Changes in fish populations • Increased runoff contamination • Increased heat island effect • Increased air pollution	• Illness—heat stress, stroke, malnutrition, water-borne disease, asthma, physical and mental disability • Exposure to elements from substandard construction • Disruption of basic service provision and access to supplies • Housing instability • Property loss and relocation • Loss of livelihoods • Community fragmentation • Exposure to flood-related toxins and wastes • Disruption in availability of potable water, food, and other supplies • Water shortages • Food shortages; higher food prices • Disruptions of electricity

Source: Adapted from Carmin and Zhang (2009); Dickson et al. (2010); Dodman and Satterthwaite (2008); Wilbanks et al. (2007).

areas of a city completely uninhabitable, or damage existing infrastructure such as transportation systems and energy plants.

For the urban poor, floods and storms can have multiple impacts. The lack of storm drainage or of solid-waste disposal in slums can worsen and extend flooding, thus increasing exposure for slum residents. Extended flooding can result in disability and death by drowning or collapsing structures, sickness transmitted by water-borne vectors, displacement, and destruction of property and livelihood. Drowning and physical injury during storm surges are a significant cause of mortality in coastal storms in South Asia and Latin America (IPCC 2007). Overcrowded slums are particularly exposed to the rapid spread of infectious diseases that are transmitted through flood waters (for example, diarrhea, cholera, typhoid, leptospirosis, and meningitis). Malaria- and dengue-carrying mosquitoes also breed in stagnant water—especially when temperatures are high. Exposed wells and broken water pipes elevate the risk of water-borne diseases. Fecal and other hazardous matter such as chemicals and heavy metals can contaminate flood-waters, leading to chronic illnesses and epidemics long after flood-waters recede. In Dar es Salaam, when residents in low-income neighborhoods were asked about major problems they face in general, 35 percent identified floods as the top problem, followed by disease and heat/increased temperatures.

Salt-water intrusion can affect coastal habitats and affect the livelihoods of populations dependent on fisheries and other coastal industries and can result in permanent damage to sensitive ecosystems. In Mombasa, Kenya, a city of 870,000 on a low-lying coastal plain, a rise in sea level of just 0.3 meters would submerge about 4,600 Ha (17 percent of the city's land area). Salt stress in Mombasa is expected to have two significant impacts. It can potentially leave large areas of agricultural lands that surround the city unproductive, as well as salinate inland waterways that supply potable water. A decrease in agricultural productivity can result in rising food prices, which would impact low-income families the most. Similarly in the poor neighborhood of Kamal Muara in Jakarta, residents rely on fishing for their livelihood. For them, salt intrusion can result in the loss of valuable wetlands, increased salination of ground water and soil, and a greater influx of diverse pollutants—all of which threaten their sources of income and their livelihoods particularly in the absence of poor with no safety nets to fall back on.

Earthquakes, Volcanoes, and Landslides

Close to 1.2 billion people (20 percent of the world's population) live in highly earthquake-prone areas (7.5 percent of the world's land area). Half of the world's cities are located on seismic fault lines. The urban population in areas with a significant probability of a major earthquake is projected to increase from 370 million in 2000 to 870 million in 2050. The urban population exposed to earthquakes is expected to increase the most in East Asia and the Pacific from 83 million in 2000 to 267 million in 2050 (Lall and Deichmann 2009). China, India, and Indonesia are the countries with the highest absolute mortality risk (ISDR 2009).

Landslides are often a result of floods and storms, or earthquakes. Approximately 2.2 million people are exposed to landslides globally. Exposure is very high in several large Asian countries, especially India, Indonesia, and China (ISDR 2009). Increased construction on steep and unstable hillsides, often by the urban poor, has contributed to landslides, intensifying the impacts of flooding and earthquakes in cities. Heavy rains in early 2011 in the states of Rio de Janeiro and São Paulo caused landslides resulting in an estimated 647 deaths and almost 6,000 people homeless (Fohla do São Paulo, January 2011).

Volcanic regions are spatially concentrated, with about 9 percent of the world's population living within a 100 kilometer range of a historically active volcano (Small and Naumann 2001). A larger proportion of people live near historically active volcanoes in Southeast Asia and Central America, and most cities exposed are in developing countries (Small and Naumann 2001; Lall and Deichmann 2009). Cities that have long experienced volcanoes report that the most important components of dealing with volcanic activity are (1) early warning and (2) advanced risk assessment, especially for vulnerable communities, facilities, and infrastructure (VSJ and IAVECI 2007). In addition to possible mud and lava flows, volcanoes emit large quantities of ash that can affect a much larger area and population through impacts on agricultural production.

Drought

With climate change, dryland cities experience extended droughts that create water scarcity and frequent sandstorms aggravated by poor infrastructure. Water shortages increase food prices, particularly affecting the urban poor, and water stored during droughts has a higher risk of contamination. Thirst, hunger, under-nutrition, protein energy malnutrition, and micronutrient deficiencies are common during drought, which have long-lasting consequences for the health and well-being of the population, particularly children (IPCC 2007). Drought is prevalent in interior and coastal regions of semiarid tropical areas. Close to 70 percent of the world's population live in drought-prone areas (38 percent of world's land area). Sub-Saharan Africa is the most affected (Dilley et al. 2005). It is estimated that 75 million to 250 million people in Africa will be exposed to water stress due to desertification induced by climate change (IIED undated). In cities, drought is also linked to a rise in infectious diseases, such as meningitis, malaria, dengue, and the West Nile Virus. In Dar es Salaam, for example, between 2 percent and 10 percent of school children living in the city are infected with malaria (De Castro et al. 2010).

Heat Waves

Climate change has resulted in extreme temperature fluctuations—aggravating a variety of existing health conditions and pollutants, and bringing about additional unhealthy changes in water and air quality. Heat waves can also contribute to an increase in fires. The IPCC predicts an increase in the frequency and intensity of heat waves in populations in high-density urban areas with poor housing, increasing heat-related deaths (IPCC 2007). Most of those who died during the heat wave in France in 2003 were the elderly, women, and poor living in the urban areas of Paris (Poumadère et al. 2005).

Such "excess deaths"—or deaths above established seasonal norms (Rabie et al. 2010)—are increasing at an alarming rate. Hot days, hot nights, and heat waves have become more frequent due to global warming, and this risk of heat-induced morbidity and mortality will increase (IPCC 2007). Cities experience more intense heat waves due to denser populations, buildings, traffic, and sparse vegetation. Climate change is expected to increase the occurrence of this "urban heat island" effect, resulting in locally acute harm to human health (Corburn 2009).

Again, the urban poor are particularly affected, as they cannot avoid exposure by remaining indoors in cool or air-conditioned surroundings. Heat is an

BOX 1.1

Increase in the Number of Heat Waves in the Mexico City Metropolitan Area (MCMA)

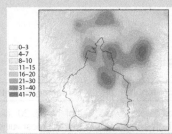 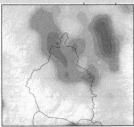

0–3
4–7
8–10
11–15
16–20
21–30
31–40
41–70

Comparison of number of heat waves in MCMA
between 1986 and 1997 and between 1998 and 2009

The temperature in MCMA is expected to rise between 2°C and 3°C by the end of the century. This temperature increase will be more noticeable during the spring months. Therefore, it is expected that heat waves (defined as two or more consecutive days with temperatures above 30°C) during this time of the year would become longer and more intense. The comparison of number of heat waves in MCMA between 1986 and 1997 and between 1998 and 2009 clearly shows an increase in frequency. The elderly population and infants are at highest risk of dehydration. Given that the number of adults above 65 is rapidly increasing (0.66 percent to 1.22 percent between the 1980s and 1990s), more people will be exposed to the damaging effects of heat waves.

Source: Leon et al. (2010).

occupational hazard for low-income residents that are reliant on outdoor labor activities such as construction, vending, and rickshaw pulling. Increased exposure can result in dehydration, heat stroke, and, in the severest of cases, death.

Efforts to Estimate Exposure in Cities

Several studies have estimated the magnitude of urban exposure to natural hazards and climate change impacts. While each study has limitations in rigorously quantifying aggregate vulnerability to climate and natural hazard impacts given the high degree of complexity and uncertainty, and none explicitly includes risk to the urban poor, they provide a useful macro-level look at risk and exposure in cities. Each study approaches urban risk from a different angle, covering different sets of cities, different types of hazards, different timeframes, and different asset measurements. That being said, all approaches confirm that such risk is increasing and that with the increasing manifestations of climate change, it will significantly worsen in the coming decades. The approaches are summarized in table 1.7; annex 2 discusses each approach.

TABLE 1.7
Major Efforts to Rank Exposure in Cities

Study	Approach	Summary of rankings
OECD ranking of port cities with high exposure and vulnerability to climate extremes	Ranks 136 port cities of over 1 million with high exposure to 1 in 100-year surge-induced floods. Exposure of population and assets circa 2005 and predictions for 2070.	14 of the top 20 cities in Asia rank most vulnerable.
Munich Re's study on megacities	Multihazard risk index for 50 of the world's largest and most economically important cities. Exposure to hazards, vulnerability of the built environment, and value of exposed property.	17 of the top 20 cities are in high-income countries, given the higher value of exposed assets.
World Wildlife Fund climate change variability in Asia	Ranks 11 large cities in Asia (mostly coastal cities), based on combined rankings of exposure, sensitivity, and adaptive capacity.	Dhaka, Jakarta, and Manila ranked highest and most vulnerable.

(continued next page)

TABLE 1.7 *continued*

Study	Approach	Summary of rankings
Earthquake disaster risk index for cities (Stanford University)	Ranks earthquake risk in cities based on hazard, exposure, vulnerability, external context, and emergency response and recovery. Methodology developed and used for sample of 10 cities.	Of the 10-city sample, Tokyo was ranked highest.
Resilient Cities: A Multi-Hazard City Risk Index (methodology report and city profiles)	A model has been developed to rank cities based on risk to population, buildings, and infrastructure using data on metropolitan elements, indices for 13 hazards, and vulnerability parameters. Current (2010) and future (2030) risk is calculated. The methodology was piloted in Bangkok, Ningbo, and Manila.	Metro Manila ranks the highest among the three pilot cities. Risk is growing for all cities in 2030 compared to 2010; risks from more frequent events (2-year return periods) is higher than less frequent events (30-year return).

Source: Author.

Notes

1. ISDR (2009) based on EMDAT data. Between 1975 and 2008, 78.2 percent of mortality in significant natural hazards occurred in only 0.3 percent of recorded events.
2. The full case studies are also available.
3. See Dickson et al. (2010).
4. United Nations, "World Urbanization Prospects," http://esa.un.org/unup/. This table covers through 2010 and thus does not include the recent earthquake and tsunami in Japan.

References

Carmin, JoAnn, and Yan F. Zhang. 2009. "Achieving Urban Climate Adaptation in Europe and Central Asia." Policy Research Working Paper 5088, World Bank, Washington, DC.

Corburn, Jason. 2009. "Cities, Climate Change and Urban Heat Island Mitigation: Localising Global Environmental Science." *Urban Studies* 46 (2): 413–427.

De Castro, M.C., Y. Yamagata, D. Mtasiwa, M. Tanner, J. Utzinger, J. Keiser, and B.H. Singer. 2004. "Integrated Urban Malaria Control: A Case Study in Dar es Salaam, Tanzania." *American Journal of Tropical Medicine and Hygiene*, 103–117.

Dickson, Eric, Judy Baker, Daniel Hoornweg, and Asmita Tiwari. 2012. "Urban Risk Assessments World Bank, Washington, DC.

Dilley, Maxx, Robert S. Chen, Uwe Deichmann, Art L. Lerner-Lam, and Margaret Arnold. 2005. *Natural Disaster Hotspots: A Global Risk Analysis.* Washington, DC: World Bank/ Columbia University.

Dodman, David, and David Satterthwaite. 2008. "Institutional Capacity, Climate Change Adaptation and the Urban Poor." *IDS Bulletin* 39(4): 67–74.

Intergovernmental Panel on Climate Change (IPCC). 2007. *IPCC Fourth Assessment Report: Climate Change 2007.*

International Federation of Red Cross and Red Cresent Societies (IFRC). 2010. *World Disasters Report: Focus on Urban Risk.* Geneva: IFRC.

International Institute for Environment and Development (IIED). 2009. *Adapting Cities to Climate Change: Understanding and Addressing the Development Challenges.* Ed. by Jane Bicknell, David Dodman and David Satterthwaite. London: Earthscan.

———. undated. *Climate Change and the Urban Poor: Risk and Resilience in 15 of the World's Most Vulnerable Cities.* London: IIED.

ISDR. 2009. *Global Assessment Report on Disaster Risk Reduction.* Geneva: UN International Strategy for Disaster Reduction.

Kinyanjui, Micahel. 2010. "Development Context and the Millennium Agenda." In *The Challenge of Slums: Global Report on Human Settlements 2003, revised and updated version (April 2010).* UN-HABITAT: Nairobi, Kenya.

Lall, S.V., and U. Deichmann. 2009. "Density and Disasters: Economics of Urban Hazard Risk." Policy Research Working Paper 5161, World Bank, Washington, DC.

Leon, C., V. Magaña, B. Graizbord, R. González, A. Damian, and F. Estrada. 2010. "Pobreza Urbana y Cambio Climático para La Ciudad de México." Unpublished, Mayor's Task Force Study, Mexico City.

McGranahan, Gordon, Deborah Balk, and Bridget Anderson. 2007. "The Rising Tide: Assessing the Risks of Climate Change and Human Settlements in Low Elevation Coastal Zones." *Environment and Urbanization* 19 (1): 17–37.

Moser, Caroline, David Satterthwaite, et al.. 2008. "Pro-Poor Climate Change Adaptation in the Urban Centres of Low- and Middle-Income Countries." Background paper for the "Social Dimensions of Climate Change" workshop, Washington, DC, March 5–6.

Poumadère, M., C. Mays, S. Le Mer, and R. Blong. 2005. "The 2003 Heat Wave in France: Dangerous Climate Change Here and Now." *Risk Analysis* 25: 1483–1494.

Small, Christopher, and Terry Naumann. 2001. "The Global Distribution of Human Population and Recent Volcanism." *Global Environmental Change Part B: Environmental Hazards* 3 (3–4): 93–109.

UN-HABITAT. 2003a. *The Challenge of Slums: Global Report on Human Settlements.* London/Sterling, VA: Earthscan Publications Ltd.

UN-HABITAT. 2003b. "Slums of the World: The Face of Urban Poverty in the New Millennium? Monitoring the Millennium Development Goal, Target 11 – World Wide Slum Dweller Estimation." Working Paper.

Volcanological Society of Japan (VSJ) and International Association of Volcanology and Chemistry of the Earth's Interior (IAVCEI). 2007. *Cities on Volcanoes 5 Conference Proceedings.* http://www.eri.u-tokyo.ac.jp/nakada/cov5_hp/documents/abstract_e.pdf

Wilbanks, Tom J., Patricia Romero Lankao, Manzhu Bao, Frans Berkhout, Sandy Cairncross, Jean-Paul Ceron, Manmohan Kapshe, Robert Muir-Wood, and Ricardo Zapata-Marti. 2007. "Industry, Settlement and Society." In *Climate Change 2007: Impacts, Adaptation and Vulnerability. Contribution of Working Group II to the Fourth Assessment Report of the Intergovernmental Panel on Climate Change*, ed. by Martin Parry, Osvaldo Canziani, Jean Palutikof, Paul van der Linden and Clair Hanson. Cambridge, UK: Cambridge University Press.

World Watch Institute. 2007. *State of the World: Our Urban Future*. New York: W.W. Norton and Company.

World Bank and United Nations. 2010. *Natural Hazards, UnNatural Disasters*. Washington, DC: World Bank.

2

Vulnerability of the Urban Poor

Key Messages

- Distinctions in spatial and location characteristics affect the nature and degree to which slum residents are impacted by natural disaster and climate change events.
- Exposure to risk by the urban poor is exacerbated by where they live within cities and their limited access to basic infrastructure and services.
- Cities typically do not have the resources or capacity to keep up with growing needs of service provision in poor urban areas.
- Land tenure, employment, financial security, and availability of social networks affect the sensitivity and adaptive capacity of the urban poor to climate change and disaster risk.

As discussed in Chapter 1, the risks in cities are on the rise as countries urbanize, particularly in cyclone-prone coastal areas and earthquake zones. This has major implications for the urban poor, with estimates that the population living in informal settlements is increasing by about 25 million per year (ISDR 2009). A number of characteristics directly relate to where and how the urban poor live and their access to basic services that increase their exposure and sensitivity to the risks associated with climate change and natural hazards. Other factors such as social networks and density can positively affect their adaptive capacity. This chapter discusses how the location, physical layout, and lack of infrastructure and basic services in slums increase exposure to risk, and how key characteristics such as tenure, employment, financial insecurity, and social networks affect their vulnerability.

Exposure: Location and Settlement Patterns of the Urban Poor

The choice of where to live within cities is driven by tradeoffs between what is affordable, proximity to income-earning opportunities, and where individuals may have social networks and kinship ties. Typically the areas affordable to the poor are those that others deem undesirable for residential purposes, or unusable for other urban activities. Slums have resulted from squatting on vacant or undeveloped lands, or from the deterioration of existing neighborhoods such as inner cities and public and industrial housing (UN-HABITAT 2003a). Many, though not all, of the urban poor live in slums that have the most visible concentrations of poor people, with lower-quality housing and services. Yet not all slum residents are poor. In many cities, such as Mumbai, where housing supply is extremely limited, the cost of housing, even for middle-income families, is unaffordable, with some living in slums.

Slum sites may be unsafe, and un-serviced, two conditions exacerbated by lack of security of tenure. Unsafe sites can be on fragile, dangerous, or polluted lands that are flood prone, on unstable soils, such as steep slopes or landfills, or are close to physical or environmental hazards such as toxic urban and industrial wastes, rail corridors, and electricity lines. Housing is typically small, overcrowded, of substandard quality, in poor structural condition, and located in highly dense areas with haphazard or irregular layouts that lack basic services. The insecurity of tenure puts the poor at constant risk of eviction, hampering residents from investing in housing improvements and efforts to provide services.

The lack of affordable land is, in many cities, attributed to inefficient land use and housing regulations, and a lack of public and private housing finance. Density regulations, such as low floor-area ratio (FAR)[1] and unaffordable minimum development and housing standards restrict the supply of land and housing and drive up prices, particularly affecting low-income groups.

Although the percentage share of urban population living in slums has decreased markedly over the last 20 years, in absolute terms the number of slum-dwellers is growing and is expected to rise due to both rural–urban migration and natural increase. It is estimated that about one-third of the urban population in developing countries—nearly 1 billion people are living in slums.[2] In Africa, the proportion of urban residents living in slums is astoundingly at 72 percent, up from 62 percent a decade ago (UN-HABITAT 2010).

Across slums, there are many different types, with important distinctions in spatial and location characteristics that affect the nature and degree to which slum residents are impacted by natural disaster and climate change.

Slum Formation

The physical formation of slums can be categorized as follows: (1) the inner city or historic core, (2) scattered pockets within the city, and (3) peri-urban areas (UN-HABITAT 2003a). Each has its own characteristics, which result in different types of vulnerability for residents.

Inner-City Slums

In many older cities, a common urbanization pattern has been an increase in commercial and manufacturing activities in the historic core, which results in deterioration of residential areas as wealthier residents move out to newer neighborhoods. Abandoned buildings have been subdivided to provide rental housing with shared amenities that often degenerate into slum conditions. Inner-city slums are highly dense, rooming houses are overcrowded, and very small apartments accommodate growing families. The older parts of most Asian and African cities, such as Delhi, Dhaka, Cairo, and Istanbul, are inner-city slums.

Although the structures are made of permanent materials, they are typically in poor condition due to deterioration over time and lack of maintenance. Absentee landlords have little incentive to maintain or redevelop the structures due to rent controls and cost, and renters lack the incentive and are too poor to invest in maintenance.[3] In an earthquake or landslide, the poor condition of such structures can amplify the destruction and damage.

Scattered Slum Pockets

Squatter settlements interspersed within a city account for much of the low-income housing in rapidly developing cities. Most low-income households illegally occupy or "squat" on vacant land close to their work place without the consent of the owner or the local authorities.[4] The land may be left vacant for several reasons: it may be reserved for public amenities, under litigation, owned by absentee landlords, or physically and environmentally hazardous. Land is informally divided, sold, leased, sub-leased to households who build dwelling units incrementally, with limited or no services (UN-HABITAT 2003a).

Although eviction in such areas is always a possibility, in many cities continued presence has given squatters a de facto right to develop and, in fact, older slums have better access to services and more permanent structures. They face little political opposition since they offer sizable vote banks. In the older slums, a vast majority of residents invest in upgrading their structures with more durable and permanent materials over time. Older slums have more owner-occupied and self-employed residents than newer, poorer settlements. However, renting and subletting from subsistence landlords, absentee landlords, developers, and rent agents is common (UN-HABITAT 2003a).

Peri-urban Slums

Slums in peri-urban areas are formed by one of three processes: squatting; deterioration of public and industrial housing that created slum estates; and illegal subdivision of land with the permission of the owner, but not of local authorities. While land is less expensive than in the inner cities, the cost of transportation can be high and travel times long, making access to work, markets, and social amenities more difficult and costly. Slum estates were typically built between the 1950s and 1970s, when many cities built public housing to rehabilitate residents of center-city slums and squatter settlements with minimal services. Although the structures are relatively recent, they were built of poor materials and construction quality. Examples include "newtowns" in Cairo (Helwan, Moktam, and Shubra), Ciudad Kenedy in Bogota, large State Housing Board housing developments constructed in almost all the major Indian cities during the 1970s and 1980s, and housing for industrial workers, such as hostels and estates of small dwellings for mine workers in Southern Africa, "chawls" built for textile industry workers in Mumbai, India, and slab blocs in the former communist countries (UN-HABITAT 2003a).

In illegal subdivisions, low-income households purchase or rent private land of relatively lower value at the periphery from developers that is developed without the consent of the local authorities, and hence is illegal. The developer may be a well-connected businessman or politician who has the resources and power to purchase, lay out, and allocate land. The layouts, however, may not meet official development standards. Since trunk infrastructure is limited in peri-urban locations, most illegal subdivisions have poor or no services. Housing conditions are typically better than adjoining rural areas and squatter settlements of the same age. Dwellings are mostly owner occupied, although renting also exists.

Spatial Contiguity and Size

There are slums laid out contiguously that are typically either physically isolated from surrounding planned neighborhoods by canals, storm drains, railway tracks, and motorways, or may be interspersed within planned residential areas. The size of slums can also vary substantially, also affecting exposure.

Although some slums are larger than many cities, medium-sized slums are more common. Kibera, in Nairobi, is a 550-acre slum with between 200,000

BOX 2.1

Locating Vulnerable Households in the Mexico City Metropolitan Area (MCMA)

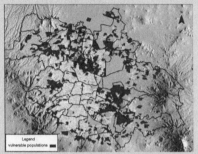

Distribution of vulnerable population in MCMA

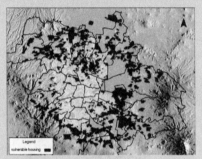

Distribution of vulnerable housing in MCMA

In preparing a socioeconomic assessment of Mexico City, two areas were selected for determining household vulnerability: population and housing characteristics. Understanding the characteristics of population and housing separately can have significant policy implications related to more effective targeting of social programs or housing upgrades. Overlaying the spatial distribution of vulnerable population and vulnerable housing also provided an expanded understanding of at-risk areas, which was critical for subsequently assessing hazard impact.

The top map was developed to assess vulnerable populations based on an index using the following indicators: percentage of adult population without formal education, percentage of population over 65 years old, percentage

(continued next page)

BOX 2.1 *continued*

of recent migrants, percentage of households headed by women, and percentage of adult population earning below the minimum wage. The analysis determined that 42 percent of the urban population is highly vulnerable from a demographic and human development point of view.

The lower map was developed to assess housing vulnerability based on an index combining indicators of roof quality, walls quality, availability of basic services, availability of a refrigerator, and security of tenure. The analysis found that 30 percent of the population (27 percent of households) lives in highly vulnerable housing units.

An overlay of housing vulnerability and population vulnerability—through a simple vulnerability matrix—shows that 27 percent of the total population of MCMA is vulnerable individuals living in vulnerable housing. It is evident also from the map above that in MCMA most vulnerable houses are located in the peri-urban areas.

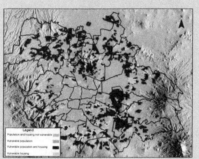

Distribution of highly vulnerable areas in MCMA

Source: Leon et al. (2010).

and 1 million inhabitants;[5] Dharavi, the largest slum in India (in Mumbai), has a population estimated between 600,000 and 1 million residing on 430 acres.[6] In Ghana, Aishaman (population 150,000), is as large as or larger than Tema, the city it is located in (population 140,000) (UN-HABITAT 2003a). These very large slums are, however, relatively uncommon. More common are medium-sized slums interspersed within a city or peri-urban slums described above.

The layout of slums may have costs and benefits in terms of destruction or damage from extreme weather or hazards. For example, if contiguous slums share the same network of services, the disruption of water supply, sanitation, drainage, and electricity can affect more slum residents. Contamination of water sources and poor solid-waste disposal can spread infectious diseases more easily over the larger area and affect more residents. At the same time, it is possible to provide safety and emergency relief to more slum households in a contiguous area through reaching one location. Equally, it is possible to efficiently provide services to more urban poor, improving their resilience to hazards.

Households in interspersed slum pockets might have a slightly higher adaptive capacity due to stronger linkages with higher-income households for whom they perform services. Their employers may be in a better position to provide emergency financial relief than other slum residents and these relationships may improve their adaptive capacity in crisis. Small slums use mostly the services of the neighboring planned areas. They illegally tap the public water supply, as well as use open public drains and public open space for sanitation and garbage disposal. These slum pockets are often overlooked or even protected by neighboring upper-income areas, since they depend on the slum residents for domestic services (UN-HABITAT 2003)—thereby improving the coping capacity of the residents to impacts of disasters.

BOX 2.2

Jardim Ana Maria: A Slum Pocket in São Paulo

Jardim Ana Maria is a slum area in São Paulo with 600 housing units in approximately 21,000 square meters. Located in the district of Brasilandia, one of the poorest in the city, Jardim Ana Maria is classified as highly and very highly vulnerable in 97 percent of its territory. More than 99 percent of the slum is under some kind of hazard; 92 percent of the area is exposed to landslides and

(continued next page)

BOX 2.2 *continued*

6 percent to washout alongside the water courses. Exposure is exacerbated by poverty and high concentrations of garbage and construction rubbish in the streets, lack of a superficial drainage system, and lack of a water supply in some of the residences. Jardim Ana Maria only began to be occupied in 1973. Today, the government of São Paulo has classified Jardim Ana Maria as a Special Interest Area, a denomination that guarantees that the area can be used only for social housing; this will prevent future evictions motivated by commercial purposes.

Source: World Bank and Diagonal Ltd. (2011).

Site Conditions

Hazardous sites, where slums are often located, may be in flood zones, low-lying dry season river beds, swamps, marshes, steep slopes, and garbage landfills. The sites may be dangerous, such as close to high-tension lines, railway tracks, or highways, or may be polluted because of being close to toxic industries. Poor conditions of structures, as well as the lack of services, compound the impact of hazards on the urban poor and increase their risks.

In São Paulo, approximately 20 percent of the land where slums are located is subject to geo-technical hazard, vulnerable to landslides and washouts. This includes 407 highly hazardous areas located in 26 subdistricts, all of which are informal settlements. Overall, more than 5 percent of slum areas are highly or very highly exposed. This means that the areas are highly prone to be affected by destructive events in the next 12 months (box 2.3).

Density and Morphology

Slum density is measured by a combination of population density and density of dwelling units and can be both a liability and an asset. It is no surprise that due to the high cost of urban land, slums have high population and dwelling density. For example, in Mumbai, 60 percent of its total population lives in slums that occupy a mere 8 percent of its total area.

Although spatial contiguity and high density might increase the adaptive capacity of the urban poor, these factors might also increase the population exposure of the urban poor to loss of life and injury, and destruction and damage to infrastructure and transportation linkages. Lack of, or poorly maintained, infrastructure in dense slums can magnify the impact of small hazards and affect

BOX 2.3

São Paulo's Geotechnical Hazard Areas and Declivity Hazard Areas

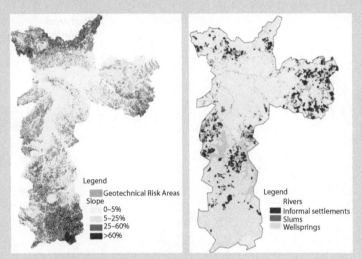

Areas ranked by their critical level and by types of settlements in São Paulo City.

	Low hazard	Medium hazard	High hazard	Very high hazard
Slums	2.92%	11.90%	**4.11%**	**1.40%**
Settlements/ allotments	0.65%	2.93%	0.97%	0.43%
Urbanized centers	4.59%	7.62%	0.56%	0.09%

Source: HABISP [Sistema de informações para habitação social] – SEHAB [Secretaria da Habitação e Desenvolvimento Urbano]; IPT [Instituto de Pesquisas Tecnológicas do Estado de São Paulo] 2010; World Bank and Diagonal Ltd. (2011).

more slum residents. As mentioned above, in dense inner-city slums, aging infrastructure and poor conditions of old, historic structures aggravate damages from hazards. Infrastructure in such areas was typically planned for a smaller population and is now inadequate. Frequent rainfall can cause drainage challenges, disruption of transportation services, and destruction or damage to roads.

BOX 2.4

Pattern between Flood-Prone Areas and Where the Poor Live in Jakarta

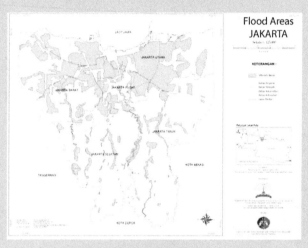

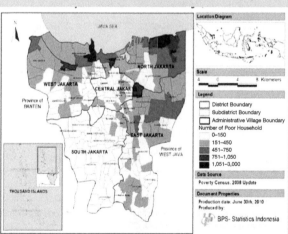

Source: World Bank (2011b). The map on the top illustrates the areas of Jakarta that would be affected by a flood with the same magnitude as the one that affected the city in 2007. The map on the bottom shows the concentration of poor households in Jakarta by subdistrict. An overlay of the two maps confirms that the poor are more likely to live in disaster-prone areas.

The economies of scale offered by the high density of slum settlements can, on the other hand, increase the adaptive capacity of cities through efficiencies in the provision of basic services.

The morphology of slums refers to the layout of slums and the distribution of built-up areas to open areas. Slums are usually characterized by irregular layouts, with very little open space in comparison to built-up areas. Haphazard layouts with minimal open space, such as those in inner-city slums, can create poorly ventilated living conditions, and extensive built-up areas increase local ambient temperatures. Irregular layouts and narrow streets that were originally suited for pedestrian traffic also limit the possible locations for water supply, sanitation services, and the collection of solid waste. During crises, irregular street networks impede relief efforts, especially in larger slums. After the Gujarat (India) earthquake of 2001, major casualties were seen in the old parts of towns where the traditional street network trapped residents and hindered rescue efforts.

Subdivisions in peripheral areas have increasingly gridiron layouts, since land is not a constraint and therefore easy to lay out; additionally, residents recognize that it is easy to install services later. Such a pattern reduces the exposure of these residents to hazards.

BOX 2.5

Exposure in Slums of South Asia and Latin America

A study of slums in six cities in Bangladesh showed that the major concentrations of slum settlements were on both sides of railway lines, low-lying riverbanks, or along embankments that have poor drainage. More than 50 percent of the slum clusters were typically fully flooded or partially flooded when the country experienced floods due to moderate-to-heavy rainfall during the rainy season (Center for Urban Studies 2006).

In Kathmandu, Nepal, a city of 1 million people located in a Himalayan valley, squatter settlements in the city are growing at an alarming rate. Most are located along the banks of its three rivers on steep slopes. Approximately 25 percent of the households flood due to inadequate drainage. The squatter settlements flood when water levels rise in the monsoon season. Some seek shelter with relatives and friends during the monsoon season as rising water inundates their homes. People who live here are also susceptible to water-borne diseases that increase when flood water stagnates in and around their homes. Solid waste is regularly thrown into the rivers, since the squatter

(continued next page)

BOX 2.5 *continued*

settlements do not have any waste-collection service. The storm-water and sewage network operates at 40 percent capacity, since it is blocked by sludge and debris. This increases the incidence of disease, exacerbated by the lack of affordable medical treatment for the urban poor.

In Bogota, Colombia, correlation of data on the location of properties, income-levels of households, and earthquake risk revealed that poor households are located closer to fault lines and face a disproportionate burden, almost twice the seismic risk compared to higher-income households (Lall and Deichmann 2009). Location of poor settlements on steep terrain increases erosion and landslide risk due to natural hazards and climate change (Lall and Deichmann 2009).

In Caracas, Venezuela, which is located in a high-risk seismic zone, high-rise buildings and densely packed apartment blocks are concentrated where shaking is expected to be highest during an earthquake. Lack of building codes and enforcement allowed residents to build on alluvial fans, which reactivated during December 1999. That month experienced over 900 millimeters of rain in a 72-hour period, triggering landslides, mudflows, and debris flows. "Barrios" or slums occupy the low-lying, rugged mountains to the east and west of the city center, where rainfall-induced debris flows are expected to be the greatest. The dwelling units in the barrios are constructed of unreinforced masonry, making them particularly vulnerable to earthquakes. Although various groups are working to repair and rebuild housing in safe locations, poor planning and code enforcement are allowing squatters to return to the alluvial fans and streambeds where most of the December 1999 destruction was concentrated (Dilley et al. 2005).

Source: Author.

Climate Change, Disaster Risk, and the Delivery of Basic Services for the Urban Poor

Access to safe shelter, water, sanitation, proper drainage, reliable transport, roads, solid-waste removal, and public health services remains an elusive goal for many of the urban poor. With rapid urbanization comes the challenge of providing basic services to a growing population, often to people with limited means and living in informal settlements. Cities typically do not have the resources or capacity to keep up with the growing need for services. Issues of informality further exacerbate the challenges, given that many governments, nongovernmental organizations (NGOs), and the private sector are reluctant to invest where residents lack secure tenure, as they perceive these investments as risky. There is also a perception that the urban poor are unable to pay for basic services, yet in many cities, the urban poor pay more than the non-poor, as they have to rely on expensive delivery systems.

A lack of basic services coupled with overcrowded living conditions reduces the resilience of the urban poor. The absence of drainage may turn a heavy rainfall into a disastrous flood. Lack of solid-waste disposal blocks drainage channels and compounds the risk of flooding. Destruction or damage to infrastructure can lead to water scarcity, contamination, and spread of disease. Infectious diseases can spread rapidly through slums. Lack of access roads can prevent relief efforts from reaching households. Lack of income and lack of access to safe housing with good provision for water, sanitation, health care, and education affects the capacity of slum residents to recover. Insecure tenure coupled with socio-spatial exclusion also reduces their access to receive information and financial assistance to cope with disasters (Lall and Deichmann 2009) (see table 1.3).

These potential impacts emphasize the urgency of providing access to clean, safe, and reliable services. Such priorities are consistent with the Millennium Development Goals and basic development goals for human settlements of the past decades—ensuring adequate shelter, provision of safe water and basic sanitation, reliable energy, proper drainage, solid-waste collection, transport, and protection from disease. The risks from disasters, climate change, and growing exposure provide added incentive for increased investments in existing and new infrastructure. As seen in recent disasters in Pakistan, Haiti, and elsewhere, such catastrophes can wipe out decades of development gains in infrastructure and service delivery. Proper investments now can protect citizens, save lives, and minimize loss and destruction in the decades to come. Some of the key issues related to the provision of safe shelter, water, drainage, solid-waste collection, roads and transport, energy, and public and environmental health to the urban poor in the context of natural hazards and climate change are discussed below.[7]

Shelter

The housing in low-income urban settlements tends to be of poor quality and located on precarious sites. While formal housing for the urban poor does exist, it is more common for housing to be self-constructed and made from low-quality materials. For squatters, the threat of eviction prevents the investment in durable materials.

New patterns in temperature and precipitation will, in some cases, alter the habitability and stability of residences, while increased frequency and intensity of natural hazards will place settlements and homes at greater risk. Although there are wide variations in impacts, the presence of substandard housing, lack of housing standards and policy enforcement, and reliance on informal service providers in most settlements result in increased risks as the climate changes.

From the perspective of managing the risk of disasters, the collapse of one poorly constructed structure can trigger the collapse of multiple houses. The accumulation of debris can block access to relief. For example, the collapse of a building after an earthquake can cause a major fire that in turn can damage other structures that had not been originally affected by the earthquake (Kunreuther and Roth 1998). Research conducted by the Architectural Institute of Japan in 1997 on the Great Hanshim-Awaji earthquake highlighted that poorly constructed houses compounded the severity of the impacts. The rubble blocked transportation networks, prevented effective fire-fighting, and made recovery more difficult (Nakagawaa, Saito, and Yamaga 2007).

The disasters in the Philippines listed in table 2.1 highlight how natural hazards in informal settlements have major impacts in informal settlements. Heavy rains, floods, mudflows, and fire often decimate homes of the urban poor.

In the wake of disasters that destroy housing in informal settlements, reconstruction and rehabilitation are complex. Support from community organizations and the government is often needed to ensure that the poor regain housing and that the new housing is more stable than the structures it replaces. However, this is not always available, particularly for those in informal settlements. For example, after Mumbai's devastating floods in 2005, the state government announced a rehabilitation package of approximately US$5 million for the flood victims (Concerned Citizens Commission 2005). The poor living in formal settlements were able to take advantage of this support, while those living in informal settlements were ineligible for the rehabilitation package (Concerned Citizens Commission 2005).

In the absence of official support to help informal settlers cope with and recover from disasters, some municipalities are making modest efforts to extend assistance. Cape Flats, for instance, is an informal settlement in Cape Town that is located below sea level and is prone to floods each winter. While the city does not provide services to this area, it has cleaned storm drains and worked with NGOs to establish emergency shelters, ensure the availability of basic relief provisions, and disseminate information so that dwellers can take their own measures, such as raising their homes and diverting flood waters (Simply Green 2009). As this example illustrates, in most instances the urban poor living in flood-prone areas have little or no assistance and therefore rely on ad hoc measures to protect their homes and well-being. A case in point is the slum of Makoko in Lagos,

TABLE 2.1
Impacts of Recent Disasters in Informal Settlements: The Philippines

Disaster	Year	Details
Trash slides at the Payatas solid-waste dump in Quezon City (metro Manila)	2000	Heavy rains from typhoons caused a 15-meter (50-foot) slope in the dump to collapse, burying hundreds of homes; 288 people were killed and several hundred families displaced. Subsequent flash floods affected the homes and livelihoods of many more people.
Landslide in Barangay Guinsaugon	2006	The whole *barangay* (district) was buried and another 80 *barangays* affected. A total of 154 deaths were recorded, 968 people reported missing, 3,742 displaced, and 18,862 affected.
Mount Mayor mudflow and floods	2006	Typhoons triggered huge floods, mudslides, and avalanches. In the Bicol region alone, at least 208 people died and another 261 were reported missing. These settlements were recovering from a previous typhoon.
Fire in the settlement of the lower Tipolo Homeowners Association in Mandaue	2007	246 structures were destroyed, leaving 913 people homeless.
Flash flood in Iloilo	2008	In the city of Iloilo, 152 of its 180 *barangays* were affected by heavy rain and flooding. Up to 500 people were killed, with 261,335 affected. Many houses were washed away and many households lost their documentation.
Flooding in Manila during typhoons Ondoy and Pepeng	2009	Typhoon Ondoy alone left 280 people dead and more than 700,000 people displaced to shelters or temporary stays with host families; more than 3 million people were affected in total.

Source: IFRC (2010).

Nigeria. To cope with the challenge of being located in a flood basin, residents have raised their homes on stilts. Similarly, in the Alaho settlement in Accra, residents respond to floods by placing barriers across their doors, raising the height of their furniture, creating elevated storage areas, and putting their homes on higher foundations (ActionAid 2006).

Water Supply and Sanitation

The delivery of a sustainable water supply and sanitation is increasingly difficult in urban areas due to (1) population growth and urbanization, (2) poor management and aging infrastructure, and (3) the impacts of climate change. A deteriorating water supply and sanitation infrastructure with poorly maintained water storage, aging treatment plants, and inefficient distribution cannot effectively serve the current population. Moreover, urban population growth will result in an increased competition for water resources and will threaten the ecosystems that supply it. This means that while urban demand for water increases, supply is being reduced. Global water consumption increased six-fold in the 20th century, and it is expected to continue growing due to expanding industrialization in urban and peri-urban areas.

Most cities in developing countries are challenged with keeping up with the growing demand. Water supply and sanitation remain particularly weak in informal settlements. For example, in Mumbai, India, of the more than 7 million residents living in informal settlements, only 5 percent have individual household connections to water. About one-half of residents use connections shared among five or more households (Water and Sanitation Program 2009, 11).

The poor routinely use nonresidential sources of supply, which can include illegal boreholes, kiosks, water-delivery trucks, and a variety of small service providers. In many cases, water obtained from these private vendors costs several times more per liter than water obtained through the municipal water system. For example, water truckers charge as much as 10 to 15 times more per unit volume than the price of public utilities, which reflects the substantially higher cost of delivering water by truck (Baker 2009). In Nairobi's Kibera slum, more than 500,000 residents get water from some 650 water kiosks, which lay pipes to connect to the city water utility and sell water to residents (Water and Sanitation Program 2009, 19). In Dar es Salam, Tanzania, only 86,000 of the city's 2.5 million residents are served by the privatized water utility (DAWASA). Alternative coping mechanisms that the poor use to offset the high costs of water from vendors include self-imposed rationing, collecting water from surface sources, and rainwater harvesting.

The situation for sanitation is even worse, with almost half of the population in developing countries without basic sanitation. Further, while progress has been made in improving access to sanitation in the last two decades, most progress has occurred in rural areas, where sanitation coverage increased 43 percent. Sanitation coverage in urban areas over the last two decades, by contrast, has improved only 5 percent (UN 2010). In São Paulo half of the residents living in informal settlements do not have access to sanitation facilities. In Dar es Salaam's Temeke municipality, 78 percent of residents report using pit latrines and the remaining population defecate in the open (Water and Sanitation Program 2009, 82).

Water supply and sanitation services will be heavily impacted by climate change, and with it, inequality in urban water distribution and contamination of available water will increase. In some regions, the unreliability of clean water and poor sanitation in low-income urban settlements will only become more acute, putting these populations at high risk. The IPCC has projected that increases in

BOX 2.6

Water Supply in Dar es Salaam

Continuous, full-pressure water supply remains a dream for the urban poor in Dar es Salaam. Water quality and reliability are poor, especially in low-income areas, where the poor frequently have to purchase water at exorbitant prices from vendors, kiosks, and neighbors. In Dar es Salaam, 60 percent of the water is lost due to poor maintenance of the water-supply network, and another 13 percent through unauthorized use and illegal taps. Only 26 percent of the water is billed (Greenhill and Wekiya 2004) and only 16 percent actually paid for.

Existing constraints to clean-water supply for the residents of Dar es Salaam's unplanned settlements will become an increasingly severe issue given both increased climatic variability (with the possibility of more or longer droughts) and the projected growth of the city's population over the coming decades. At present the city's water demand already far outstrips its water-treatment capability. Existing treatment capacity is 282,000 m³ per day; water demand in 2007 was 412,000 m³ per day. Demand is projected to rise to 964,000 m³ per day by 2032 (DAWASA 2008). A study of 45 of Dar es Salaam's wards, containing 84 percent of the city's population, found that the percentage of informal residents without access to improved drinking water ranged from 37.8 percent to 90 percent, with a mean of 71.8 percent (Penrose et al. 2010). Unpredictable water supply has led poorer residents to try to adapt to the situation by diversifying sources (often expensive) and reducing consumption. The considerable cost of a piped water connection continues to pose an obstacle for poorer households; only 8 percent of the city's residents had access to piped water.

Sources: Greenhill and Wekiya (2004); and Penrose et al. (2010).

average global temperatures, sea-level rise, and in some areas, more frequent and intense floods and droughts will affect water availability for urban water-supply systems. Higher temperatures and reduced precipitation are expected to cause supply shortages due to the slower replenishment rates of groundwater aquifers and reduced surface water (Danilenko et al. 2010).Combined with a lack of sanitation, the urban poor frequently suffer from contaminated water sources during dry periods (Stephens 1996, 25). Drinking water is also more vulnerable to contamination due to stagnant water remaining in settlements, and because flooding will mobilize more pathogens and contaminants. Floods can carry contaminated

Figure 2.1 Percentage of Urban Population Using Improved Sanitation (2008)

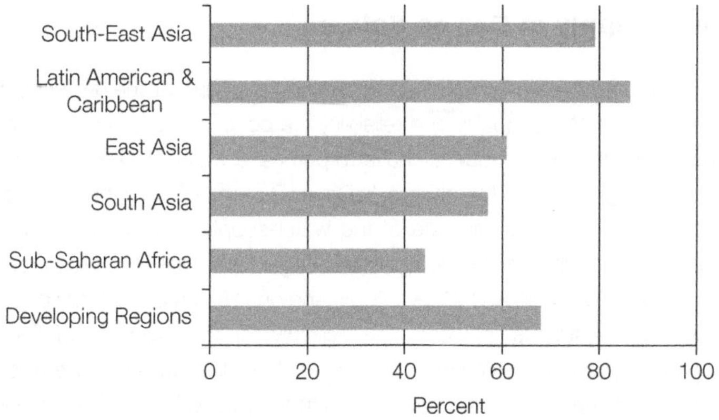

Source: UN (2010).

water containing wastes and toxic chemicals into living spaces. The incidence of diarrhea may be around 10 percent higher in some countries by 2030 (McMichael et al. 2006). In Kampala, Uganda, recent outbreaks of cholera, dysentery, and diarrhea have been attributed to flooding.[8]

While short- and medium-term measures, such as water rationing or altering of design parameters, may allow urban water utilities to cope with the effects of climate change, long-term impacts of climate change are likely to surpass current design allowances. Compounding the effects of climate change and urbanization, many cities fail to properly maintain and rehabilitate water utility networks for lack of financial resources.

Drainage

The lack of proper drainage can lead to devastating flooding. The urban poor are particularly vulnerable because their homes are frequently located in low-lying areas, with little or no access to drainage. For example, in Dhaka, Bangladesh, only 10 percent of slum dwellers had sufficient drainage to avoid water-logging during heavy rains (Islam 2005). In most low-income settlements, inadequately maintained storm drains and poor waste-disposal practices prevent drainage systems from working during heavy rains, often resulting in flooding. Stagnant floodwater provides an ideal breeding ground for parasites, which may lead to an increase in malaria and other vector-transmitted diseases. In Phnom Penh (1.3 million inhabitants) (Heinonen 2008), some 176,000 of the urban poor live

---

BOX 2.7

Water Scarcity in Mexico City

Despite major infrastructural investments to funnel water resources toward industrial and population centers, water scarcity remains in places such as Mexico City (Mumme and Lybecker 2002, 313). In these areas, overexploitation of ground water has led to land subsidence, salinization, and pollution of ground water (Peritore,1999). Uneven subsidence changes the gradients of water delivery, drainage, and sewage networks, which further contaminates ground and surface water (Peritore, 147). Leaky and insufficient water supply and drainage infrastructure are complicated by the subsidence of Mexico City at a rate of 45 centimeters a year. It is estimated that 77 percent of Mexican rivers are polluted to the point that they pose a risk to human health (Mumme and Lybecker, 312). Treatment is required for most Mexican surface water before it is considered potable, and fecal contamination is considered responsible for gastrointestinal illness in one-third of the Mexican population (Peritore, 147).

Source: Leon et al. 2010.

---

in housing that floods regularly due to heavy rainfall and clogged drains; this population is highly exposed to water-borne diseases and may be increasingly so as climate change advances (ADB 2008). In Jakarta, a city highly vulnerable to sea-level rise, problems of public health related to poor drainage and standing water are severe. A study in informal settlements in the northern part of the city reported diarrheal incidence at 342 episodes per 1,000 people, and 43 percent of children under five were infected with at least one type of intestinal worms (Harpham, Garner, and Surjadi 1990).

With increases in flooding due to climate change as discussed in Chapter 1, proper drainage becomes increasingly important. Policy makers and planners can minimize the consequences of flooding through structural, social, economic, and administrative measures taken now. Storm-water drainage overlaps with other services, such as solid-waste disposal and Integrated Urban Water Management. Additionally, drainage can benefit from sustainable and natural drainage systems.

Solid Waste

In many poor urban areas, solid-waste management presents huge challenges. While the urban poor may generate less waste than their more affluent neighbors, they are much more likely to suffer the consequences of inadequate waste management. Typically, up to two-thirds of the solid waste generated is not collected, and most often municipal authorities focus their limited budget on solid-waste collection in neighborhoods with wealth and political power (Zurbrügg 2002, 1). Even in places like Brazil, where urban waste collection is relatively high (80 percent), waste disposal is often inadequate, occurring in open dumps that contaminate soil and water and adversely affect the health and safety of the sur-rounding, often poor, population (IBGE 2003).

Solids, whether they are the sediments from land development or the solid waste produced by human populations, decrease the flow of rivers. In urban areas with inadequate services, solid waste can block storm-water drains, impeding the flow of water from the impacted area and increasing pollution. In addition, solid waste contributes to general environmental degradation and increases disease vectors. In the case of many cities, solid-waste disposal and drainage improvements are included in general urban upgrading programs and in some cases, such as Ouagadougou (UN-HABITAT 2008) and several communities in Liberia, improvements in solid-waste disposal and drainage were also used as a vehicle for job creation.

Good solid-waste management is also important for mitigating climate change. Nearly 5 percent of global greenhouse gas (GHG) emissions (1,460 $mtCO_2e$) in 2010 came from post-consumer waste (Hoornweg et al. 2010, 40).

Investments in solid-waste management can also be a small but catalytic source of revenue. For instance, the Dar es Salaam City Council closed the Mtoni solid-waste dumpsite and, in collaboration with a private company, created mechanisms for tapping and flaring the gases produced at the dump. Together they invested over US$1.25 million in 2008. The partnership was able to sell the 13,895 tons of carbon that had been flared at a cost of US$15–25 per ton.

Roads and Transport

Access to roads and transport services are critical for mobility to jobs, markets, health, education, and, during extreme weather, to safety. Often the quality of roads in urban slums is very low, hampering service provision, and, during floods or other disasters, preventing emergency vehicles from getting to residents.

Roads can be washed out, intense heat can warp and crack pavement, and increased precipitation can cause subsidence. In Ethiopia, where extensive modeling has been done, increased precipitation due to climate change is expected to both decrease the lifespan of unpaved roads and increase the maintenance needs and costs for paved roads (World Bank 2010). The condition of pedestrian paths and roads in slums, which are usually unpaved, is already often poor and will only further deteriorate with increased extreme weather. In Dar es Salaam, roads become impossible to navigate during the rainy season, when the increasing number and depth of holes can completely block vehicles (Olvera et al. 2002). Daily trips on foot also become much more difficult during rains, when people are cut off from their neighborhoods and bridges or roads collapse. During the 2010 earthquake in Port au Prince, Haiti, the lack of access roads between streets hindered relief efforts. Relief vehicles had difficulty entering the patchwork of unmarked "corridors" (IFRC 2010).

Squatter settlements are surrounded by planned developments, and most are well connected to public transportation networks. However, the interior of large slums may be poorly connected and do not have any transportation services (UN-HABITAT 2003a). Slums in peri-urban areas typically must rely on public transport, which is often limited or unaffordable. Slum residents in peri-urban areas may spend a substantial portion of their income, up to 30 percent, on transportation to jobs, markets, and social amenities; some walk as much as 3 to 4 hours a day to reach their places of employment (UN-HABITAT 2003a). This limits employment opportunities and can contribute to social exclusion. The economic and social costs associated with transport are particularly relevant when assessing the tradeoffs for policy related to relocating slum residents to safer locations, which may be in peri-urban areas as is discussed in Chapter 3.

Energy

Energy services are critical to raising productivity, creating opportunities at the household level for income generation, and contributing to improved health and education. The poor's access to safe, affordable, and reliable services is still relatively low in many cities. Many rely on illegal connections and inefficient or dangerous sources. The majority of the urban poor rely on burning biomass (wood, charcoal, agriculture, and animal waste) for cooking.

Traditional cook stoves worsen indoor air pollution and respiratory health. Depending on the fuel used, traditional cook stoves also contribute to climate change and deforestation (World Bank 2011). In such cases, improved cook stoves would decrease indoor air pollution and also contribute to mitigating climate change. The use of cook stoves is common in countries across the developing world, including India and China, where projects to introduce improved cook stoves are underway. In Dar es Salaam, the city administration has pioneered the production of briquettes made of recycled trash, replacing charcoal as fuel for family cooking stoves. As a result, the use of wood and related air pollution has been dramatically reduced.[9] In India, a government subsidy program has reduced the price of 8 million stoves by 50 percent (World Bank 2010a, 312), with impacts both on air pollution and on the health of the urban poor (World Bank 2003).

Globally, a new Alliance for Clean Cook Stoves, led by the United Nations, was established in 2010 to improve low-quality cook stoves that present environmental and health risks. This initiative is important for climate change because studies suggest that black carbon, such as the particulates emitted as soot from rudimentary cook stoves, may have contributed fully 13 percent of the warming of the Arctic since 1976.[10]

Much like other infrastructure, climate change and extreme weather are anticipated to have significant impacts on energy infrastructure, as the latter will be vulnerable to flood and wind damage. Meanwhile, heat and cold waves are expected to produce shifts in energy demand in response to building design and internal temperature control. Even in high- and middle-income countries, the increased demand for air conditioning during heat waves can cause widespread blackouts. The high temperatures can prove fatal for the elderly, very young, and urban poor—many of whom have no access to air conditioning.[11] In Delhi, rising temperatures and the energy demand for cooling are being cited as signs that the National Capital Region could become unsustainable, despite rapid economic growth.[12] Similarly, there is significant overlap between the energy and water sectors. In areas dependent on hydropower, droughts will affect energy generation. In the other direction, cities that already use energy-intensive pumps to convey their water supply over long distances may face additional challenges with increasing drought or competing energy demands. An example would be Mexico City, which uses pumps to carry a third of its water supply up and over 1,000-meter peaks.[13] To the extent that the urban poor rely on energy services for cooking, heating, lighting, and home-based businesses, they will similarly be affected by these changes.

Public and Environmental Health

Many impacts of climate change and natural hazards on the urban poor are most notable in risks to public health. Exposure to changing weather patterns in temperature, precipitation, sea-level rise, and more frequent earthquakes and landslides have direct consequences for people's health: morbidity and mortality. Many communicable diseases are highly sensitive to changing temperatures and precipitation. These include vector-borne diseases, such as malaria and dengue, and water-borne diseases, such as diarrhea and cholera. The pathogens that cause these diseases thrive in living conditions characteristic of those typically found in slums. Worse, their impact is also likely to be more severe in populations with a preexisting burden of disease (IPCC 2007).

In Dar es Salaam, accessing clean water and sanitation are major problems for the poor, contributing to widespread illness, including cholera, malaria, lymphatic falorisi, and diarrhea, particularly during floods. Since the first major cholera epidemic was reported in southern Tanzania in 1977, cholera has spread to most regions of the country and has remained a chronic and widespread problem in Dar es Salaam. In 2006, 14,297 cases, including 254 deaths (1.8 percent case fatality rate), were reported from 16 of Tanzania's 21 regions. Dar es Salaam represented 62.7 percent of the total cases and 101 deaths (39.8 percent of total deaths) (Penrose, Werema, and Ryan 2010; WHO 2008).

While research on the impact of climate change on vulnerable populations is still in early stages, the link between urban poverty and ill-health is already well established. In its Fourth Assessment Report, the IPCC has warned that changing weather patterns are altering the distribution of some infectious-disease vectors and worsening existing health conditions. The report also predicts that adverse health impacts of climate change will be greatest in low-income countries, and the urban poor in all countries will be at greater risk apart from the elderly, children, and coastal populations (IPCC 2007). The urban poor are more prone to diseases such as diarrhea, tuberculosis, dengue, malaria, pneumonia, cholera, and HIV/AIDS (Montgomery 2009; Harpham 2009; Mercado et al. 2007; Cattaneo et al. 2007). In cities, the poor tend to live in low-income settlements or slums with inadequate access to clean water and sanitation facilities, drainage, and solid-waste management, which exposes them to a "double burden" of both communicable and noncommunicable diseases[14] causing disability and death (Harpham 2009). Despite their proximity to better health-care facilities than people in rural areas, the urban poor often do not have access to quality health care, as services are unaffordable or facilities are inaccessible. They also die disproportionately of both infectious and chronic, degenerative diseases (Montgomery et al. 2004).

Climate change is expected to expose 90 million more people in Africa to malaria by 2030—a 14 percent increase—because of expanded mosquito breeding grounds and because the disease is now spreading to higher altitudes.[15] Dengue fever is expanding in its geographic range: climate change is expected to double the proportion of the world's population at risk, from 30 percent to 60 percent by 2070 (World Bank 2010b, 97).

Emergency Services

Emergency services include measures to respond to disasters and catastrophes, including both preparedness and emergency response and recovery. The lack of, or limited, emergency services in developing countries often is crippling to citizens and economies. A study of natural hazards in Mediterranean countries noted that disasters in the Southern European countries have had the lowest levels of fatalities, as well as the lowest livelihood and economic loss, attributed to the presence of preventive measures and disaster-management

BOX 2.8

Incidents of Dengue in Jakarta

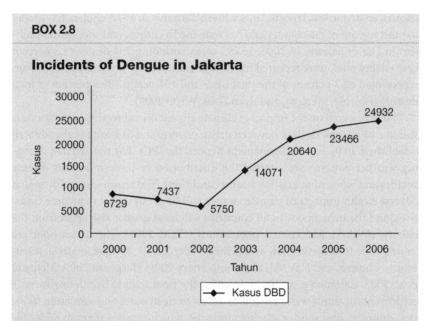

Changes in rainfall patterns and increasing temperatures are a significant health hazard for the urban population, particularly in the area of water- and mosquito-borne diseases. While often nonfatal when adequately treated, dengue has a disproportionate impact on the poor, who have lower less access to medical care. In Jakarta there has been a significant increase in recorded cases of dengue in recent years attributed to increases in rainfall, humidity, and temperature. The correlation between monthly rainfall and dengue cases was the strongest, where one study has estimated that every 9.73 mm increase in monthly rainfall resulted in an additional 67 cases of dengue. The correlations with increased temperatures and humidity were positive, although less strong. Increase in cases of dengue fever is only one indicator of how global meteorological changes are affecting the spread of diseases in Jakarta.

Source: World Bank (2011b).

preparedness. In contrast, North Africa and Turkey had the most debilitating impacts (Brauch 2003).

One of the core institutional indicators of emergency preparedness is the presence of national, regional, and sector-level disaster-management plans. Although these are important tools, the presence of plans alone does not ensure that a country, region, or city is able to adequately respond when disaster strikes.

Mumbai, for instance, has a comprehensive disaster-management plan that lists different calamities that can affect the city and identifies those areas most at risk. It also contains provisions to reduce the impact of disasters through infrastructure development, communication and public information, and land-use policies and planning, as well as maps out protocols to be followed when a disaster occurs (Concerned Citizens Commission 2005). Despite the plan, when the 2005 floods hit the city, it became clear that disaster-management strategies such as early-warning systems had not been implemented and first responders did not have the equipment or training to act (Concerned Citizens Commission 2005).

While slums and informal settlements are not always able to obtain government support when emergencies arise, communities, NGOs, and the private sector respond in various ways. The private sector has begun to engage with the public and NGOs in providing services and warning systems. International organizations such as the Red Cross, Oxfam, and Save the Children Fund provide shelter, food, and other forms of humanitarian aid in disasters, when governments cannot or do not act quickly enough (Beamon and Balcik 2008). At the most basic level, social networks and social capital are critical aspects of emergency response. In moments of extreme events, local community members support one another by providing information and by working together to address impacts. For example, flood management is often handled by sand-bagging. Such approaches are often effective in emergency scenarios, but are not substitutes for the levels of prevention that can be achieved through infrastructure and emergency services.

Other Key Issues Affecting the Vulnerability of the Urban Poor

Several factors related to the characteristics of the urban poor affect their sensitivity and adaptive capacity to climate change and disaster risk, impacting vulnerability. Among these are security of tenure, employment and financial insecurity, and social networks.

Security of Tenure

More than a quarter of the world's urban populations experience various levels of tenure insecurity, ranging from some level of legality to full illegality (for example, unauthorized squatting) (UN-HABITAT 2007). Insecure tenure and protection from forced evictions are key to obtaining public infrastructure services—municipalities are reluctant to provide infrastructure to slum households, in the absence of property rights, especially in unplanned settlements or on public land. Security of tenure is also critical to self-investments in property and service improvements that are critical for ad hoc adaptation of the urban poor. In Dhaka, Bangladesh, residents, donors, NGOs, and government report lack of tenure security as a key constraint to service delivery. With the constant threat of evictions, government agencies, NGOs, and donors are reluctant to invest capital in erecting permanent structures that residents may stand to lose if evicted (World Bank 2005). This has obvious implications on vulnerability.

Forced evictions are the most extreme manifestation of tenure insecurity. At least 2 million people, mostly those with the worst housing, are forcibly evicted by local government authorities every year. Recent data reveals that forced evictions worldwide have increased during the last decade, especially in Africa and Asia (UN-HABITAT 2007). The most common reasons cited for

---

BOX 2.9

Settlements and Environmentally Sensitive Lands

Parks, gardens, natural areas, and recreational spaces are highly valued in most cities. As a result, informal settlements that encroach upon urban parks, forests, waterways, and wetlands often are seen as posing threats to natural resources. The common responses by local governments to these settlements are displacement and relocation. As a case in point is an informal settlement in Mumbai that grew over the years and ultimately encroached upon the city's Borivali National Park, the only park in India within a metropolis. This national park contains two of the city's sources of drinking water and is home to a variety of flora and fauna. The Bombay High Court ruled to evict and resettle the residents, because of their location (Bavadam 2003). As a further example, after the 2005 Mumbai flood, the local government targeted some informal settlements that had encroached upon a narrow point of the Mithi River and planned to evict the residents and construct a park in that area. At the same time, the encroachment of the high-income Bandra-Kurla Complex, which was constructed over the mangrove ecosystem of the Mithi River (Concerned Citizens Commission 2005) was overlooked. These examples illustrate how local government interventions based on relocation are used to protect resources, although not necessarily in an equitable way. (Bartlett et al. 2009).

Source: Carmin, Roberts, and Anguelovski (2009).

forced evictions are infrastructure projects, international mega-events, and urban beautification.

Employment and Financial Security of the Urban Poor

While the urban economy provides many income and employment opportunities, the poor tend to be marginalized on many fronts and often face low incomes, limited (mostly informal) sources of livelihood, lack of social insurance, and limited access to credit markets. For some, especially those living in peri-urban areas, accessing jobs is difficult. For others, the negative stigma associated with living in certain neighborhoods provides a barrier to entering the formal job market.

Climate change and natural hazards could significantly affect access to livelihoods for the urban poor. For example, slum entrepreneurs operate outside of formal markets and typically do not have insurance against their assets. Hazards such as floods, mudslides, hurricanes, and storms, especially if increasing in frequency or severity, can easily destroy the physical assets of these businesses as well as homes, leaving residents destitute.

Urban agriculture accounts for a substantial percentage of employment in some cities with links to commercial food and ornamental plant production, development of small agro-food industries, marketing of agricultural products, input supply, and waste-recycling enterprises. Urban agriculture could be affected by climate change in obvious ways related to water shortages, flooding, and heat stresses, but also has an increasing role to play for both climate-change adaptation and mitigation with implications for job creation. Urban agriculture can contribute to overall food security, particularly in providing emergency food in disasters when supply chains do not function. Green rooftops can contribute to improved air quality, and rainwater-harvesting systems can help lessen the effects of flooding. Urban agriculture can also help to build resilience by keeping environmentally sensitive and dangerous lands from being used for illegal residential development.

Social Networks

Traditionally, vulnerable individuals and communities have managed risk through ad hoc coping techniques that draw on their local knowledge of hazards and community resources. There is substantial literature that discusses ad hoc adaptation to illustrate the strength of social capital. In slums where social networks and kinship ties are stronger, communities are more resilient. Older communities have stronger social networks than newer settlements, where residents may be more transient. Active internal leadership in close-knit communities can organize relief and rehabilitation more effectively and efficiently. This is especially the case for fast-onset events that require temporary relocation; at these times, residents rely on their existing social capital and existing networks. A study on adaptation by the poor in Mombasa, Kenya, and Esteli, Nicaragua, provides examples (World Bank 2010b). When slum dwellers in Esteli are forced to leave their home in time of emergency, they take refuge in churches and with friends and relatives in other areas. Charitable citizens provide basic needs for those evacuated, and police protect their homes—often their most valuable asset (World Bank 2010b). These systems of mutual support significantly enhance community resilience to disasters and climate change.

In these two cities, community organizations are actively involved in adapting to extreme weather. Adaptation at the household and business level is slightly more common, but community-scale adaptation occurs in Mombasa in approximately 80 percent of extreme weather events (World Bank 2010b). Communities that lack social capital have more limited capacity to respond to climate change and disasters. A community's level of social capital depends on an array of characteristics, including length of tenure or settlement and pattern of occupation of an area (Moser and Satterthwaite 2010; Moser and Felton 2007).

Extended family networks, as part of the larger social network, often go beyond the urban arena to rural households. In such networks, urban relatives are often called on for financial support in times of drought or other difficulty. In addition, rural family members may move to join urban-dwelling relatives during droughts or floods (Raleigh and Jordan 2010). This means that changing weather patterns and extreme events in far-reaching regions also have an impact on urban households.

The study also found that the asset that the poor value and tend to protect the most during extreme events is their house. Other important assets were businesses and electrical appliances. Most households were resourceful at developing resilience measures (for example, 91% of the households implement some kind of adaptation action before severe weather event, 100 percent during the event and 91 percent afterward). Furthermore, the study revealed that the most critical dimension of vulnerability of the poor was weak or unclear tenure rights, and that owner occupiers tend to invest more resources in adaptation measures than tenants, especially in reinforcing the house before heavy rains.

Notably, such social networks do vary from community to community. A study of marginalized populations in Mumbai, India, following the 2005 floods found that around 97 percent of the households that undertook reconstruction of their damaged houses depended on their past savings (Hallegatte et al. 2010). Only 1.7 percent of the households said they secured the money for reconstruction from family members, and the reminder relied on loans from money lenders and other sources.

Ad hoc Adaptation and Risk of Maladaptation

Some of the coping mechanisms used by the poor also reflect a short-term perspective by individuals or communities who may be accustomed to living with risk from recurrent hazards and cannot rely on government protection (Douglas et al. 2008). Examples of ad hoc adaptation in Accra, Kampala, Lagos, and Maputo following heavy flooding in 2006 show that individuals resorted to using concrete blocks and furniture to raise valuables above the reach of flood waters, creating small barriers to prevent the flood waters from entering their home, or when this was unavoidable, creating openings to channel flood waters through their homes as quickly as possible. Those individuals who lacked safe places for their assets or vulnerable family members moved away from the impacted area to stay with family or in public buildings (Douglas et al. 2008). In low-income areas in Jakarta vulnerable to flooding along the coast, residents have raised their homes on stilts to accommodate rising sea levels and land subsidence. Residents in one close-knit neighborhood report working together to repair the government-constructed sea wall, or fixing boats used for fishing. While ad hoc adaptation may save lives and assets in the short term, its unregulated nature creates the possibility for maladaptation—where a shift in vulnerability from one group to another may deliver a short-term gain, at the cost of creating long-term, higher vulnerability such as impacts on future generations.

TABLE 2.2
Adaptation Strategies Applied during Heavy Rain

Asset holder	Before	Mombasa Strategies During	After
Tenants	• Repair roof • Build stronger foundations • Dig trenches around houses • Clear drainage	• Seal leaking areas • Vacate flooding houses • Open up passage routes	• Block water passage routes • Repair houses
Owner occupied	• Make water drains • Repair houses • Build concrete skirting around houses • Seal holes and leakages • Build barriers at entrance to houses • Build strong houses	• Unblock and clear drains • Move to safer houses • Remove water from house	• Rebuild and repair

Household asset	Before/continuous	Esteli During	After
Plots or sites	• Level the land • Build terraces • Plant local trees • Dig trenches • Build drainage channels	• Spread dry soil and gravel • Build stone dykes • Dig trenches around plots • Open up drainage passages	• Plant damp-resistant tress • Replace eroded ground with new soil and stones • Build stone dykes • Repair fences • Replant trees and plants
Houses	• Clean ditches • Replace plastic and zinc • Replace wooden planks • Build stone dykes • Reinforce foundations • Build steps with tires	• Block leaks • Collect leakages • Secure zinc roofs with stones • Spread sawdust • Dig drainage ditches	• Repair leaks • Mend roofs • Reinforce foundations • Maintain drainage ditches
Latrines/showers and washstands	• Build and maintain • Abandon and eliminate saturated latrines • Improve absorbency with tires • Tie down and secure	• Dig ditches • Channel water away from houses	• Repair structure • Replace poles and plastic • Reinforce with tires • Dig new holes

Source: World Bank (2010b).

Notes

1. FAR, the floor-area ratio, determines the total amount of floor space (including all levels) that can be built on a plot of land.

2. Slum estimates are calculated by UN-HABITAT based on the definition of a group of individuals living under the same roof in an urban area lacking at least one of the following five conditions: access to improved water supply; access to improved sanitation facilities; sufficient living area (not more than three people sharing the same room); structural quality and durability of dwellings; and security of tenure. If a home has one or all five of these conditions, they would be classified as a slum household (UN-HABITAT 2008). While there are major deficiencies with this approach to measuring slums—such as a lack of the degree of deprivation experienced by a given household or community, and inability to capture improvements of individual deficiencies over time—these estimates provide a basis for understanding the scope of shelter deprivation in urban areas globally.

3. Rent control introduced in many countries during and after World War II freezes rents at levels that are affordable to low-income families, but that do not relate to the value or replacement cost of the accommodation, or to the economic cost of adequately maintaining the building and its services; owners remove value from the building by withdrawing maintenance (UN-HABITAT 2003a).

4. Occupation can be a rapid, organized invasion at one end, and incremental growth at the other. Initially, squatting may have been the result of authorities tolerating post-independence inflow of migrants to cities in Asia and Africa. In many cases, squatting eventually becomes a profitable business in connivance with politicians, police, and land racketeers. Squatter housing is not free. An entry fee is charged by an agent who controls land subdivision (UN-HABITAT 2003a).

5. http://siteresources.worldbank.org/WBI/Resources/213798-1278955272198/Putting_Nairobi_Slums_on_the_Map.pdf.

6. http://www.time.com/time/asia/covers/501060619/slum.html.

7. Much has been written on basic services from a sectoral perspective; this section highlights key issues related to the urban poor, and provides context for the chapter that follows on building adaptive capacity and resilience.

8. IIED (2009, 15).

9. http://wbi.worldbank.org/wbi/stories/dar-es-salaam-mayor-"some-will-be-talking-and-some-will-be-doing"-global-video-dialogue-expl.

10. Author's calculations from World Bank (2010a, 312). Black carbon is estimated to have accounted for as much as 70 percent of this warming effect, and cook stoves in the developing world account for 18 percent of that black carbon (18 percent of 70 percent is 13 percent).

11. As mentioned in the adaptation plans for New York City and Paris.

12. Revi (2008) as cited in Satterthwaite (2007).

13. Romero-Lankao (2007), as cited in Satterthwaite (2007).

14. Communicable diseases are caused by pathogenic microorganisms, such as bacteria, viruses, parasites, or fungi. They can be spread, directly or indirectly, from one person to another. Communicable diseases prevalent in developing countries include diarrhea, viral hepatitis, typhoid fever, HIV/AIDS, tuberculosis, and

vector-borne infectious diseases, especially malaria, dengue fever, and chikungunya. Noncommunicable diseases, or NCD, are not contagious. Examples of NCD include cardiovascular diseases, cancer, diabetes, and allergies.
15. Hay et al. (2006) cited in World Bank (2009, 3).

References

ActionAid. 2006. *Unjust Waters. Climate change, Flooding and the Protection of Poor Urban Communities: Experiences from Six African Cities.* Johannesburg: ActionAid International.

Asian Development Bank (ADB). 2008. *Urban Innovations: Partnerships for a Cleaner City: Community-based Environmental Improvements in Phnom Penh.* ADB. http://www.adb.org/Documents/Urban-Development/Environmental-Improvements.pdf.

Baker, Judy, ed. 2009. *Opportunities and Challenges for Small Scale Private Service Providers in Electricity and Water Supply.* Washington, DC: World Bank, PPIAF.

Bartlett, Sheridan, David Dodman, Jorgelina Hardoy, David Satterthwaite, and Cecilia Tacoli. 2009. "Social Aspects of Climate Change in Urban Areas in Low- and Middle-Income Nations." Contribution to the World Bank Fifth Urban Research Symposium Cities and Climate Change: Responding to an Urgent Agenda.

Bavadam, Lyla. 2003. "Encroaching on a Lifeline." *Frontline* 20(4). http://www.hinduonnet.com/fline/fline 2004/stories/20030228002609200.htm.

Beamon, Benita M., and Burcu Balcik. 2008. "Performance Measurement in Humanitarian Supply Chains." *International Journal of Public Sector Management* 1 (21): 4–25.

Brauch. 2003. "Urbanization And Natural Disasters In The Mediterranean: Population Growth And Climate Change in the 21st Century." In *Building Safer Cities: The Future of Disaster Risk*, ed. A. Kreimer, M. Arnold, and A. Carlin. Washington, DC: World Bank.

Carmin, JoAnn. 2010. "Variations in Urban Climate Adaptation Planning: Implications for Action." Paper presented at the International Climate Change Adaptation Conference, Gold Coast, Australia.

———, Debra Roberts, and Isabelle Anguelovski. 2009. "Planning Climate Resilient Cities: Early Lessons from Early Adapters." Paper presented at the Fifth Urban Research Symposium "Cities and Climate Change: Responding to an Urgent Agenda," Marseille, France.

Cattaneo, M., S. Giliani, P. Gertler, S. Martinez, and R. Titiunik, 2007. "Housing, Health and Happiness." Policy Research Working Paper 4214, World Bank, Washington, DC.

Center for Urban Studies. 2006. *Slums of Urban Bangladesh – Mapping and Census.*

Concerned Citizen's Commission. 2005. *Mumbai Marooned: An Enquiry into the Mumbai Floods,* 2005 Full Report. Mumbai: Conservation Action Trust, 115. http://cat.org.in/index.php/site/article/concernedcitizens-commission-an-enquiry-into-mumbais-floods-2005/.

Danilenko, Alexander, Eric Dickson, and Michael Jacobsen. 2010. *Climate Change and Urban Water Utilities: Challenges and Opportunities.* Water Working Notes. Washington, DC: World Bank.

Dar es Salaam Water Supply and Sewerage Agency (DAWASA). 2008. "Development of a Strategic Water Supply Plan for Dar es Salaam,Water Supply Improvement Plan."

Final Report Prepared by Dr. Ahmen Abdel Warith Consulting Engineers in association with DCL and Norplan, for DAWASA. Dar es Salaam, June.

Dharmavaran, Soumya, 2011, Courting Hazards: Where the Urban Poor Live, Processed.

Dilley, Maxx, Robert S. Chen, Uwe Deichmann, Art L. Lerner-Lam, and Margaret Arnold. 2005. *Natural Disaster Hotspots: A Global Risk Analysis.* Washington, DC: World Bank/ Columbia University.

Douglas, Ian, Kurshid Alam, Maryanne Maghenda, Yasmin Mcdonnell, Louise Mclean, and Jack Campbell. 2008. "Unjust Waters: Climate Change, Flooding and the Urban Poor in Africa." *Environment and Urbanization* 20 (1): 187–205.

Greenhill, R., and Wekiya, I. 2004. *Turning off the Taps: Donor Conditionality and Water Privatization in Dar es Salaam, Tanzania.* London: ActionAid.

Hallegatte, Stéphane, Nicola Ranger, Sumana Bhattacharya, Murthy Bachu, Satya Priya, K. Dhore, Farhat Rafique, P. Mathur, Nicolas Naville, Fanny Henriet, Anand Patwardhan, K. Narayanan, Subimal Ghosh, Subhankar Karmakar, Unmesh Patnaik, Abhijat Abhayankar, Sanjib Pohit, Jan Corfee-Morlot, Celine Herweijer. 2010. "Flood Risks, Climate Change Impacts and Adaptation Benefits in Mumbai." OECD Environmental Working Paper 27.

Harpham. 2009. "Urban Health in Developing Countries: What Do We Know and Where Do We Go?" *Health & Place* 15 (1): 107–116.

Harpham, Trudy, Paul Garner, and Charles Surjadi. 1990. "Planning for Child Health in a Poor Urban Environment—The Case of Jakarta, Indonesia," *Environment and Urbanization* 2 (2): 80.

Hay et al. 2006. "The Malaria Atlas Project: Developing Global Maps of Malaria Risk." *PLoS Med* 3(12).

Heinonen, Ulla. 2008. "Millennium Development Goals and Phnom Penh: Is the City on Track to Meet the Goals?" Water Resources Laboratory, Helsinki University of Technology, Finland.

Hoornweg, Daniel, Mila Freire, Marcus J. Lee, Perinaz Bhada-Tata, Belinda Yuen, 2010. *Cities and Climate Change, Responding to an Urgent Agenda.* Washington, DC: World Bank.

Instituto Brasileiro de Geografia e Estatística (IBGE). 2003. "National Survey of Domicile Samplings." Ministry of Planning, Budget and Management, Federal Government of Brazil.

Intergovernmental Panel on Climate Change (IPCC). 2007. *IPCC Fourth Assessment Report: Climate Change 2007.*

International Federation of Red Cross and Red Crescent Societies (IFRC). 2010. *World Disasters Report: Focus on Urban Risk.* Geneva: IFRC.

International Strategy for Disaster Reduction (ISDR). 2009. *Global Assessment Report on Disaster Risk Reduction.* Geneva: UN International Strategy for Disaster Reduction.

Islam, N. 2005. *Dhaka Now: Contemporary Urban Development.* Dhaka: Bangladesh Geographical Society.

Katich, Kristina, 2011, The Impacts of Climate Change and Disasters on Urban Serices, Processed.

Kreimer, Alcira, Margaret Arnold, and Anne Carlin, eds. *Building Safer Cities: The Future of Disaster Risk.* 2003. Washington, DC: World Bank.

Kunreuther, Howard, and Richard J. Roth. 1998. *Paying the Price: The Status and Role of Insurance against Natural Disasters in the United States.* Joseph Henry Press.

Lall, Somik, and Uwe Deichmann. 2009. "Density and Disasters: Economics of Urban Hazard Risk." Policy Research Working Paper 5161, World Bank, Washington, DC.

Leon, C., V. Magaña, B. Graizbord, R. González, A. Damian, and F. Estrada. 2010. "Pobreza Urbana y Cambio Climático para La Ciudad de México." Unpublished, Mayor's Task Force Study, Mexico City.

McMichael et al. 2006. "Climate Change and Human Health: Present and Future Risks." *The Lancet* 367(9513): 859–869.

Mercado S., K. Havemann, M. Sami, and H. Ueda. 2007. "Urban Poverty: An Urgent Public Health Issue." *Urban Health* 84 (1): 7–15.

Montgomery, Mark, 2009. "Urban Poverty and Health in Developing Countries." *Population Bulletin* 64 (2).

Montgomery et al. 2004. In *Cities Transformed: Demographic Change and Its Implications in the Developing World*, ed. M. Montgomery, R. Stren, B. Cohen, and H. Reed. Washington, DC: National Academies Press.

Moser, Caroline, and Andrew Felton. 2007. "Intergenerational Asset Accumulation and Poverty Reduction in Guayaquil, Ecuador, 1978-2004." In *Reducing Global Poverty: The Case for Asset Accumulation*, ed. Caroline Moser. Washington, DC: Brookings Institution Press.

Moser, Caroline, and David Satterthwaite. 2010. "Towards Pro-Poor Adaptation to Climate Change in the Urban Centres of Low- and Middle-Income Countries." In *Social Dimensions of Climate Change: Equity and Vulnerability in a Warming World*, ed. R. Mearns and A. Norton, 231–258. Washington, DC: World Bank.

Mumme and Lybecker. 2002. "Environmental Capacity in Mexico: An Assessment." In *Capacity Building in National Environmental Policy*, ed. Helmut Weidner and Martin Jänicke.

Nakagawa, Masayuki, Makoto Saito, and Hisaka Yamaga. 2007. "Earthquake Risk and Housing Rents: Evidence from the Tokyo Metropolitan Area." *Regional Science and Urban Economics* 37: 87–99.

Olvera, L. Diaz, D. Plat, and P. Pochet. 2002. "Transportation and Access to Urban Services in Dar es Salaam." In *Transportation*.

Penrose, K., M.C. Castro, J. Werema, and E. Ryan. 2010. "Informal Urban Settlements and Cholera Risk in Dar es Salaam, Tanzania." *PLoS Neglected Tropical Disease* 4(3).

Peritore, Patrick. 1999. *Third World Environmentalism, Case Studies from the Global South.* Gainesville, Florida: University Press of Florida.

Raleigh, Clionadh, and Lisa Jordan. 2010. "Climate Change and Migration: Emerging Patterns in the Developing World." In *Social Dimensions of Climate Change: Equity and Vulnerability in a Warming World*.

Revi. 2008. "Climate Change Risk: An Adaptation and Mitigation Agenda for Indian Cities." Environment and Urbanization 20(1): **207-229.**

Romero-Lankao, Patricia. 2007. "How Do Local Governments in Mexico City Manage Global Warming?" *Local Environment: The International Journal of Justice and Sustainability* 12: 519–535.

Satterthwaite, David. 2007. "The Urban Challenge Revisited." *Environment* 49 (9): 6–16.

Simply Green. 2009. "The Cape Prepares for Extreme Weather and Flooding." May 3. http://www.simplygreen.co.za/local-stories/latest/the-cape-prepares-for-extreme-weather-and-flooding.html.

Stephens, C. 1996. "Healthy Cities or Unhealthy Islands? The Health and Social Implications of Urban Inequality." *Environment and Urbanization.*

United Nations. 2010. *The Millennium Development Goals Report 2010.* United Nations: New York.

UN-HABITAT. 2003a. *The Challenge of Slums: Global Report on Human Settlements.* London/Sterling, VA: Earthscan Publications Ltd.

———. 2003b. "Slums of the World: The Face of Urban Poverty in the New Millennium? Monitoring the Millennium Development Goal, Target 11—World Wide Slum Dweller Estimation," Working Paper.

———. 2007. *Enhancing Urban Security and Safety.*

———. 2007. *Global Report on Human Settlements.*

———. 2008. *Harmonious Cities: State of the World's Cities 2008/9.* London/Sterling, VA: Earthscan Publications Ltd.

———. 2010. *Cities for All, Bridging the Urban Divide: State of the World's Cities, 2010/2011.*

Water and Sanitation Program. 2009. *Global Experiences on Expanding Services to the Urban Poor.*

World Bank. 2005. *Dhaka Urban Poverty Assessment.* Washington DC: World Bank.

———. 2009. *World Development Report 2010: Development and Climate Change.* Washington DC: World Bank.

———. 2010a. *Ethiopia Economic of Adaptation to Climate Change.* World Bank: Washington, DC.

———. 2010b. *Pro-Poor Adaptation to Climate Change in Urban Centers: Case Studies of Vulnerability and Resilience in Kenya and Nicaragua.* Washington, DC: World Bank.

———. 2011a. *Black Carbon and Climate Change.* Washington, DC: World Bank.

———. 2011b. *Jakarta: Urban Challenges in a Changing Climate.* Jakarta: World Bank.

World Bank and Diagonal Ltd. 2011. *Climate Change, Disaster Risk Management and the Urban Poor: São Paulo, processed.*

World Health Organization (WHO), Global Task Force on Cholera Control. 2008. *Cholera Country Profile, United Republic of Tanzania.*

Zurbrügg, Christian, 2002. "Urban Solid Waste Management in Low-Income Countries of Asia: How to Cope with the Garbage Crisis." Presented at the Scientific Committee on Problems of the Environment (SCOPE) Urban Solid Waste Management Review Session, Durban, South Africa, November.

3

Building Resilience for the Urban Poor

Key Messages

- City governments are the drivers for addressing risks, through the provision of public infrastructure, delivery of basic services, and mainstreaming climate-change adaptation and disaster-risk reduction into urban planning and management practices.
- Stakeholders will need to balance a number of difficult policy tradeoffs among risk reduction, urban development, and poverty reduction in decision making.
- Better policies for land-use planning and management will have the biggest impact on risk reduction.
- Investments in risk reduction will have the greatest impact when implemented in partnership with communities.

The challenges of improving living conditions for the urban poor through better service delivery are not new; however, the risks from climate change and increasing exposure to natural hazards accentuate the growing urgency in proactively addressing them. Despite these existing challenges, there is much accumulated experience in efforts to improve living conditions for the urban poor, yet many cities have not been able to achieve these goals largely due to the pace of urbanization, ineffective policies, resource constraints, lack of political will, and weak capacity.

This chapter underscores several recommended actions based on experience to help cities build resilience for those at greatest risk. These recommendations are rooted in the need for strong institutions for better urban planning and management, and sustainable urban policies that consider the positive and negative outcomes of the difficult decisions city officials must make.

In implementing these actions, it is city governments that are the drivers for addressing risks, by providing public infrastructure, delivering basic services, and mainstreaming climate-change adaptation and disaster-risk reduction into urban planning and management practices. Such investments will have the biggest impact when implemented in partnership with communities that have much to contribute to the process.

The recommended actions are grouped in five main areas discussed in this chapter. These include (1) assessing risk at the city and community level to inform decision making and action planning; (2) integrating climate change and disaster risk reduction policies for the poor into urban planning and management; (3) balancing policy tradeoffs among risk reduction, urban development, and poverty reduction in decision making; (4) strengthening institutional capacity to deliver basic services and reduce vulnerability to climate and disaster risk; and (5) bridging communities and local governments to work together on local solutions.

Assessing Risk at the City and Community Levels to Inform Decision Making and Action Planning

The case studies carried out as part of this report have demonstrated the importance of understanding hazards, and socioeconomic and institutional risks, for any city as an important first step to developing plans in order to adapt and reduce the risk of disaster.

Assessing Risk

A risk assessment can define the nature of risks, answer questions about the characteristics of potential hazards, and identify the vulnerabilities of communities and potential exposure to given hazards. Risk evaluation helps in prioritizing measures of risk, giving due consideration to the probability and impact of potential events, the cost-effectiveness of the measures, and resource availability.

Relevant and up-to-date information can allow all stakeholders to assess risk and make informed policy and investment decisions. Such information will affect zoning, property markets, location choices, and adaptation investments. Investing in regular data collection is necessary for monitoring changes over time and continually updating risk-reduction plans. All four of the cities in the Mayor's Task Force mentioned a lack of data for assessing risk. This has ranged from information gaps related to the location of the urban poor, socioeconomic and housing data for the poor, subsidence maps, and data on climate hazards and measurement of risk and potential losses.

Cities are approaching risk assessments in different ways, with some working on them in a holistic fashion and others carrying out sector-level assessments one at a time. Tools are being developed to help cities identify risks, initiate planning, and establish adaptation priorities. One such approach is the Urban Risk Assessment recently developed by the World Bank in partnership with Global Facility for Disaster Reduction and Recovery (GFDRR), United Nations Environmental Programme (UNEP), UN-HABITAT, and others (box 3.1). This is the approach used for the case studies carried out for this report. Note that in carrying out risk assessments, local analysis of natural hazards is not always sufficient for assessing risk given the ripple effects of network systems within cities. Impacts in one location can lead to effects that go way beyond the directly affected area. For example, a localized flood can shut down electricity in an entire city, stop all public transport systems, and completely paralyze economic activity.

Mapping informal settlements can be a first step to assessing risk for the urban poor. In a growing number of communities, the poor themselves are carrying out this work. In Cuttack, India, community-driven data gathering includes the preparation of digital maps at the city scale for city authorities with input from an NGO.[1] The work begins with residents mapping their communities with a GPS device, commenting on boundaries and characteristics (risk profile, services, etc.), which help the visiting NGO team understand the settlement. Points marked with the GPS are uploaded to Google Earth and, when aggregated into a citywide map, provide the location and boundaries of all informal settlements, as well as their risk profile.

The process of carrying out a risk assessment can be as important as the results, particularly with regard to building coalitions among stakeholders. The experiences from the Dar es Salaam, Jakarta, Mexico City, and São Paulo cases point to a few lessons outlined in box 3.2.

Action Planning

Once a risk assessment is carried out, the critical step of identifying priorities and action planning will follow. As with assessments, workbooks and tools have been (or are being) developed to assist cities in initiating planning for adaptation and risk reduction. Most of these emphasize standard planning approaches, such as building support within government departments, building a team, conducting assessments, identifying actions, and implementing and monitoring actions.

BOX 3.1

Urban Risk Assessment

The Urban Risk Assessment (URA) is a flexible approach that facilitates improved understanding of a city's risks from disasters and climate change, which has been developed by the World Bank in partnership with GFDRR, UNEP, UN-HABITAT, and others. It is a somewhat standardized cost-effective tool intended to harmonize how information is gathered and analyzed related to disaster and climate risk at the city level, and to identify areas and populations that are most vulnerable.

The URA is based on three main pillars: institutional, hazard impact, and socioeconomic assessment. For each pillar, there are three levels of assessment: primary, secondary, and tertiary. The URA allows for customization in how it is applied, depending on need, available resources, institutional capacity, available information, and time. Through a phased approach, where each assessment level is linked to progressively more complex and detailed tasks, city managers may select the appropriate series of components from each pillar that individually and collectively enhance the understanding of risk in a given city. The approach is structured to integrate both rapid onset events, such as floods or landslides, which are more typically the purview of the disaster risk- management community, and slow onset hazards, such as drought or sea level rise typically associated with a longer-term change in climate trends.

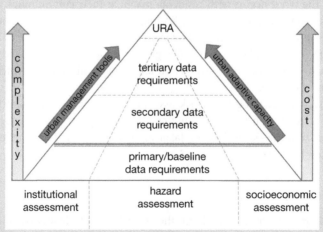

The urban risk assessment is ideally undertaken as a part of a cycle of assessing risk, developing and implementing risk-management plans, monitoring, and reviewing over a planning cycle. The URA has been used by the four cities of the Mayor's Task Force.

Source: Dickson, Baker, Hoornweg, and Tiwari. (2012).

BOX 3.2

Lessons Learned from Carrying out City-level Risk Assessments under the Mayor's Task Force

1. High-level support from the mayors and heads of key agencies was essential to giving priority and support to the work. Working-level focal points were key to ensuring accountability and getting the work done.
2. In all of the cities, an interagency working group was set up to carry out the risk assessments. This included agencies working on urban development, service provision, poverty reduction, disaster management, and climate change. In some cases, this was the first time these agencies worked together, which created synergies for a more integrated and comprehensive risk assessment and began the process for adaptation planning. However, it is unclear that these interagency working groups will be sustained without a more formal working arrangement.
3. In some of the cities, there was a big disconnect between knowledge at the institutional and at the community level. This was addressed by involving city officials in site visits to poor neighborhoods, and in two cases, involving stakeholders in the workshops. Communicating in a language that all stakeholders could understand was fundamental. In that regard, producing materials in a simple format and local language was important for communicating results. In Jakarta and Mexico City, short films have been produced for broad dissemination of key messages.
4. Across the four cities, accessing data, maps, and climate projections was problematic. Information is scattered across many different agencies, departments, organizations, and research institutions, with some reluctant to share data. Enormous effort went into collecting the information made available. To benefit from and sustain this effort, setting up a permanent institutional "home" to maintain and update this interagency information in each city would be beneficial for any future work.
5. The risk assessments were perceived as a useful framework for understanding climate change, disaster risk, and impacts on residents. The multidimensional approach to assessing hazards, and socioeconomic and institutional risks, brought together key issues in a comprehensive way. This was found, however, to be only the first step. Stakeholder workshops held in all of the cities were useful in discussing key issues, but follow-up will be needed to integrate these findings into planning for adaptation and risk reduction across city agencies.

Source: Author.

BOX 3.3

Developing Action Plans in Vietnam, New York City, and Mexico City

One of the tools developed and currently being used in three cities in Vietnam (Hanoi, Dong Hoi, and Can Tho) is the Local Resilience Action Plan (LRAP).[a] The LRAP is a planning document that helps a city to assess alternative options for adaptation and risk reduction, with economic assessment of the costs and benefits of each. It includes an inventory of planned capital investments and policy changes to address high-risk areas, gap analysis, and multistakeholder priority-setting based on comparison of alternatives in light of limited budgets and fundraising prospects. The action plan will result in a strategic set of short-term (less than 1-year), medium-term (1- to 3-year), and long-term (more than 3-year) adaptation priorities for project investment with specific costs, timelines, and responsible actors. In the case of Can Tho, the outcomes of the LRAP process are currently being integrated into local urban planning.

Stakeholders work to establish priorities, highlighting those actions that are most critical to undertake in relation to the available funding and capacity for implementation. Other factors, such as financial feasibility, political and technical complexity, social issues, and distributional and equity issues, are also considered. Once priorities are established and an action plan is developed, detailed plans for each project (ranked by priority), including objectives, cost parameters, and a plan of implementation, are prepared. When considering implementation, the city may decide to treat risks differently in different areas of the city, with the following options: (1) eliminate or avoid; (2) transfer or share (example through insurance); (3) mitigate (through structural interventions); and (4) accept and manage the risk.

New York City provides an interesting example of moving from risk assessment to action planning to implementation. In 2008 Mayor Michael Bloomberg tasked the New York City Climate Change Adaptation Task Force with developing a plan to increase the resilience of the city's critical infrastructure. The task force comprised 40 city, state, federal, and private sector infrastructure operators and regulators with the goal of identifying climate risks to the city's critical infrastructure and developing strategies to mitigate these risks.

Once the risk analysis was completed, an extensive process of identifying, developing, and prioritizing actions was carried out. The task force focused on improving current buildings, amending building design and other regulatory

(continued next page)

BOX 3.3 *continued*

codes, as well as the strategic placement of public facilities. It adopted a risk-based approach to climate action, and uses Flexible Adaptation Pathways to address the anticipated risks, compensating for the uncertainty of climate impacts (NYCPCC 2010). The task force was supported by a panel of technical experts, which was also convened by the mayor.

New York City is working on site-specific adaptation plans through a community planning process with stakeholder groups. The first two case studies worked with vulnerable waterfront communities and involved local universities and nongovernmental organizations to create a process for planning neighborhood climate adaptation. Recognizing that risk and adaptation solutions will vary based on location and resources, the goal was to produce a standardized process to use in waterfront communities throughout the city.

Mexico City's experience is also notable as the first city in Latin America to introduce a local climate action program (Mexico City's Climate Action Program [MCCAP], 2008–2012, which is part of a 15-year green plan in which Mexico City is investing US$1 billion a year, approximately 9 percent of the yearly budget). The MCCAP aims to (1) reduce CO_2 emissions by 7 million tons in the period 2008–2012 and (2) develop a Climate Change Adaptation Program for the federal district and fully begin its implementation in 2012. In implementation, the government uses various policy instruments, including regulation, economic incentives, voluntary carbon markets, education and information campaigns, and direct resources from the city budget.

The Inter-Institutional Climate Change Commission of Mexico City is in charge of coordinating and evaluating the MCCAP. This commission includes representatives from all the administrative units of the federal district. Its responsibilities are to design, encourage, and coordinate policies to mitigate the effects of climate change in Mexico City; to evaluate, approve, and disseminate related projects; to develop financial strategies that generate revenue; and to coordinate actions and policies with other programs.

A main challenge of the MCCAP has been institutional coordination. Multiple agencies are executing a series of actions with limited communication or information exchange. Further exacerbating the open exchange of information is that each agency has its own information platform. An important step to improving coordination would be to use a common interface, which all government agencies could use for data storage and use.

[a] See World Bank, (2010b).

Source: Author.

Developing comprehensive plans that incorporate climate change and disaster risk reduction can be daunting, as cities already are overburdened and struggling to achieve existing goals. That being said, for those countries that have worked on developing plans, some lessons have been learned and guidance developed. First, assessments provide important information for establishing priorities. Second, the orientation of the tools being developed demonstrates the importance of assessing natural systems and hazard risk as well as institutional capacity and the vulnerability of settlements and subpopulations. Third, assessments developed by consultants are less effective than those developed by or in cooperation with city departments and stakeholders (Carmin 2010).

Integrating Climate Change and Disaster Risk Reduction Policies for the Poor into Urban Planning and Management

Ideally any adaptation or risk-reduction plan will be integrated with urban planning and management. Policies to address climate and disaster risk have links to many sectors and thus come with important synergies that are best captured through system-wide approaches. Given the risks for the urban poor that have been highlighted in this report, integrating climate change and policies for disaster risk reduction into urban planning for upgrading or preventing slums is imperative.

Diverse cities have incorporated disaster and climate-change risk into their planning, with positive outcomes and important lessons. Among these are Boston, Cape Town, Ho Chi Minh City, London, Quito, Rotterdam, and Toronto (Birkman et al. 2010). At a minimum, these cities have identified risk-prone areas and through urban planning discouraged new construction in these areas. Similarly, Istanbul, Ho Chi Minh City, and Cape Town called for resettlement of communities in the most risk-prone areas, in addition to improved construction and regulation of low-income and informal housing. Of the more proactive approaches, both Boston and Rotterdam encouraged new methods of construction to cope with anticipated flooding, elevating buildings and creating floating communities, respectively. Several cities, including Boston, Toronto, Halifax, and Rotterdam, encouraged the use of green infrastructure to mitigate risk. The plans that featured the most comprehensive urban planning to combat climate change are the ones developed for London, New York, Quito, Halifax, and Toronto. Examples from developing countries with a focus on improving slums are almost nonexistent, which is not surprising given that few countries have citywide urban plans that fully address informal settlements let alone integrating policies to make them resilient.

Disaster Risk Reduction in Istanbul

Rebuilding after a disaster is frequently used as an opportunity to improve land use and construction quality. Following the 1999 Marmara earthquake in Turkey, the Istanbul Metropolitan Municipality prepared the Earthquake Master Plan for Istanbul in cooperation with local universities (Metropolitan Municipality of Istanbul 2003). Among many elements, the plan includes an assessment of current vulnerabilities, guidelines on the rehabilitation of existing buildings, and an outline of the urban planning issues necessary to mitigate seismic risk in Istanbul. The document created a Strategic Plan for Disaster Mitigation in Istanbul (SPDMI), with the primary goal of reducing seismic impacts and the secondary goal of improving environmental quality.

The SPDMI identified problems associated with planning laws in the Istanbul area that it would seek to improve. First, it identified the lack of mandatory regional planning, which would prevent the cohesive development at the macro level. Second, the coverage and scale of some local plans directly contradict other laws at the metropolitan scale. Additionally, disaster risk mitigation was lacking in available plans, as well as a general tolerance of illegal construction in vulnerable areas. In relation to the built environment, the SPDMI identified an abundance of bureaucratic obstacles in construction, and a lack of a coherent building code, which both encouraged illegal development and substandard construction. Estimates are that 80 percent of the buildings are occupied and potentially renovated without permits. The recommendations for these challenges encouraged the empowerment of metropolitan authorities and the regional seismic commission to assess disaster risks and prepare strategic plans through a disaster-management lens.

In relation to the physical footprint and structures within the city, the SPDMI categorized construction according to when the structures were built, who built them (including the permits required), and where these structures were located relative to infrastructure and natural hazards. The SPDMI then identified priority areas for intervention using three steps. First, a location quotient was calculated for the percentage of buildings expected to be heavily damaged (BEHD) in each district. Second, data produced by the Japan International Cooperation Agency on hazard probability, reflecting the density of each BEHD, was analyzed to calculate the standard number of units per hectare. Third, the SPDMI multiplied these values by the building and population densities to gain a clear idea of which areas would suffer the greatest economic or human losses due to an earthquake.

Using this information, the SPDMI identified the safest and most beneficial areas for development and retrofitting, and laid out three levels of plans for action. At the macro level, the need to create a national strategy on the spatial basics of social and economic growth was identified, mandating the use of regional plans. Within the regional framework, the environmental assets of the metropolitan areas were identified as serving a hazard-mitigation role. In addition, the national plan identified peripheral areas near Istanbul for resettling high-risk, high-density urban communities. At the mezzo and micro levels, the SPDMI identifies municipal planning agencies that will manage urban redevelopment, with a special focus on the low-risk land readjustment areas for urban facility placement.

Climate Change Adaptation in London

The Greater London Authority released the draft London Climate Change Adaptation Strategy in 2010, with the key actions of improving management of surface water flooding, developing an urban greening program, and retrofitting 1.2 million homes for more efficient water and energy use by 2015 (Greater London Authority 2010). To reduce flood risks in London, the strategy calls for mapping current flood areas and using climate projections to understand how climate change could increase the size of flood-prone areas in the future. In addition, the plan aims to increase green spaces, constructing wetlands, and to use sustainable urban drainage systems in the city to mitigate flooding. To counteract the effect of urban heat islands and heat waves, the strategy encourages planting trees and creating green spaces to provide shade. Also, the vegetation will provide insulation during winter. The strategy also calls for all new development to use passive-cooling rather than mechanical-cooling systems. Spatial planning, using the projected flood maps, will determine where development should not occur, and where existing structures should be removed. The strategy recognizes that development pressures may necessitate the development of flood-prone areas; however, the Greater London Authority and London boroughs will use planning to reduce flood risk.

Quito Climate Change Strategy

In Quito, Ecuador, the city has used its ecological footprint as a tool to plan for water resources and natural-hazard risks of the city (City of Quito 2010). Through population growth and decreased precipitation, the ecosystem of Quito is already suffering from water scarcity. This is expected to get worse as higher temperatures begin to affect the mountain glaciers, which provide the city with water. Currently, the city has prepared vegetation maps, climate and forest-fire maps, and watershed models, as well as having analyzed the socioeconomic demographics of the city. The city has already begun to relocate families living in high-risk areas and to integrate climate impacts into sustainable plans for land use, including slope and hillside management. Upcoming activities include analysis of vulnerability for all sectors, analysis of land use and land-use changes, and creation of an information system on climate change that includes a virtual platform on forest fires' risk management. In relation to green space, the city also plans to create ecological corridors and to explore REDD+ afforestation as a potential adaptation mechanism with financial benefits.

Mainstreaming Climate Change in Halifax

The Halifax Region Municipality (HRM) collaborated with the Canadian Sustainable Environment Management Office and ClimAdapt, a network of regional private-sector companies with climate-adaptation expertise, to produce the Climate SMART (Sustainable Mitigation and Adaptation Risk Toolkit) series. Climate SMART includes documents aimed at mainstreaming concerns about climate change into municipal planning and decision making. Among these documents, there is a *Climate Change Risk Management Strategy for HRM*, as well as a *Developer's Risk Management Guide*. These two documents guide both the public and private sector in concerns about physical development through a risk-management approach to prevent, tolerate, and share risk in the built environment. Both reports encourage the use of natural ecosystem responses to climate concerns. In relation to coastal and storm-related flooding, the *Climate Change Risk Management Strategy for HRM* encourages the use of LIDAR (light detection and ranging) technology to establish precise elevation for coastal-inundation models, improved urban-design criteria for infrastructure, and urban greening (Halifax Regional Municipality 2007b).

The city has established new precipitation return periods for use in municipal physical planning to reflect the expected increase in storm intensity and frequency. This information is being used to analyze current land use, zoning, and settlement patterns. For the private sector, the *Developer's Risk Management Guide* encourages four strategies to deal with the effects of climate change (Halifax Regional Municipality 2007a). First, the strategy calls for prevention, toleration, and sharing of loss through the use of natural systems (in the form of green belts) and proactive planning to mitigate precipitation and heat affects. Second, it calls for the change of land use to accommodate and possibly take advantage of expected climate changes. Third, the strategy calls for relocation of planned development to areas expected to be less vulnerable to climate. Finally, the plan encourages restoration and retrofitting of developments following damage or climactic change.

Toronto's Wet Weather Flow Master Plan

Much like Halifax, Toronto officials expect climate change to bring heat waves and intense precipitation. In recent years, Toronto has experienced a record number of days with average temperatures over 30°C, leading the city to issue 18 extreme heat alerts (as of 2008) (Toronto Environmental Office 2008). In addition to rec-ommending future adaptation actions, the Toronto plan listed several ongoing programs that are currently helping the city adjust to risks and make it more sustainable. Toronto has established a 25-year Wet Weather Flow Master Plan, designed to reduce flooding and impacts on area streams due to severe precipita-tion. This plan encourages the use of permeable paving and rain barrels to reduce runoff. The city is currently studying the tree canopy and working to double the urban tree cover, including by greening surface parking lots in order to increase shade and reduce heat and runoff. In addition, the city is providing tax incentives to encourage the greening or use of reflective paint on area roofs. Finally, Toronto is engaging local neighborhoods in the "Live Green Toronto" project. As in New York, they are using feedback from local communities to inform land-use policy and greening initiatives.

Jakarta Risk Planning

Jakarta's plan for 2010–2030 calls for incorporating risk reduction into long-term spatial planning for the city. Such approaches include restoring mangrove forests, improving public facilities and mass transit, refining building and environmental regulations that consider hazard risk, redesigning technology and engineering in disaster areas, and improving provision of open space for anticipated increases in intense rainfall. The city has also established a dedicated body for disaster-risk reduction in 2010, which is intended to help with planning and mainstreaming at the neighborhood level. A Kelurahan Empowerment Initiative is under way in five neighborhoods to develop Local Resilience Action Plans (LRAP) with local and community leaders in Jakarta.[2]

Green Infrastructure and Ecological Services to Reduce Risk

In several examples above, green infrastructure and ecological services are being used to mitigate flood and heat risks as part of adaptation planning. There is a growing recognition that natural drainage systems are the most effective at mitigating flood risk, rather than passing the risk to communities downstream. The United Kingdom Climate Impacts Programme has projects that aim to improve knowledge on climate impacts, including the urban-focused Adap-tation Strategies for Climate Change in the Urban Environment (ASCCUE). ASCCUE explores options for climate adaptation through urban-design and strategic planning, and the potential of urban green space in flood and heat mitigation (Gill et al. 2007). Incorporating land cover, sustainable urban drain-age techniques, and green roofs, the ASCCUE explored the potential impacts of green installations in Manchester. The sheeting of water over buildings and paved surfaces prevents the rain from entering the ground, thereby interrupting the local hydrological cycle.

The Manchester study found that green roofs reduced the total runoff by 18 millimeters for anywhere between 0.1 and 1.0 percent, depending on the building type covered. While this percentage may seem small, at the urban scale, the runoff reduction could have a significant impact. Aiming to counteract the effects of urban heat islands, green land cover in high-density residential areas and the town center were found to maintain maximum surface temperatures at or below the 1961–1990 baseline for the next 70 years. This encouraging estimate demonstrates the huge impact and importance of urban greening. Finally, the Manchester study recognized that storage will be an important way to respond to extra precipitation, and explored options such as point infiltration, swales, and retention ponds in order to use the water during droughts. Public parks and the restoration of rivers are other options being practiced in various urban sites where urban planners and water managers are recognizing that the previous practices of encroaching upon and enclosing urban water ways are exacerbating flash flooding downstream.

While one of the earliest recognized successes may be Curitiba, Brazil, there are a handful of newer cases in Spain, the Philippines, Chile, and Korea. In Barcelona, the flash-flood prone Besos River was restored to a meandering low-flow channel within a wider floodway of constructed wetlands (Martin-Vide 2001). Intense urbanization in the 1960s had led to the encroachment of 300,000 poor residents into the original Besos floodplain. Planning for river restoration began in the mid-1990s in an effort to improve the environmental quality of the city, control floods, and provide a green recreation space for the impacted municipalities. The Marikina River in Marikina City, the Philippines, is another example; uncontrolled encroachment and the unregulated disposal of waste had created a festering waterway in the center of the city (Yu and Sajor 2008). Begun in 1993, the Save the Marikina River program operated over more than a decade, removing informal settlements, reducing dumping, and establishing a recreational park around the river for flood control. While complicated, the removal and relocation of informal settlements proved justified, and 10 years later, the affected communities were satisfied with their safer houses and improved service provision.

Currently under construction, Parque La Aguada in Santiago, Chile, restores the city's main ecological corridor in an effort to revitalize an abandoned and neglected industrial area (Allard and Rojas 2010). Focused around the Zanjón de la Aguada, a seasonable stream, the flood park will cover 60 hectares of river bank, providing recreational areas during the dry season. As part of the Santiago Inner Ring Initiative, the Aguada Flood Park will "daylight" a 4-kilometer stretch of the stream, which is no longer able to handle the high-intensity flows of the rainy season. In addition, the park aims to trigger economic and social development for the adjacent communities. Similarly, the 2005 Cheonggye-cheon Restoration Project has created a 6-kilometer public recreation space centered on a seasonal stream in the central business district in Seoul, Korea.[3] During a period of rapid economic growth, the stream was transformed into a culvert to make space for transportation infrastructure. In a US$900 million effort to improve the environmental quality of Seoul, the metropolitan government removed concrete surfaces and elevated highways to release the historic stream and create a park and floodway, thereby revitalizing the adjacent neighborhoods.

Balancing Policy Tradeoffs among Risk Reduction, Urban Development, and Poverty Reduction in Decision Making

Policy decisions typically involve difficult decisions with both positive and negative outcomes that local decision makers and stakeholders must carefully weigh. Urban systems have long time scales and cannot be physically changed easily, thus decisions made now will have impacts for decades to come. This is due to (1) the long life span of urban infrastructure and buildings, which can be as much as one hundred years or more for high-value buildings, bridges, or water systems; and (2) the location decisions of infrastructure and buildings, which typically go well beyond their life span. For example, when railways reach their replacement time, they are almost always replaced at the same location. In the same way, new urban development is a somewhat irreversible choice, as it is economically and politically difficult to relocate people.

The most instrumental policy area is land-use planning and management. As cities in developing countries grow, they often expand into marginal areas such as flood plains, water catchments, and steep hillsides. Poor urban-planning and management policies exacerbate this. At the city scale, there is a need for land-use planning to consider flood, seismic, and other hazard zones when determining where new development should be permitted. Efficient transport systems can increase land supply in new areas by enabling access and mobility, thus reducing incentives to develop in vulnerable locations. Preventing building and settlements in high-risk areas can save lives and prevent destruction. A framework for regularizing land tenure, including partial or incremental solutions, can spawn investments and encourage improvements in infrastructure. Proactive policies aimed at preventing new slums, which may involve changes in the legal and regulatory framework and draw on the lessons of past experiences with sites and services projects, can help to curtail the rapid growth of new slums on vulnerable lands. In some cases, governments and municipalities would acquire land for block-level infrastructure rights of way around the peripheries of rapidly growing cities.

Such policies are, however, controversial. The high demand for land and resources, and the influence that private land speculators and developers often have, can reduce the effectiveness of formal policy and planning practices (Birkmann et al. 2010). In megacities where land use plans do exist, they are rarely coordinated across jurisdictions or levels of government. Even within a city, responsibilities for land and associated services may be scattered among several entities, hindering coordination of land management.

Policy Tradeoffs

In identifying policy choices and actions that cities can consider when addressing climate change, disaster risk, and the urban poor, it is important to understand the positive co-benefits as well as possible negative consequences of each. From an operational perspective, governments must make these policy choices in the context of broader priorities, which include quality of life for city residents, economic competitiveness and attractiveness for investors, other environmental goals such as greenhouse gas emissions and protection of natural areas, public health, and social concerns such as equity and social capital. Key policies and actions in five areas aimed at reducing risk for the urban poor are highlighted below, with the positive co-benefits and possible negative consequences of each summarized in table 3.1.

The first policy area involves the tradeoffs between protection for many areas against extensive risk versus protection for few areas against intensive risk. Some investments such as basic services will have more immediate welfare and economic gains, but this may mean delaying other investments such as drainage or levees that will increase resilience to large shocks in the longer term. There are co-benefits for some policy choices, such as planning regulations for land use where the policy outcomes will have positive impacts on reducing both extensive and intensive risk.

Second are the complex tradeoffs between investing in upgrading at-risk informal settlements versus relocating populations to safer areas. Studies show that slum dwellers gain more from slum upgrading than from relocation (World Bank 2006). It is unclear, however, whether these analyses consider natural risks, including extreme events. In higher-risk locations, providing additional services (energy, housing, water, drainage, and sanitation) may increase exposure through attracting more inhabitants and increasing the value of the assets at risk. Institutional changes (for example, secure land tenure) may lead inhabitants to invest in their dwellings and related contents, increasing assets at risk and losses in case of disaster.

In balancing these tradeoffs, a policy response is to define an acceptable risk level via a political process with as much local participation as possible. Below

TABLE 3.1
Consequences of Risk-Reduction Policies and Actions in Urban Areas

Risk reduction policy	Actions	Positive Co-benefits	Potential negative consequences
1. Protection for many areas against extensive risk (versus few areas against intensive risk)	Investments in basic services such as water, sanitation, waste, drainage, and transport in poor areas Investments in early-warning systems and insurance Regulations to mitigate increases in exposure through land-use planning, zoning, and building norms Delay large, costly investments against extreme events, such as drainage, levees, embankments, urban transport, and buildings	Large quality-of-life benefits from improved basic services Most cost-effective, given that most risks for urban poor are extensive Improvements in city economy from increases in productivity and competitiveness Reduction in overall risk from frequent events Reductions in local air and water pollution Large health co-benefits Improvements in social equity from pro-poor investments	Increase in vulnerability to most extreme events Increase in population and asset risk
2. In situ upgrading in at-risk informal settlements (versus relocation to safer areas)	Investments in basic services in at-risk informal settlements Avoid more costly investments in dykes and drainage systems Avoid relocation to new areas (could be cost-neutral)	Similar benefits as listed in 1 Residents may benefit from location choice close to jobs and services Avoid new urbanization, and reduce urban sprawl and destruction of preserved areas Avoid negative social impacts of relocation programs (loss of jobs, social networks, culture)	Investments may further attract people to high-risk areas and increase population and assets at risk Increase in vulnerability to extreme events Poor population investments made at risk of extreme weather; risk of poverty trap if disasters are too frequent

3. Zoning to prevent occupation of at-risk areas	Regulations to prevent development, investments, and housing in at-risk areas	Reduction in overall risk and potential losses Decrease in population and assets at risk (that is, smaller likelihood of large-scale disasters with significant effects) Avoid negative health effects from occupying unsafe or polluted land Protect mainly poorest households, which generally occupy the most at-risk areas	Decrease in overall available land, increase in land pressure, and general increase in housing and office-space prices in the city Possible acceleration of urban sprawl; soil consumption and water-proofing; loss in natural areas and biodiversity; competition with agriculture May increase travel distances in city and commuting times Environmental concerns from additional mobility needs and energy consumption Perverse incentive of attracting illegal settlements in no-building zones
4. Develop new, less risky land with efficient transport	Invest in urban infrastructure and basic services in new areas Invest in new transportation networks that are efficient and affordable (train, metro, dedicated bus line, highways)	Create new urban area with provision of basic services and high accessibility Increase in available land, reduction in land pressure, and general reduction in housing prices in city; development and competitiveness benefits Reduced pressure to urbanize at-risk areas (flood, landslide, subsidence) in city centers; reduction in overall risk and average losses Avoid undesired development in natural areas and ecosystem losses Improve access to adequate housing and basic services; poverty reduction benefits	Increased car use, energy consumption, local and noise pollution and congestion, particularly if based on individual-vehicle transport Environmental concerns from additional energy consumption High cost of new infrastructure (transport and other services) Accelerated urban sprawl, with higher cost to provide public services; possible higher property taxes Additional soil water-proofing, increased runoff, and possible increase in flood risks Accelerated urban sprawl; loss in natural areas and biodiversity; competition with agriculture Risk for poor to be relocated, causing social segregation

(continued next page)

Table 3.1 *continued*

Risk reduction policy	Actions	Positive Co-benefits	Potential negative consequences
5. Promote dense urbanization	Containment policies that determine where growth can and cannot happen	Shift to public transport, reducing noise and traffic Lower cost of providing public services (water and sanitation, electricity, education, health) Gain in competitiveness through reduced energy expenditures and lower taxes Higher-density zoning to avoid development in at-risk areas Reduce mobility needs and energy consumption Reduced urban sprawl and protected natural areas; increased competition with agriculture Improved social equity through reducing segregation	Reduced access to housing, dwelling size Reduction in available land for construction, increase in construction costs, increase in housing prices in city; possible reduction in competitiveness Potentially larger urban heat island and larger vulnerability to heat waves Possible increase in natural hazard risk if containment land-use plans do not control for additional density in flood-prone or landslide areas

Source: Adapted from Bigio and Hallegatte, 2011.

such risk level, slum upgrading is considered an appropriate approach. Beyond this risk level, population relocation is preferable. Alternatively, higher levels of risk can be reduced with more costly investments that protect the site against systemic risks, such as dykes and drainage systems, but in this case the overall costs of in situ upgrading may go beyond the costs of relocation.

Third are zoning regulations that can be used to prevent development and housing in high-risk areas. Zoning regulations, however, also involve tradeoffs. Depending on how large the areas in a city are at risk, such regulations will reduce the overall land available, raising prices and thus making it most difficult for low-income residents. Another potential issue is that even if zoning regulations are in place, it is difficult to enforce them. As with other policy choices, it is necessary to define an acceptable risk level through consultation with local participation.

The fourth policy area is the development of new land with efficient and affordable transportation and local services. The location of transport infrastructure, its nature (public and private), and transport pricing have enormous impacts on city structure and characteristics, particularly on housing prices and access to jobs and services. The concentration of poverty on marginal land in, or close to, city centers is mainly driven by proximity to jobs and services, particularly in the absence of transport systems. Investing in affordable transport can open up new areas on safe land and reduce land prices, improving overall housing options. Possible negative outcomes of such policies, if not well managed through urban planning, can result in urban sprawl.

Fifth are policies aimed at promoting dense urbanization through containment. Such policies determine where growth can and cannot happen in a city and can reduce environmental concerns through reduced mobility needs and energy consumption for transportation, land consumption, and risk similar to zoning regulations. However, these policies also reduce the amount of available land, increasing land pressure and prices, making it more difficult for poor households to access housing, and increasing incentives to settle in at-risk areas.

Incorporating Policy Tradeoffs and Uncertainty in Decision Making

Decisions and investments in public-service provision, disaster risk reduction, and adaptation to climate change will have consequences for many decades, given the longevity of many infrastructure investments. Yet these decisions are particularly sensitive to changes in climate conditions, where there is much uncertainty. This makes decision making particularly complex and has invoked some new approaches to decision making.

Climate Sensitivity and Uncertainty

Most buildings are supposed to last up to one hundred years and will have to cope in 2100 with climate conditions that, according to most climate models, will be radically different from current ones. When designing a building, architects and engineers thus have to be aware of and account for expected future changes. Taking the example of Paris, many climate models project that the climate conditions in 2070, in the absence of ambitious mitigation policies, will be comparable to those found today in the south of Spain. Obviously, buildings are designed differently in Paris and in the south of Spain, and this should be taken into account. Building norms applied today in France to reduce heating energy consumption in winter may even become counter-productive if they do not take into account the risk of high energy consumption from air conditioning in summer a few decades from now. Similarly, when planning for adaptation in water, adjustments must be made for changes in water trends (rainfall, runoff, etc.) (Milly et al. 2008). With more than US$500 billion invested every year in this sector, a strong case is made for incorporating the climate model to optimize strategies, policies, and efficiency.

With regard to risk management, Nicholls et al. (2007) demonstrate that, in 2070, up to 140 million people and US$35,000 billion of assets could depend on flood protection in large port cities around the world because of the combined effect of population growth, urbanization, economic growth, and rise in sea level. Previous coastal-defense projects (for example, the Thames River barrier) have, however, shown that implementing coastal protection infrastructure typically has a lead-time of 30 years or more. Also, urbanization plans are very able to influence flooding risk, but they can do so only over many decades. This inertia suggests that action must begin today to protect coastal cities and to manage flood risks from impacts expected by mid-century, which may be affected by rise in sea level, extreme weather, and other manifestations of climate change.

Climate change and sea-level rise are also concerns that need to be accounted for in providing basic services. Sanitation and drainage systems need to take into account how precipitation patterns will change in the future. The provision of drinking water should be based on sources that will remain viable in the future; thus it is important to analyze how demands from various water usages, including irrigated agriculture, will change over time, ensuring that the proposed investments are robust over the long term.

A particular challenge is the dramatic increase in uncertainty of future climate conditions. In the past, the climate parameters pertinent to most activities could be observed and measured, and with specific objectives, statistical analyses and optimization algorithms were able to produce "best" designs as a function of known climate conditions (for example, dike heights as a function of the return time of certain storm surges, or building characteristics as a function of typical

TABLE 3.2
Sectors for which Climate Change Should Be Incorporated Due to Time Scale or Sensitivity to Climate Conditions

Sector	Time scale (years)	Sensitivity
Water infrastructures (e.g., dams, reservoirs)	30–200	+++
Land-use planning (e.g., in flood plain or coastal areas)	>100	+++
Coastline and flood defenses (e.g., dikes, sea walls)	>50	+++
Building and housing (e.g., insulation, windows)	30–150	++
Transportation infrastructure (e.g., port, bridges)	30–200	+
Urbanism (e.g., urban density, parks)	>100	+
Energy production (e.g., nuclear plants)	20–70	+

Source: Hallegatte (2009).

Note: Sensitivity is estimated empirically. +++ = high sensitivity; ++ = medium sensitivity; + = low sensitivity.

temperature levels). In the future, however, substantial climate uncertainty makes such methods more difficult. As an illustration of this uncertainty, there is still disagreement among climate models about whether precipitation in West Africa will increase or decrease in response to global warming. It means that while water management needs to take into account future changes in climate conditions, it is not known if this change will be an increase of a decrease in rainfall. Clearly, this uncertainty represents an important obstacle to the design of water management.

More generally, climate uncertainty can be an obstacle for all investment decisions that are climate sensitive and have a long lifetime. This problem is particularly acute for water, land-use planning, and coastline and flood defenses (Hallegatte 2009).

Decision-Making Tools

Some of the existing decision-making tools, such as cost-benefit and cost-effectiveness analysis, may not be viable with large uncertainty. These methods require a quantified assessment of the likelihoods of the different possible outcomes, which in most cases cannot be estimated.

Robust Decision Making

Given this uncertainty, new tools for decision making are emerging that are based on the concept that, over the long term, the priority is to avoid irreversible choices that can lock in undesirable or even unacceptable situations. For instance, developing low-lying coastal areas with the current uncertainty on future sea-level rise is dangerous, as it can lead to a difficult choice between expensive protection and retreat in the future. If such a situation is considered undesirable or unacceptable, and while the uncertainty is so large, it is preferable to develop only the areas that are not too vulnerable in case pessimistic scenarios in the rise of sea level are confirmed. This is the basic concept of robust decision making. While traditional decision making seeks to predict the future and pick the best option for that particular future, robust decision making will instead identify the choices that are robust over many alternative views of the future.

To help with the prioritization and decision making, robust, multicriteria decision-making tools can be useful. This approach can be used to ensure that any given policy has no unacceptable consequences for stakeholders. The approach helps build policy mixes that are robust in most possible future scenarios. The application of robust decision-making strategies can be lengthy, requiring the involvement of many stakeholders, including city officials, multiple agencies, private developers, and community residents. Such decision making, however, can help stakeholders assess their own choices toward higher resilience and lower vulnerability.

BOX 3.4

Decision Making for Adaptation Planning in Chicago

The City of Chicago offers an example of a how a systematic process can aid in decision making. Initially the likelihood of different types of impacts affecting the city were identified and then narrowed down to issues with the highest risk. In Chicago, the focus was on extreme heat, extreme precipitation, damage to infrastructure, and degradation of ecosystems. A list of options for each issue that could be pursued was then identified. The initial list of 150 adaptation activities was then narrowed down by evaluating the benefits and costs, as well as the time horizon and barriers that were anticipated to be encountered during implementation. Based on this analysis, activities that were expected to prevent impacts in a short time span and would not be inhibited by many barriers were classified as "must do." In contrast, those that would have benefits, but were likely to encounter numerous barriers or a long time horizon were classified as "investigate further," while others that were costly were labeled as "watch." By analyzing options in this way, the City of Chicago was able to identify a bounded set of adaptation activities for each of the four focal areas (Coffee et al. 2010). In addition, they evaluated the priorities and capacities of individual departments so that implementation would be realistic (Parzen, 2009).

One approach, which focuses on avoiding irreversible choices that can lead to large regrets, bases decisions on scenario analysis (for example, Schwartz 1996). In theory this approach results in the most robust solution, that which is most insensitive to future climate conditions (Lempert et al. 2006; Lempert and Collins 2007). These methods are consistent with those commonly used to manage exchange-rate risks, energy-cost uncertainty, research and development outcomes, and many other situations that cannot be forecast with certainty. Such robust decision-making methods have already been applied in much long-term planning, including water management in California (Groves and Lempert 2007;

BOX 3.5

Robust Decision Making for Road Design in a Flood-Prone Area

An illustration of robust decision making applies to a local government assessment of designing a road in a flood-prone area. The key challenge is a lack of information on the future intensity and frequency of flooding. In addition, basic data is unavailable on the future climate and patterns of flooding in the region, the volume for future traffic, and future land-use patterns. All this uncertainty could threaten long-term performance of the road.

In such a scenario, robust decision making in the choice of road design could be used by the government through sequentially doing the following:

- Choosing the candidate strategy or the basic "business as usual" design, as well as the performance objective of the road.
- Identifying all the future combinations of conditions that might cause the road to fail to meet its objective (for example, X rise in sea level, Y increase in rainfall, and Z traffic volume will cause the road's level of service to be unacceptable).
- Identifying design options that address the unacceptable possibility of suspending service on the road.
- Finally, selecting the design option that performs well compared to the alternatives over a wide range of futures.

In this case, robust decision making has helped the government identify design options to reduce unacceptable vulnerability and understand tradeoffs among those options.

Source: Lempert and Kalra (2011).

Groves et al. 2007). For most decision makers, the novelty will be to apply these methods to climate conditions. This requires users of climate information to collaborate more closely with climate scientists and to adapt their decision-making methods to climate change.

Strengthening Institutional Capacity to Deliver Basic Services and Reduce Vulnerability to Climate and Disaster Risk

Cities have a range of institutional structures and capacity for dealing with service delivery, disasters, and climate change. The institutions typically involved with the response and management of disasters include departments of public health, security, police, fire, and those that serve vulnerable populations like the elderly and young. Plans often provide a structure through which departments communicate with one another, and many cities prepare by running simulations.

The institutional arrangements to cope with and plan for climate change, particularly adaptation, are somewhat less developed, as it is a relatively new field of policy and planning. Furthermore, the institutional structures for delivering services to the urban poor have the longest history, yet in many cities they are weak. A major constraint has been capacity as local governments struggle with inadequate staffing, technical skills, or financial resources. This is further complicated in many places by the lack of legal tenure, which means that governments are reluctant or unable to invest in services in informal areas.

In all four of the cities studied, the institutional arrangements for urban planning, climate change, disaster risk, and poverty are fairly complex. Jakarta's city government is highly decentralized, with 267 *lurah* or urban ward leaders.[4] The Mexico City Metropolitan Area comprises the 16 boroughs of Mexico City and 34 municipalities of the State of Mexico, for a total of 50 geopolitical and administrative units that must coordinate among themselves. In the São Paulo Metropolitan Area there are 39 municipalities, while the City of São Paulo is divided into 31 administrative divisions (subprefectures) and 96 districts. Dar es Salaam probably has the simplest structure, in part reflecting the smaller size. The city is managed by the Dar es Salaam City Council (DCC) and the Municipal Councils of Temeke, Kinondoni, and Ilala, which are under the Ministry of Regional Administration and Local Government. Each municipality has individual technical and administrative departments. Coordination across municipalities and with national agencies is limited.

Other cities have areas that lack strong formal institutions, where informal institutions such as NGOs and CBOs play an important role in responding to the needs of the urban poor. In many cities these informal institutions address gaps in service delivery, and at times are the first responders in disaster events. In Mombasa, local religious organizations are recognized as key players when extreme events occur and facilitate evacuation, emergency relief assistance, and provisional shelter. The earthquake in Haiti in 2010 saw the emergence of volunteer technology communities, who mobilized through the Global Earth Observation Catastrophe Assessment Network (GEO-CAN) to develop a comprehensive and rigorous damage analysis to assist with relief and recovery efforts (GFDRR 2011).

Learning from Successful Examples

There are numerous examples where progress has been made in addressing risks for the poor through programs to upgrade slums, improvements to service delivery in slums, emergency warning systems, knowledge generation, and other initiatives. Such efforts were implemented with strong political commitment, community participation, and institutional support.

In Dar es Salaam, the local government has successfully implemented the *Community Infrastructure Upgrading Program*, which has targeted unplanned areas in three municipalities (World Bank 2011b). Through a structured process, communities have prioritized technical improvements in roads, drains, and public toilets. The new community infrastructure allows safe access to homes on a regular and emergency basis, and improved drainage dramatically decreases flooding in the affected areas.

A relatively well-known effort in Pakistan, through the Orangi Pilot Project Research and Training Institute, supports local governments as well as slum dwellers in building capacity for the planning, implementation, and financing of basic sanitation—at far lower costs than government-built infrastructure. These efforts have brought major benefits to large sections of the urban poor in more than 300 communities in Karachi.

In São Paulo, the "Summer Rainfall Operation" is a city plan that brings together the Housing, Transport, Urban Infrastructure, Social Assistance, and Sub-districts Coordination Secretariats led by the Emergency Management Agency, which targets risk areas during the summer when heavy rainfall is common. When heavy rainfall approaches, the Emergency Management Agency issues an alarm to the various agencies, which respond through prevention (evacuating residents in high-risk areas), search and rescue in flood or landslide zones, and restoration of affected areas. Water and sanitation authorities repair water pipes, while social assistants verify housing conditions and if necessary direct people to temporary shelters while the Housing Secretariat arranges for "rent allowance" or allocates housing for the needy. Health authorities disseminate public information on how to avoid endemic diseases spread by water and of symptoms requiring medical attention.

Mexico City has been proactive in initiating climate-change programs and is the first in Latin America to launch a local climate-change strategy. Furthermore, the city has established the distinguished Virtual Center on Climate Change for Mexico City to contribute to increased and improved knowledge on the impact of climate change in the Metropolitan Area, as well as to the formulation and implementation of public policies.

A number of institutions have developed approaches to monitor changes and disseminate information about changes in weather patterns and the natural environment as part of ongoing risk assessment. These measures often are established through monitoring stations sponsored by national governments. Early-warning systems are critical to ensuring awareness of natural hazards and to promoting timely response, including evacuation. Several approaches have been used, involving the urban poor in the Caribbean, Africa, and Southeast Asia, such as local courses, tone alert radio, emergency alert system, presentations and briefings, and reverse 911 (Pulwarty 2007; Van Aalst, Cannon, and Burton 2008). Low-tech measures such as brochures, public service announcements, and direct contact with local residents also are important to fostering awareness and response in poor communities (National Research Council 2007). For example, heat-warning systems used to alert urban populations of extreme heat generally include a communications component that depends on public service announcements in urban areas (Health Canada 2010).

Safety nets can be critical in building resilience for the urban poor, as well as in post-disaster recovery. Safety nets have traditionally focused on the chronic poor through targeted cash transfers (both conditional and unconditional), workfare programs, and in-kind transfers. In Bangladesh, under the National Disaster Management Prevention Strategy, an early-warning system triggered safety nets in response to Cyclone Sidr in 2007 (Pelham, Clay, and Braunholz 2011). The program began distributing cash, rice, and house-building grants even before the main impacts of the cyclone were felt.

Programs can be designed to also assist at-risk households and communities to help people cope with hazards. For example, social funds, community-driven development, and slum upgrading can be designed to support adaptation and risk reduction in low-income communities by scaling up their work on actions most relevant for creating resilience, such as improving drainage, water supply, and sanitation, and setting up community-maintenance programs. Indonesia's National Community Empowerment Program (PNPM), which operates in all urban areas of the country, finances investments in flood prevention, water retention and storage, and slope stabilization to prevent landslides as well as building emergency evacuation routes.

Such programs have been instrumental in post-disaster recovery as well. In Indonesia, efforts were rapidly mobilized following the disasters in Aceh (2004 tsunami), Yogyakarta, and Central Java (2006 earthquake), and most recently in Central Java (2010 Mt. Merapi eruption), via community-driven development. On the very day the government says it is safe for residents to return to their neighborhoods, trained facilitators already working in the communities are available to work with beneficiaries in identifying needs, preparing community settlement plans, and allocating block grants. The key is to have programs in place before the onset of natural disasters, with flexible targeting, flexible financing, and flexible implementation arrangements.

At the institutional level, success translates to good leadership, good governance, and good management. These elements can be built through changes in incentives to promote reform and improve performance, for example, through better accountability, financial management, and coordination across agencies, with structured rewards. Other methods that have proven successful are professional certification programs for municipal staff that elevate, professionalize, and promote their development.

Capacity Building

Several programs are available to provide advice to decision makers such as city technicians and city managers, as well as key actors in civil society, on topics related to sustainable development, climate change, disaster risk, and reduction of urban poverty. These programs range in levels of engagement and development, but all have the common goal of building capacity among decision makers at the city level.

Universities and research centers equally provide an important vehicle for building capacity in developing countries through training future policy makers and practitioners, and through targeted executive training programs. Accordingly, it is useful for such institutions to partner with international researchers to ensure the transfer of current knowledge, approaches, and technologies.

Also, much capacity building can happen as cities learn from each other. Successful experiences include city and local government networks at the country, regional, and international level, training programs, and knowledge exchange through twinning and other programs that allow cities to share knowledge and information.

Bridging Communities and Local Governments to Work Together on Local Solutions

The urban poor are clearly on the front line in addressing the impacts of climate change and disaster risk. Much is already happening at the household and

TABLE 3.3
Capacity Programs Aimed at Knowledge Sharing, Education, and Training for Urban Resilience

Agency/program	Capacity building
African Centre for Cities (ACC)	Interdisciplinary research and teaching program for sustainable urbanization in Africa
C-40	Establishing activity-specific subcommittees, which include city resilience planning and focus on unique needs of port cities
International City/County Management Administration (ICMA)	Provides knowledge-based assistance in disaster mitigation and preparedness for vulnerable communities, and recovery and restoration of basic municipal services
International Institute for Environment and Development (IIED)—capacity strengthening of least developing countries for adaptation to climate change network	Experts work to strengthen organizations through publications and capacity-building workshops, mostly in Africa and South Asia, and active support for Conference of the Parties (COP) negotiations
International Strategy for Disaster Reduction (ISDR)—My City Is Getting Ready Campaign	Focuses on raising political commitment to disaster risk reduction and climate change adaptation among local governments, including high-profile media and public-awareness activities, and develops technical tools for capacity building
International Organization for Standardization	Development of ISO 31000—principles and guidelines for risk management
Local governments for sustainability (ICLEI)	Works with cities globally to conduct climate resiliency studies and develop adaptation plans
Rockefeller Foundation	Asian Cities Climate Change Resilience Network (ACCRN) helps cities to develop adaptation plans with civil society (10 cities in Vietnam, Indonesia, and Thailand)
United Cities and Local Governments/ Metropolis	UCLG represents and defends interests of local governments on world stage. In area of cities and climate change, Metropolis is working on range of projects and knowledge products
World Bank Group • Urbanization Knowledge Partnership (UKP) and Green Growth Knowledge Platform	New platforms that include provisions for peer-to-peer exchange and knowledge sharing
• World Bank Institute	Global capacity-building programs include: • E-Learning Safe and Resilient Cities Course, Cities and Climate Change • Networking • Mentoring • On-Demand Knowledge and Capacity Building

Source: Author.

community levels that local governments can draw upon (World Bank 2010a). Such actions include repairing roofs, building stronger foundations, digging trenches, clearing drainage and ditches, repairing leaks, channeling water, and planting trees. These efforts are especially important for cities that have limited capacity and resources.

At the same time, much of what is needed to reduce risk in low-income urban communities depends on the availability of infrastructure that residents cannot provide themselves. Storm and surface drainage, road and path networks, links to water networks, and health-care services require specialized skills and substantial resources that communities may not have.

Despite the obvious benefits of partnerships between local governments and communities, this does not always happen, in part due to negative perceptions particularly around policies related to informal settlements. There are, however, good examples of partnerships between community organizations and local governments in working in poor urban communities on risk reduction. An important component of these partnerships is good communication.

In the Philippines, a partnership between a grass-roots organization, the Philippines Homeless People's Federation (PHPF), and local governments has worked to secure land tenure, build or improve homes, and increasingly to design and implement strategies to reduce risk (PHPF 2010). Following the devastation caused by Typhoon Frank in 2008, the local government in the city of Iloilo worked closely with PHPF in technical working groups, mapping of high-risk areas, and identification and prioritization of communities to be given post-disaster assistance.

In one of the oldest and largest slums in Jakarta, Kampung Melayu, residents have responded to an increase in the severity and frequency of flooding by developing an early-warning flood system. Neighborhood and village heads receive SMS messages on their mobile phones from flood-gate areas upriver when the water level is getting high. They can then spread the news in the community by broadcasting from the minaret of the local mosque, so that residents can prepare for the coming inundation (see box 3.2).

One of the more complex but impressive examples is in Quelimane City, Mozambique, where local communities have partnered with the City Council and several international organizations to work on upgrading communities particularly affected by cyclical floods (City Council of Quelimane 2006; Cities Alliance 2008; Grimard 2006–2008). The city and community worked together on developing an upgrading strategy that had a special focus on water and sanitation conditions. In implementing the strategy, the City Council provided an in-kind contribution of US$100,000 by providing office space, equipment, a meeting room, technical and administrative staff, and vehicles. The community provided an in-kind contribution of US$150,000 by providing subsidized labor, conducting awareness campaigns, forming operational management teams, and reducing their plot size, or, in extreme cases, moving to another area because of improvement works. UN-HABITAT, the World Bank, the Danish International Development Agency (DANIDA), UNICEF, and WaterAid together contributed US$440,000 in cash and in-kind. Other in-kind contributions totaling US$30,000 were secured from a state water-supply institution, and from a private-sector firm that made its trucks available during weekends in exchange for paying only for fuel and the driver.

Community-based resources are integral to providing health services to the urban poor, which are important for prevention and environmental health interventions to ensure a safe and clean environment for residents and to prevent the outbreak of disease. For example, "preventive advocacy," an approach through which at-risk groups promote prevention-based messages within their communities and social networks, has been effective in decreasing risk for communicable disease (Weibel 1988). Local opinion leaders, or informal leaders who are well-connected and well-regarded in a neighborhood, often are able to effectively diffuse ideas and information more effectively than other interventions (Valente and Davis 1999). Local community groups and partnerships also play integral roles in monitoring and advocating for public health services.

With regard to environmental health interventions, some local communities use low-tech methods of monitoring pollution in order to inform policy makers of toxic releases or establish cooperative agreements with industrial facilities (O'Rourke 2002). NGOs such as Global Community Monitor train communities, particularly those that are disempowered and situated next to polluting facilities, to understand the impacts of pollution on their health and train them to monitor and document soil and air quality. Others both work with and advocate on behalf of these communities at the local and national levels, while still others use their international position and ties to provide support through advocacy and media campaigns.

Among the lessons learned from experience of partnerships between communities and local governments are that such cooperation can be facilitated through mutually recognizing the role that each group plays; improving the dialogue to dispel misunderstandings; and understanding and recognizing what is happening at the local level and forming partnerships with local organizations.

For the poor, understanding what the city can and cannot provide and what its constraints are is a first step. Strong community groups and detailed community-level information systems can be extremely effective for initiating engagement in such partnerships. For local governments, this means recognizing the contribution that the urban poor make to a city's economy and society and involving them in discussions about needs and priorities. Local participation is crucial to ensure that the approach taken suits the needs of residents,

BOX 3.6

Locally Organized Early-Warning System in Kampung Melayu in Jakarta

Kampung Melayu is one of the largest and oldest kampungs (villages) in Jakarta. It is situated along the banks of the Ciliwung River, which has been flooding with increasing intensity over the past 10 years, according to residents. The community is made up of a mix of formal and informal settlements. Some areas, notably those further from the riverbanks, comprise formal housing, while others, particularly the areas closer to the river, are less formal, characterized by more tenuous housing construction. Due to the increasing severity of the flooding, sometimes up to 4 meters of water, as often as ten times per month, people have adapted by moving to the second floor of their homes, leaving the bottom levels empty, and using the space for cottage industries and cooking only when it is dry. An early-warning flood system has been established in the

(continued next page)

BOX 3.6 *continued*

community: the Rukun Warga and Rukun Tetangga (neighborhood and village heads) receive mobile-phone SMS messages from flood-gate areas upriver in Depok when the water level is getting high. They can then spread the news in the kampung, usually by broadcasting from the minaret of the local mosque, so residents can prepare for the coming inundation. This is a powerful, locally organized example of how residents in communities are connecting through their own means to more sophisticated and established water- management technology at the regional level.

Source: World Bank (2011a).

and in ensuring quality standards. Many of the examples of local government-community organization partnerships in Africa and Asia have been initiated by federations of slum dwellers who are engaged in initiatives to upgrade slums, secure land tenure, develop new housing that low-income households can afford, and improve provision of infrastructure and services.

Notes

1. This is drawn from Livengood (2001) and from field visits to Cuttack by David Satterthwaite in June and October 2010.
2. The body is called Badan Penanggulangan Bencana Daerah (BPBD) (World Bank 2011a).
3. http://english.sisul.or.kr/grobal/cheonggye/eng/WebContent/index.html.
4. A lurah is the urban ward leader under the mayor of the city; there are more than 70,000 in Indonesia.

References

Allard, Pablo, and Jose Rojas. 2010. *The Aguada Flood-Park: Recovering a Post-Industrial Urban Stream in Santiago de Chile.* http://www.holcimfoundation.org/Portals/1/docs/F07/WK-Grn/F07-WK-Grn-.

Bigio, Anthony and Stephane Hallegatte. 2011. "Planning Policy, Synergies and Tradeoffs for Urban Risk Management, Climate Change Adaptation and Poverty Reduction," Mimeo.

Birkmann, Jörn, Matthias Garschagen, Frauke Kraas, and Nguyen Quang. 2010. "Adaptive Urban Governance: New Challenges for the Second Generation of Urban Adaptation Strategies to Climate Change." *Sustainability Science* 5: 185–206.

Carmin, JoAnn. 2010. "Variations in Urban Climate Adaptation Planning: Implications for Action." Paper presented at the International Climate Change Adaptation Conference, Gold Coast, Australia.

Carmin, JoAnn, Sabrina McCormick, Sai Balakrishnan, and Eric Chu. 2011. Institutions and Governance in a Changing Climate: Implications for Service Provision for the Urban Poor, processed.

Cities Alliance. 2008. Comments on Progress Report, Improving Water and Sanitation in Quelimane City. P101077.

City Council of Quelimane. 2006. Improving Water and Sanitation in Quelimane City, Mozambique.

City of Quito. 2010. "Estrategia Quiteña ante el cambio climatico." Dirreccion metropolitana ambiental. Quito, Municipio del Districto Metropolitano de Quito. http://www.quitoambiente.gov.ec.

Coffee, Joyce E., Julia Parzen, Mark Wagstaff, and Richard S. Lewis. 2010. "Preparing for a Changing Climate: The Chicago Climate Action Plan's Adaptation Strategy." Journal of Great Lakes Research 36: 115–117.

Dickson, Eric, Judy Baker, and Dan Hoornweg. 2012. Urban Risk Assessments: An Approach for Understanding Disaster and Climate Risk in Cities. Washington, DC: World Bank.

Gill, S.E., J.F. Handley, A.R. Ennos, and S. Pauleit. 2007. "Adapting Cities for Climate Change: The Role of Green Infrastructure." Built Environment 33 (1).

Global Facility for Disaster Reduction and Recovery (GFDRR). 2011. Volunteer Technology Communities: Open Development. GFDRR: Washington DC.

Greater London Authority. 2010. The London Climate Change Adaptation Strategy, Draft Report. London: Greater London Authority. http://www.london.gov.uk/climatechange/strategy.

Grimard, Alain. 2006–2008. Grant Progress Report, Improving Water and Sanitation in Quelimane City. P101077.

Groves, D.G., and R.J. Lempert. 2007. "A New Analytic Method for Finding Policy-Relevant Scenarios." Global Environmental Change 17: 73–85.

Groves, D.G., D. Knopman, R. Lempert, S. Berry, and L. Wainfan. 2007. Presenting Uncertainty About Climate Change to Water Resource Managers—Summary of Workshops with the Inland Empire Utilities Agency. RAND: Santa Monica, CA.

Halifax Regional Municipality (HRM). 2007a. Climate Change Risk Management Strategy for HRM. HRM: Halifax. http://www.halifax.ca/climate/.

———. 2007b. HRM Climate Smart: Climate Change: Developer's Risk Management Guide. HRM: Halifax. http://www.halifax.ca/climate/documents/DevelopersGuidetoRisk Managment.pdf.

Hallegatte, S. 2009. "Strategies to Adapt to an Uncertain Climate Change." Global Environmental Change 19: 240–247.

Health Canada. 2010. "Communicating the Health Risks of Extreme Heat Events: Toolkit for Public Health and Emergency Management Officials." Canada.

Katich, Kristina. 2011. Beyond Assessment, A Review of Global Best Practices Addressing Climate Change and Disaster Management for the Urban Poor, processed.

Lempert, R.J., and M.T. Collins. 2007. "Managing the Risk of Uncertain Thresholds Responses: Comparison of Robust, Optimum, and Precautionary Approaches." Risk Analysis 27: 1009–1026.

Lempert, R.J., D.G. Groves, S.W. Popper, and S.C. Bankes. 2006. "A General, Analytic Method for Generating Robust Strategies and Narrative Scenarios." *Management Science* 52 (4): 514–528.

Lempert, Robert J., and Nidhi Kalra. 2011. "Managing Climate Risks in Developing Countries with Robust Decision Making." In *World Resources Report*, Washington, DC: World Resources Institute.

Livengood, Avery. 2011. "Enabling Participatory Planning with GIS: A Case Study of Settlement Mapping in Cuttack, India." *Environment and Urbanization* 23 (2).

Martin-Vide, J.P. 2001. "Restoration of an Urban River in Barcelona, Spain." *Environmental Engineering and Policy* 2: 113–119.

Metropolitan Municipality of Istanbul Planning and Construction Directoriat Geotechnical and Earthquake Investigation Department. 2003. *Earthquake Masterplan for Istanbul*. http://www.ibb.gov.tr/en-US/SubSites/IstanbulEarthquake/Pages/IstanbulEarthquakeMasterPlan.aspx.

Milly, P.C.D., J. Betancourt, M. Falkenmark, R.M. Hirsch, Z.W. Kundzewicz, D.P. Lettenmaier, and R.J. Stouffer. 2008. "Climate Change: Stationarity Is Dead: Whither Water Management?" *Science* 319 (5863): 573.

National Research Council. 2007. *Tools and Methods for Estimating Populations at Risk from Natural Disasters and Complex Humanitarian Crises*. Washington, DC: National Academies Press.

New York City Panel on Climate Change (NYCPCC). 2010. *Climate Change Adaptation in New York City: Building a Risk Management Response*. Ed. C. Rosenzweig and W. Solecki. Annals of the New York Academy of Sciences, Vol. 1196. Wiley-Blackwell.

Nicholls, R.J., et al. 2007. *Ranking Port Cities with High Exposure and Vulnerability to Climate Change: Exposure Estimates*. Environment Working Paper 1. OECD.

O'Rourke, Dara. 2002. "Community-Driven Regulation: Toward an Improved Model of Environmental Regulation in Vietnam." In *Livable Cities: Urban Struggles for Livelihood and Sustainability*. Ed. Peter Evans. Berkeley: University of California Press.

Parzen, Julia. 2009. *Lessons Learned: Creating the Chicago Climate Action Plan*. Chicago: City of Chicago.

Pelham, L., E. Clay, and T. Braunholz. 2011. "Natural Disasters, What Is the Role of Safety Nets?" Social Protection Discussion Paper, World Bank, Washington, D.C.

Philippines Homeless People's Federations (PHPF). 2010. "Addressing Vulnerabilities through Support Mechanisms: HPFPI's Ground Experience in Enabling the Poor to Implement Community-rooted Interventions on Disaster Response and Risk Reduction." Background paper prepared for the 2011 *Global Assessment Report on Disaster Risk Reduction*.

Pulwarty, Roger. 2007. "Communicating Agroclimatological Information, Including Forecasts for Agricultural Decision." In *Guide to Agrometeorological Practices*. World Meterological Organization.

Satterthwaite, David. 2011. How Local Governments Work with Communities in the Delivery of Basic Services, processed.

Schwartz, P. 1996. *The Art of the Long View*. New York: Double Day.

Shah, Fatima, and Federica Ranghieri, 2012. A Workbook for Urban Resilience in the Face of Disasters, Adapting Experiences from Vietnam's Cities to other Cities World Bank, Washington, DC.

Toronto Environmental Office. 2008. *Ahead of the Storm: Preparing Toronto for Climate Change.* Toronto. http://www.toronto.ca/teo/pdf/ahead_of_the_storm.pdf.

Valente, Thomas W., and Rebecca L. Davis. 1999. "Accelerating the Diffusion of Innovations Using Opinion Leaders." *Annals of the American Academy of Political and Social Science* 566: 55–67.

Van Aalst, Maarten K., Terry Cannon, and Ian Burton. 2008. "Community Level Adaptation to Climate Change: The Potential Role of Participatory Community Risk Assessment." *Global Environmental Change: Human and Policy Dimensions* 1(18): 165–179.

Weibel, W. Wayne. 1988. *Combining Ethnographic and Epidemiologic Methods in Targeted AIDS Interventions: The Chicago Model.* Rockville, MD: National Institute on Drug Abuse.

World Bank. 2006. *Morocco, Poverty and Social Impact Analysis of the National Slum Upgrading Program.* Washington, DC: World Bank.

———. 2010a. *Pro-Poor Adaptation to Climate change in Urban Centers: Case Studies of Vulnerability and Resilience in Kenya and Nicaragua.* World Bank: Washington, DC.

———. 2011a. *Jakarta: Urban Challenges in a Changing Climate.* Jakarta: World Bank.

———. 2011b, *Urban Poverty & Climate Change in Dar es Salaam, Tanzania; A Case Study,* processed.

Yu, Carlyne Z., and Edsel E. Sajor. 2008. *Urban River Rehabilitation: A Case Study in Marikina City, Philippines.* http://www.wepa-db.net/pdf/0810forum/paper35.pdf.

4

Opening New Finance Opportunities for Cities to Address Pro-poor Adaptation and Risk Reduction

Key Messages

- Adaptation and risk reduction costs include physical investments, such as urban infrastructure and basic services in slum areas, as well as investments in information systems, safety nets, and capacity building.
- There is no common established method for estimating the costs of adaptation in a broadly comparable, standardized manner at the city level.
- The available climate funds are modest compared with the needs of developing countries; therefore these funds are mainly catalytic.
- A combination of public and private resources is needed in order to finance investments that contribute to building resilience for the poor.

The analysis of the risks for the urban poor associated with climate change and natural hazards point to significant financing needs for cities. The costs of adaptation and risk reduction include physical investments, such as urban infrastructure and basic services in slum areas, but equally important are investments in good information systems and tools for integrating climate change and disaster-risk management into urban planning, safety nets, and capacity building to help local governments better deliver services and manage risk for their residents.

Existing approaches to financing investments that contribute to building resilience are reviewed in this chapter, with an aim to identify potential opportunities for scaling up such investments. While many of the current instruments are not explicitly designed for adaptation, risk reduction, or to be pro-poor, with some program modifications, resources can be directed to address the growing needs in this intersection of climate change, disaster risk, and the urban poor.

Costing Adaptation and Risk Reduction

When reviewing potential financing needs for climate adaptation and disaster risk reduction in cities, it is important to consider that not all investments are necessarily high and some can have more direct impacts on the poor than others. Large-scale city-wide infrastructure investments such as seawalls, embankments, or levees for flood protection, or measures to make roads, ports, and power-generation facilities more resilient to extreme events, may be necessary in many cities over time, but they are expensive and will not improve conditions for those living with the current impacts of the more frequent less extreme events.

Smaller-scale investments in drainage and improvements in basic infrastructure need not be expensive, and are catalytic in building resilience for the urban poor. Programs to upgrade slums take a neighborhood approach and, in addition to local infrastructure improvements, often include social programs aimed at community development. Such programs are most effective when coupled with policies that tackle difficult issues related to land.

At the city level, there is as yet no common established method for estimating the costs of adaptation in a broadly comparable, standardized manner. Estimating the costs of adaptation is particularly difficult, for several reasons. Adaptation strategies rely on what scenario is chosen (for example, the rate of climate change), the valuation approach and indirect costs, temporal variation dependent on the discount rate, and uncertainty—all dependent on a specific location (European Environment Agency 2007).

One approach used is to assess the cost of potential damages, and then accordingly estimate costs of prevention. The recent study on *Climate Risks and Adaptation in Asian Coastal Megacities: A Synthesis Report* (World Bank 2010b) estimates that the costs from major flooding in Bangkok, Ho Chi Minh City, and Manila are expected to run into billions of dollars over the next few decades, putting the estimated costs of the additional damage from climate change in the range of 2 percent to 6 percent of regional gross domestic product (GDP).

Another example of a subnational cost estimate is the adaptation cost curve for Florida (see figure 4.1), which disaggregates adaptation measures and helps in prioritization. Activities below the cost-effective line in light gray

Figure 4.1 Adaptation Cost Curve: Florida Test Case

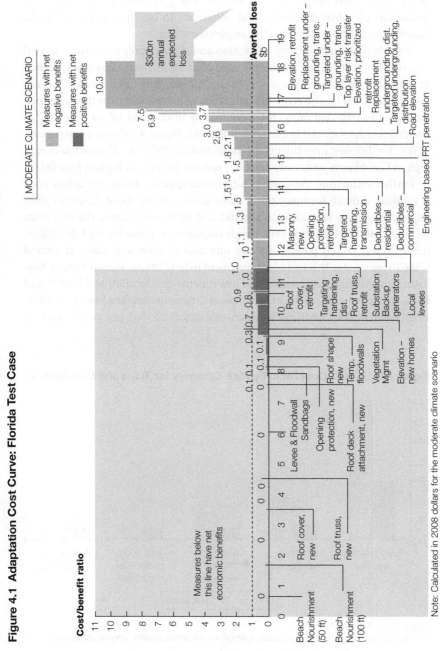

Note: Calculated in 2008 dollars for the moderate climate scenario

Source: ECA Working Group (2010).

are cost-effective. One consideration not fully reflected in this approach is the social aspect or community linkages associated with many adaptation measures. Adaptation efforts, such as early-warning systems, preservation and protection of vulnerable lands, and adherence to land-use plans, generally require "socialization" for effective implementation.

A study on climate change adaptation and disaster preparedness in coastal cities of North Africa calculates estimated costs for infrastructure works related to resilience and action plans for Tunis, Tunisia, and Casablanca, Morocco (World Bank 2011). The economic efficiency of investments was then captured through a benefit/cost ratio (B/C), comparing discounted values over time to avoided damages against implementation costs. Figure 4.2 shows a comparison of B/C for different investments for Tunis and Casablanca. Efficiency is overall high in Casablanca, with early-warning systems having the highest benefits.

Further estimating the costs of adaptation specifically for the urban poor is similarly difficult for many of the same reasons listed above. Costs for slum improvements are very location specific, and even within cities, the unit costs can vary substantially. However, rough estimates prepared by the UN Millennium Project (2005) put the average unit cost of slum upgrading at around US$670 per capita. This includes investment in land titling, access to water, sanitation and sewage treatment, social investments in education and health, and home improvements. This cost is comparable to estimates for a bundle of infrastructure services to Africa's medium-size cities, US$663 per capita, and for

Figure 4.2 Benefit-Cost Ratio by Risk Category for Tunis and Casablanca

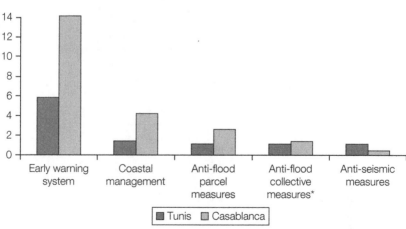

Source: World Bank (2011).
*Anti-flood collective measures include urban drainage and integrated water-management planning.

large cities, a lower cost of US$325 per capita, which reflects the importance of density in infrastructure cost (World Bank 2010a). Using these averages along with estimated slum population, one could approximate a back-of-the-envelope cost for slum improvements for a given city.

Sources of Financing for Adaptation and Risk Reduction

Financing for investments that contribute to building resilience for the poor should, in theory, be covered by a combination of public and private resources. Infrastructure investments generate benefits for the whole city and thus should be financed by public funds. Housing, home improvements, and land titling are considered private goods and thus financed by beneficiaries.

Cities in developing countries currently rely on national and local tax revenues, the private sector, public-private partnerships, and loans and concessional sources through the World Bank and other multilateral development banks to

TABLE 4.1
Current Sources of Financing and Instruments for Climate Change, Disaster Risk, and Slum Improvements

Source of financing	Instruments	Pro-poor benefits: direct (D) or indirect (I)
Government revenues and expenditures	Taxes	I
	Targeted subsidies	D
	Land-based financing	D
Multilateral development banks and donors	Investment and policy loans	D
	Grants	D
Risk-management instruments	Insurance	I
	Catastrophe bond platform (MultiCat)	I
	Partial credit and partial risk guarantees	I
	Micro-insurance	D
Carbon markets	Citywide approach	I
	City-based emissions trading systems	I
	Carbon-linked bonds	I
Private sector	Individual and community savings funds	D
	Public-Private Partnerships	D
	Microfinance	D
	Results-based financing	D

Source: Author.

finance infrastructure and social needs. Existing programs provide smaller grants or technical assistance for projects and programs at the city level. In practice, such resources are vastly insufficient to meet the service needs of the population, particularly in slums.

In countries that have carried out large efforts to upgrade slums, most of the funding has come from central governments through transfers to local government, and from donors. A typical package is financed by about 40 percent to 50 percent from the central government in the form of grants or loans to subnational localities, another 40 percent from foreign loans or grants, 5 percent from localities, up to 10 percent from beneficiaries and communities, and 3 percent from cities (World Bank, Approaches to Urban Slums, 2008). Local governments typically contribute with land.

Government Revenues and Expenditures

Revenues raised by governments through taxes, fees, and charges are a basic means of funding public expenditures, but do face constraints. Governments at all levels are usually reluctant or unable to increase taxes or reduce existing subsidies, both measures being politically unpopular. In lower-income settings, and where the formal economy is small, revenue raising can be difficult or limited. In decentralized countries, with increased functions and responsibilities for local governments, greater revenue-raising authority should be given commensurately to local governments. In the absence of such revenue authority, there would need to be significant transfers from higher levels of government.

Taxes, fees, and charges can be designed with specific policy objectives in mind and some can be designed with climate-related or pro-poor benefits, such as in the urban-land use, buildings, and transportation sectors. Taxes are a potentially powerful tool, especially property tax. Fees and charges are ideal for funding local services, where specific beneficiaries, such as the poor, can be targeted. Fees are particularly effective when they recover full costs and when fees are paid according to individual or household use, as these give residents incentives for more efficient use of resources.

Land is the most important asset for generating resources in cities. Land-based instruments include betterment levies, development land sales, value capture, sale of development rights, developer exactions, and impact fees. Most of the land-based instruments generate revenues upfront, reducing the need for borrowing. Land-based revenues have been used for infrastructure projects supported by the private sector, such as the metro in São Paulo, and the installation of public infrastructure in exchange for desert land in Cairo. When such approaches are used for slum areas, they risk increasing land values to a point that becomes unaffordable for the poor, pricing them out of the market.

In Bogota and Porte Alegre, approaches have been designed to ensure that the increases in land prices generated by government interventions are used to finance the housing program itself (Smolka2008).

Multilateral Development Banks and Donors

Government revenues alone cannot fund all actions related to climate and disaster risks, particularly the new or incremental costs associated with climate change. For this reason, and particularly in developing countries, loans and sources of concessional finance have an important role. From the city perspective, access to resources at the international level is often complicated, not least because of historical arrangements that primarily targeted national governments. Relevant financing is available through climate change, disaster risk, and urban development.

Climate Change

There have been proposals for substantial amounts of assistance for adaptation activities through external assistance, though these funds have been limited and are not explicitly targeted for cities. The available climate funds are modest compared with the needs of developing countries. Annex 1 summarizes sources of climate finance and their relevance in the urban context. An example of how the Clean Technology Fund's Investment Plan for Thailand included an urban transformation component for Bangkok is illustrated in box 4.1. More detailed information on most of the sources can be obtained from the joint UNDP/World Bank Climate Finance Options website.[1] In using such resources, one can design programs with a focus on the urban poor. For example, in the case of Bangkok, in developing the bus rapid transport system, priority can be given to ensuring access and affordability for those living in urban slums.

The progress achieved to date with climate finance demonstrates the potential catalytic role of public finance—its ability to leverage both climate and development finance for climate action. This includes the piloting of innovative approaches that combine resources to maximize synergies, explore new opportunities to expand the scope for market mechanisms, and strengthen capacity to facilitate access to and effective use of resources (World Bank 2010c). Box 4.2 describes the example of Mexico's Urban Transport Transformation Program, in which financial resources from different sources were combined to fund the entire program.

The World Bank Group offers various concessional finance instruments that national governments can channel for urban climate action, such as the International Development Association for low-income countries, and budget support in the form of Development Policy Loans (DPL). Recent climate

BOX 4.1

Bangkok's GHG Emissions and the Clean Technology Fund

The Clean Technology Fund Investment Plan for Thailand was approved in December 2009 and includes a significant component for "urban transformation" in Bangkok due to the city's unique position in the country. Thailand's energy consumption is concentrated in the Bangkok Metropolitan Region and directly contributes to the city's GHG emissions.

On average, Bangkok is less dense than other East Asian cities, and its urban form is currently locked in by its transportation system. An analysis undertaken as part of World Bank work on the international standard for city GHG emissions found that, at 10.6 tons of carbon dioxide equivalent, Bangkok's residents generate more GHG emissions per capita than the global average for city dwellers. Prior to the CTF Investment Plan, the Bangkok Metropolitan Administration (BMA) had already launched its Action Plan on Global Warming Mitigation, with a target to reduce the city's emissions by 15 percent. With the CTF, Bangkok was thus able to enhance its GHG-mitigation program based on a credible and verifiable emissions baseline. The CTF is providing $70 million for urban transformation in Bangkok, to co-finance the development of a bus rapid-transit system for the city. CTF support is also co-financing investments in energy efficiency for BMA facilities and public spaces, focusing on electrical appliances and air conditioning.

Source: World Bank.

change-related DPLs include Mexico (with transportation policy actions in Mexico City), Indonesia (with climate-change DPLs expected), and Brazil (with a focus on standalone climate-change policy in Rio de Janeiro and São Paulo). Other multilateral development banks and bilateral development agencies have similar concessional instruments.

Disaster Risk Reduction and Recovery

In funding for disaster risk reduction and recovery for the urban poor, there is more experience than with climate-adaptation programs for the urban poor. The 2010 Haiti earthquake left more than 1.5 million people homeless in a country with a 70 percent slum prevalence rate (IFRC 2010). With immense funding needs, governments and international partners pledged more than US$5 billion to rebuild Haiti soon after the earthquake, with many of the costs for urban

---

BOX 4.2

Combining Resources to Maximize Synergies: Supporting Mexico's Urban Low-Carbon Transformation

The objective of the Mexico Urban Transport Transformation Program is to change urban transport in Mexican cities to a lower-carbon growth path by improving its quality and sustainability and by upgrading related elements of the urban transport system. The project is ambitious in its design and scope and, if successful, will have a transformative impact on the urban transport sector in Mexico. It builds on a World Bank loan of $200 million and an additional Clean Technology Fund concessional loan of $200 million. These resources will be channeled through the Banco Nacional de Obras, which will then provide the participating municipalities with this loan funding. Combined with funding from the National Trust for Infrastructure, this will make up to $900 million available. The private sector and the municipalities themselves are expected to contribute up to $300 million and $150 million, respectively. An estimate of the potential for carbon revenue payments could run to approximately $50 million additional funds. Urban areas that complete and propose integrated transport plans will be eligible for funds.

Source: World Bank.

---

rebuilding in Port-au-Prince.[2] The extremity and magnitude of the Haiti earthquake make it an outlier, with funding not always as easily accessible for post-disaster urban reconstruction.

Urban Development and Slum Upgrading

Lending for urban development is on the rise at the World Bank and other multilateral development banks, though the amounts are still very low relative to the need generated in cities by rapid urbanization. Overall lending by the World Bank during the fiscal years 2000–2009 was approximately US$15 billion (World Bank 2010d). The proportion of that going to slum upgrading is approximately 20 percent, or some US$2.8 billion invested during the period through some 40 projects, with most in Sub-Saharan Africa and Latin America and the Caribbean.

Finally, there are financing and technical assistance programs designed to provide catalytic resources for cities, which one way or another relate to building resilience for the urban poor. Some of those available through the World Bank are listed in table 4.2.

TABLE 4.2
Summary of Catalytic Financing and Technical Assistance Programs at the World Bank

Financing program	Brief description
Citywlde approach to carbon finance	Enhancing cities' access to carbon finance, by aggregating emissions reductions from multiple sectors within a city, to overcome barriers such as high transaction costs and small volumes.
Carbon market development guarantee	A proposed guarantee instrument to facilitate forward contracts between buyers of carbon credits and cities (as sellers). Buyers will provide upfront payments for future delivery of carbon credits. The Bank will provide guarantees to buyers, underpinned by indemnity agreements with respective national governments. Provides early cash flow to cities given significant upfront investments needed to generate carbon credits.
PPIAF Sub-National Technical Assistance (SNTA) program	Grants to cities improve their creditworthiness and access to market-based financing, with a specific focus on publicly owned utilities. Complemented by technical assistance on private-sector potential in infrastructure.
Gobal Facility for Disaster Reduction and Recovery (GFDRR) Track II Financing for Disaster Risk Reduction Mainstreaming	Financing for national disaster risk reduction and climate change adaptation programs – this is usually channeled nationally and for GFDRR priority countries, but a window will be made available for cities (tbc).
Cities Alliance Catalytic Fund	Grant support for projects that strengthen and promote the role of cities in poverty reduction and sustainable urban development.
Global Partnership on Output-Based Aid (GPOBA) technical assistance funding	Technical assistance activities that support the design, implementation, and evaluation of output-based aid (OBA) projects. Sectors relevant to cities include water and sanitation, energy, and transport.

Source: Author.

Risk-Management Instruments

Insurance and other risk-management instruments serve an important function for cities and countries when disaster does strike. Globally, private insurers do provide coverage for a wide range of risks, but not all risks are fully covered for various reasons: insurers may be willing to cover certain risks, but the potential clients deem the premiums too expensive; or insurers may simply be unwilling to take on risks that they view as being too great. These instruments are generally for upper- and middle-income families, large businesses, and wealthy governments, but not for the urban poor. The urban poor often do not have access to insurance products, and even if they did, the transaction costs of filing and verifying claims would be very high.

The World Bank has developed a catastrophe bond issuance platform—the MultiCat Program—that allows governments to use a standard framework to buy parametric insurance on affordable terms. Box 4.3 describes the experience with MultiCat in Mexico. For implementation in cities, a Global MultiCat bond issue for cities would pool a large number of exposed areas or cities and risks, considerably reducing insurance costs through diversification. Working with such a pool, identified donors and cities would pay the insurance premiums. The unique risk-return profile associated with the pool would attract interest from a wide variety of investors. Estimates show that a three-year $250-million Global MultiCat placed in capital markets could provide $50 million in coverage against earthquakes, hurricanes, or floods to each member of a group of some 40 cities.

BOX 4.3

MultiCat Mexico

Background: The Mexican government in 2006 insured its catastrophe reserve fund, the Fondo de Desastres Naturales (FONDEN), against natural disasters with a mix of reinsurance and a catastrophe bond. The resulting contract was linked to a parametric trigger in terms of magnitude and depth of seismicity for the three-year period 2007–09. In 2008, the Mexican government spent US$1.2 billion from the reserve fund to cover rescue and rebuilding operations after Hurricanes Stan and Wilma. In collaboration with the World Bank, Mexico developed and successfully established the catastrophe bond MultiCat Mexico in 2009, with the World Bank acting as arranger.

Limitations: The coverage from FONDEN is the fraction of the coverage that is taken care of by the federal government. Mexican states are also supposed to support a fraction of the post-disaster expenses; the instrument does not give these Mexican states access to reinsurance markets. In addition, the preparation of the MultiCat Mexico was possible thanks to the technical expertise existing in the Mexican Ministry of Finance. Such technical expertise would need to be developed by any participating government either before or during the preparation of a MultiCat issue.

Source: World Bank.

MDBs can also support financing in cities by offering credit enhancements to facilitate access to broader credit by governments. With a partial credit guarantee (PCG), the guarantor shares the risk of debt service default with the lenders on a predetermined basis. The PCG programs funded by the Global Environment Facility (GEF) for energy efficiency investments typically provide for a 30 percent to 50 percent guarantee on loans made by participating financial institutions. A partial risk guarantee insures private lenders or investors/project companies (through shareholder loans) against the risk of a government (or government-owned entity) failing to perform its contractual obligation with respect to the private project.

The World Bank offers both partial credit and partial risk guarantee products. Each can be structured to meet the specific needs of the project investors and government and can require a counter-guarantee from the sovereign government (see, for example, the proposed carbon market development guarantee instrument in table 4.3). On the other hand, the Multilateral Investment Guarantee Agency of the World Bank Group offers standard cross-border risk insurance without an explicit counter-guarantee from the government.

Microfinance can also be used to finance risk reduction and recovery by the poor. Microfinance has been used to improve resilience through housing improvements and livelihood assets. In low-income communities in El Salvador, self-insurance includes encouraging family members to migrate to provide remittance income, and stockpiling building materials that can be either used or resold (World Watch Institute 2007). One study estimated that residents spend approximately 9 percent of their income on risk-reduction measures. At the community level, many contribute to community emergency funds or join religious institutions that traditionally offer post-disaster help.

In Manizales, Colombia, the city has arranged for insurance coverage to cover the urban poor through municipal tax collection. Any city resident may purchase insurance coverage for his or her property, and once 30 percent of the insurable buildings participate, the insurance coverage is extended to tax-exempted properties, including properties with a value of 25 monthly salaries or less (estimated at US$3,400) (Velasquez 2010). Despite the municipal administration collecting a handling fee of 6 percent, the insurance company has a direct contractual relationship with the individual taxpayer and bears responsibility for all the claims.

Carbon Markets and Related Instruments

Carbon finance refers to the use of the flexible mechanisms of the Kyoto Protocol, including the Clean Development Mechanism (CDM) and Joint Implementation, as well as voluntary programs outside of the United Nations Framework

TABLE 4.3
Main Instruments for Financing Climate Action in the Urban Context

		Climate-specific additional resources under the aegis of UNFCCC
Adaptation fund US$300–600 million by 2012 adaptation-fund.org	A	The overall goal of all adaptation projects and programs financed under the fund will be to support concrete adaptation activities that reduce the adverse effects of climate change facing communities, countries, and sectors. Can be implemented at the city level. Applications through national designated authorities and implementation through accredited multilateral or national implementing entities.
Global Environment Facility (GEF) US$1.35 billion over 2011–14 gefweb.org	M (A)	Largest source of grant-financed mitigation resources. Strategic Pilot on Adaptation (SPA) is a funding allocation within the GEF Trust Fund to support pilot and demonstration projects that address local adaptation needs and generate global environmental benefits in all GEF focal areas. Cities can initiate new projects or be implementation partners with national agencies.
UNFCCC GEF-administered special funds LDCF: US$223 million SCCF: US$148 million gefweb.org Green Climate Fund	A M&A	Least Developed Countries Fund (LDCF) helps to prepare and finance implementation of national adaptation programs of action (NAPAs) to address the most urgent adaptation needs in the least developed countries. Special Climate Change Fund (SCCF) supports adaptation and mitigation projects in all developing countries, with a large emphasis on adaptation. First agreed to in the Copenhagen Accord at COP-15, with the stated goal of mobilizing $100 billion annually by 2020 to address the needs of developing countries. The details of this fund are still under discussion.
		Resources from the carbon market
Size of 11 carbon funds and facilities: US$2.5billion **World Bank Carbon Partnership Facility (CPF)** US$100 million	M	Cities can access CDM funds through certified emission reduction (CER). CPF can support cities in preparing CDM projects. World Bank Treasury can support in monetizing CERs.

(continued next page)

TABLE 4.3 *continued*

		Dedicated concessional funding (ODA) from the DAC community
Climate investment funds US$6.4 billion climateinvestmentfunds.org/	M	The Clean Technology Fund (US$4.5 billion programmed for 13 investment plans) finances scaled-up demonstration, deployment, and transfer of low-carbon technologies. Major urban mitigation (transport and energy) investments in Bangkok and Mexico City; others are possible, provided more funds are pledged for programming.
World Bank administered, implemented by MDBs	A M	The Strategic Climate Fund: (1) Pilot Program for Climate Resilience (PPCR—US$1 billion programmed for nine pilot countries and two regions) helps build climate resilience in core development; (2) Forest Investment Program (FIP—US$587 million for eight pilot countries); (3) program to Scale up Renewable Energy for Low-Income Countries (SREP—US$318 million for six pilot countries). Urban upstream planning support and city-based investments are possible to integrate into national plans now being formulated in agreed pilot countries.
Reduced Emissions from Deforestation and Forest Degradation (REDD) programs US$4 billion in pledges as Fast Start Finance following the Copenhagen Accord		Two major REDD funds fully or partially run by the World Bank, the Forest Carbon Partnership Facility (FCPF), and the Forest Investment Program (FIP, under the Climate Investment Funds) have already received over US$700 million in pledges for pilot programs in forested developing countries, and are currently commencing implementation. Cook-stove programs can still be integrated into country strategies and implementation plans for reducing deforestation. Their impact at the urban level is in reducing greenhouse gas and black-carbon emissions in low-income areas with corresponding health co-benefits.
Examples of other climate funds and their volumes: US$10 billion US$1.6 billion US$180 million annually US$580 million US$180 million US$160 million US$135 million US$100 million	M&A M&A M&A M&A M&A A M&A M	Cities can access these funds through cooperation in the national programming process: Cool Earth Partnership (Japan) Environmental Transformation Fund—International Window (UK) International Climate Initiative (Germany) Climate and Forest Initiative (Norway) International Forest Carbon Initiative (Australia) Global Climate Change Alliance (European Commission) International Climate Change Adaptation Initiative (Australia) UNDP-Spain MDG Achievement Fund

		Examples of non-climate-specific support from donors and MDBs
Global Facility for Disaster Reduction and Recovery (GFDRR)	A	Partnership within the UN International Strategy for Disaster Reduction (ISDR) initiative, focusing on building capacities to enhance disaster resilience and adaptive capacities in changing climate. About two-thirds of GFDRR's assistance has primarily focused on climate change adaptation; that is more than US$27 million in nearly 90 countries worldwide. GFDRR support has leveraged an additional US$17 million of co-financing from development partners and greater amounts from World Bank investments. The GFDRR Technical Assistance Fund is global, established through contributions of GFDRR partners into a multi-donor trust fund. The Callable Fund is a fund-in-readiness to be activated when disaster strikes. This multi-donor trust fund provides an innovative approach in that donors enter into an agreement with the World Bank *before* a natural disaster to support the Callable Fund; however, actual funds are mobilized *after* a natural disaster through a Call for Funds.
International Development Association (IDA) World Bank core concessional loans for low-income countries	A (M)	To be developed as part of national initiatives and with national authorities: – Development policy operations to build resilience into city budgets – Adaptation at city level – Mitigation at city level
IBRD, MDB, and bilateral core funds	A M	Stand-alone or in combination with climate-specific funds city-based adaptation and mitigation as part of national programs and with national authorities.
Trust funds and partnerships; guarantees	M A	Grant financing for knowledge products, capacity building, upstream project work/pilots; partial risk guarantees to support development, adoption, and application of clean-energy technologies, including those not fully commercialized, in client countries.
Climate insurance products World Bank Treasury, etc., fee-based or donor supported	A	Risk financing strategy development MultiCAT products with cities with parameter-based triggers CAT swaps for extreme flood risk, etc. Multicity insurance products for risk sharing and lower cost

(continued next page)

TABLE 4.3 *continued*

Climate bonds World Bank Treasury, etc., fee-based or donor supported	**M** **A**	Bonds against city CERs or NAMAs Advice on monetizing carbon bonds
Public-private partnerships		World Bank Public-Private Infrastructure Advisory Facility (PPIAF) or similar schemes can provide technical assistance and match-making in planning and making operational urban NAMAs by improving an enabling environment and strategic public intervention conducive to long-term private-sector commitment.
Private sector		IFC and other MDB private-sector arms can provide technical assistance and financial support to investors in climate-resilient infrastructure or low-carbon technologies through a combination of risk management and other concessional instruments, bringing the cost to a level attractive for long-term private investment.

Source: www.climatefinanceoptions.org.

Note: A = Adaptation; M = Mitigation; UNFCCC = United Nations Framework Convention on Climate Change.

Convention on Climate Change (UNFCCC). Registered projects resulting in GHG emission reductions located in developing countries or economies in transition obtain certified emission reductions (CERs) that can be traded in the market, thereby providing a performance-based revenue stream to the project. The World Bank's Carbon Partnership Facility can support cities in improving their overall market readiness, in developing emissions-trading projects, and in acquiring CERs for the market CDM methodologies cover 15 sectors, including waste, energy, and transport, which cover many typical projects in cities.

For cities with limited budgets, carbon finance can help justify the effort of coordinating with various stakeholders (including their own departments) and help deal with the higher cost of choosing a lower-emission technology. Moreover, carbon-finance revenues can be directed for pro-poor objectives, such as investments to build resilience in poor urban areas. One illustration is the case of São Paulo, highlighted in box 4.4.

The *citywide approach to carbon finance* is designed to help cities overcome some of the barriers to CDM projects at the city level, including small projects and high transaction costs. Typical projects in cities, except for waste-management projects in large cities, yield small volumes of CERs. Furthermore, repeated clearances are needed from the same city for different projects—which can be time consuming and cumbersome. Clear and standardized baselines for GHG emissions are a prerequisite for this citywide approach. The World Bank has piloted this approach in Amman, Jordan, and endorsement from national governments was obtained in a Decision of the Parties at COP-16 in Cancun in December 2010. Approval by the CDM Executive Board was pending at the time of writing.

Other market-related instruments for carbon include city-based emissions trading systems (ETSs, see box 4.5) and carbon-linked bonds. The World Bank is currently working in two middle-income countries on new carbon-linked bonds that would contribute to financing a program of emissions-reduction projects. Such bonds could be issued through different structures in which the World Bank helps to select the best financial firms as partners and reaches out to investors interested in emissions-reduction projects. City governments with energy-efficiency projects that could generate flows of measurable GHG abatement over time, potentially eligible for the CDM or for future ETSs, could obtain funding on very attractive terms through such structures. Again, these funds could be used for building resilience for the urban poor.

The Private Sector

Private companies—ranging from small businesses selling water through kiosks or providing road maintenance to local and international operators with solid

BOX 4.4

Landfill Gas-to-Energy Projects in São Paulo

Through a public bidding process, the City of São Paulo gave a concession to the holding company Biogas to install thermoelectric power plants to burn biogases emitted by decaying waste from the Bandeirantes and São Joao landfills. This generates the equivalent of 7 percent of the electricity consumed in the city. Each facility now generates more than 175,000 MW/h, enough to supply power to 600,000 residents for 10 years. It is estimated that 11 million tons of CO_2-equivalent will be abated by 2012.

Both landfills were approved as Clean Development Mechanism (CDM). According to the concession agreement, 100 percent of the energy and 50 percent of the carbon credits produced by the landfills belong to Biogas Co. to be traded in the market, while the City of São Paulo has the right to sell the other half of carbon credits at public auctions. In September 2007, the city held the first auction, raising about US$18 million (at US$22 per ton) from the Bandeirantes landfill CERs generated between December 2003 and December 2006. A second auction, held in September 2008, offered CERs from both landfills and collected more than US$19 million (at US$28 per ton).

In addition to mitigating climate change, São Paulo's projects to convert landfill gas to energy also aim to revitalize the surrounding low-income communities. In 2009, two public plazas, Cuitegi and Mogeiro, near the Bandeirantes landfill, were inaugurated. Cuitegi Plaza has 2,300m² of leisure area, playgrounds, and seating. Minor road works were also completed to facilitate mobility within the local community. The Mogeiro Plaza has 6,897m² of leisure area and offers a walking path, exercise equipment, playground, seating, and community space.

Source: C40 Case Study.

expertise and substantial financial resources—can play a key role in providing infrastructure and services in urban areas. Developing efficient public-private partnerships (PPPs) that recognize the strengths of both the private and public sectors is an important part of the solution. An enabling policy environment and strategic investments through public funds can be designed to attract private funds.

The experience with PPPs for improving infrastructure and services in urban slums has mainly been through components of larger projects that

BOX 4.5

Tokyo's Emissions Trading System

Emissions trading is a market-based approach for addressing air pollution problems, also known as "cap-and-trade." Emissions-trading schemes for greenhouse gases (GHGs) include the European Union's ETS and the Regional Greenhouse Gas Initiative in the northeastern United States. At the city-level, however, ETSs in cities such as Chicago, Los Angeles, and Santiago de Chile have the primary objective of improving air quality, where some of the air pollutants covered also are GHGs.

The world's first city-level carbon dioxide (CO_2) cap-and-trade program, with the primary objective of mitigating climate change, was launched in Tokyo in April 2010. Tokyo's ETS covers energy-related CO_2, involving around 1,340 large installations including industrial factories, public facilities, educational institutions, and commercial buildings. With this ETS, the Tokyo Metropolitan Government aims to reduce CO_2 emissions by at least 6 percent during the first compliance period (2010–2014), with the ultimate goal of a 25 percent reduction below 2000 levels by 2020.

Source: World Bank.

may include an entire utility (water, sewerage, electricity, transport) within a certain city or region. Municipal governments may hire a private company to extend the water and sanitation network to new parts of the city including slum communities (a service contract). Or, they may include in a concession the commitment to extend service to certain slum communities, which obliges the private company to recover the costs of service provision and initial investment from their customers, including the slum dwellers. In Port Vila, Vanuatu, a concession contract successfully extended free potable water to poor areas through cross subsidies from wealthier areas. In Manila, the concessionaires Mayniland Water Services and Manila Water Company use a variety of internal programs and partnerships with NGOs, community organizations, and small entrepreneurs to increase water distribution to slums.[3] Municipalities have discovered that involving the private sector in public utilities and works is not without its problems, but as cities continue to consider public-private partnerships as ways to improve public services, service expansion to slums can be brought to the negotiating table and integrated into PPP contracts (box 4.6).[4]

BOX 4.6

Getting Private Water Utilities into Slums: Metro Manila Water Concessions

Metro Manila's water authority was privatized in 1997 with the intention of solving problems of inefficiency and financial shortfalls. Two 25-year concession contracts were signed, one with Manila Water Company (composed of Ayala and International Water) to cover the eastern zone of the city and a second with Maynilad Water Services (Benpres and Ondeo) to cover the western zone. Both concessionaires are required to expand service coverage to between 77 percent and 87 percent by 2001 and between 95 percent and 98 percent by 2021. To achieve this, both companies have had to devise strategies to profitably extend water services to slums.

Although the concession agreement allows for the installation of one public standpipe per 475 people in depressed areas, both companies have worked to establish other types of connections that bring water closer to people's homes and ensure greater revenue for the companies. Manila Water has introduced group taps for two to five households to share a single connection registration and water bill. The company has also introduced community-managed water connections in which a community association is responsible for a master meter and installs and manages a distribution network to blocks or individuals. Manila Water also permits private companies to buy water for resale through private distribution networks, which the contractor must take responsibility for maintaining.

Maynilad has actively sought out partnerships with NGOs to extend individual household connections, preferred by customers in all income groups, to slums. Its Bayan Tubig (Water for the Community) program waives the land-title requirement in slums and integrates payment of the connection fee into the first 6, 12, or 24 monthly water bills. NGOs, such as the Swiss chapter of Médecins San Frontières and the local LINGAP Foundation in Malabon, get communities involved to support ownership of the program through information, education, and community campaigns and assistance to the poorest families through microfinance. Maynilad additionally will contract with community-based associations to provide billing and collection services, which further localizes value creation in household water provision.

(continued next page)

BOX 4.6 *continued*

The companies have enhanced their image and have decreased non-revenue water through formalizing water provision arrangements in slums where many people had been receiving water through illegal connections and public standpipes. Through their contract with the local government and their partnerships with NGOs and community associations, these two private water utilities are promoting access to safe, reliable potable water in the poorest areas in Metro Manila.

Sources: Baker and McClain (2009), based on Weitz and Franceys (2002). See also Franceys and Weitz (2003).

In several cities in India, capital has been mobilized for slum improvements through credit guarantees and bonds (Baker and McClain 2009). In India, the Ahmedabad Municipal Corporation issued the first municipal bond in 1998 without a central government guarantee for the purpose of financing a citywide water and sanitation project that included many slum areas and the Slum Networking Project "Parivartan." In 2005, municipal governments around Bangalore built on Ahmedabad's success with a bond issue called the Greater Bangalore Water and Sanitation Pooled Facility that combined the commitments of eight city governments. In both cases, the success of the bond sales depended on the municipal governments' having previously demonstrated a revenue surplus and received a sufficiently high credit-rating to ensure an interest rate in line with the government's projections of future ability to pay, among other conditions. The ability of municipal governments to mobilize domestic capital greatly enhances the scale at which municipal governments can engage in development. Ahmedabad's four municipal bond issues raised $89.5 million between 1998 and 2006. The Greater Bangalore Facility raised over $23 million, with the assistance of a $780,000 partial credit guarantee from USAID, essentially mobilizing over $29 in domestic capital for every dollar donated (Painter 2006, 19–20).

At the household level, the urban poor use microfinance particularly for purchasing and improving houses, which often contribute to resilience. Housing microfinance typically comprises small loans (from $550 to $5,000) of limited maturing (6 months to 3 years), generally without collateral (Freire, forthcoming). A number of commercial banks, financial cooperatives, and NGOs specialize in microfinance for low-income residents. Mibanco, for example, is one of the largest microfinance institutions in Latin America, with 70,000 active borrowers, and Grameen Bank in Bangladesh has delivered 600,000 housing loans since it was established. In general, all of these institutions show performance rates above housing loans in the banking industry (Biswas 2003). A further application of microfinance is the Local Development Program (PRODEL) in Nicaragua, which lends to community groups for small infrastructure projects.

Initiatives at the community level focus on finance for housing and infra-structure, which are growing in significance. These funds involve savings at the community level, which are leveraged to access funds from national government donors. For example, the Jamii Bora Trust Low Cost Housing Scheme in Kenya raised funds through members' savings, market finance, and donations to pur-chase 293 acres of private land and to construct houses. Members then finance their housing units ($3,000) with loans from the trust at about $45 per month. Monthly fees of $7 are charged for maintenance (UN-HABITAT). Other exam-ples exist in Cambodia, Thailand, the Philippines, and India.

Results-based Financing

Results-based financing (RBF) is an umbrella term for mechanisms that disburse funds only after pre-set results have been achieved. Disbursements are normally made on the basis of independent verification of these results. This has the effect of transferring performance risk from the subsidy provider to the service pro-vider, thus improving the likelihood that desired results are achieved. RBF is rel-evant at two levels: the investment level and the consumer level.

At the level of the investment, RBF can be thought of as results-based viabil-ity gap funding. Such payments depend on there being sufficient pre-financing capability. Pre-agreed results must be specific enough to be verifiable. This should lead to transparent and more effective use of subsidy funds. Different stages of delivering the desired service—such as financial closure of projects, initial works, completion of works, and delivery of performance—can all be verified and lead to payments.

For the consumer, results-based payments focused on delivering basic services to low-income individuals are termed output-based aid (OBA). OBA is normally designed to support the upfront costs of delivering basic and reliable services to the poor. Examples include electricity and water connections. Operating costs are normally not subsidized, and are expected to be affordable to the consumer to ensure sustainability of the investment. The level of subsidies, delivered after the "output" has been verified, is normally set based on unit costing from indepen-dent experts. The costs could also be set using competitive bidding. The objective of this costing is to determine the "efficient" cost. The actual level of subsidy is then set after taking into account household affordability.

In low-income communities in western Jakarta, an arrangement developed through the Global Partnership on Output Based Aid (GPOBA), the city government, and the local water utility, PALYJA, subsidizes the cost of water-supply connections for almost 12,000 households in poor areas, including 2,200 in informal settlements where PALYJA had previously not been authorized to provide services (Menzies and Setiono 2010). Concessionaires are given grants for the cost of installing connections to the networks, provisional on two measureable outputs—the provision of a working household connection, and the delivery of acceptable service for three months. While the project has faced some difficult challenges in implementation related to water availability, and problems dealing with existing informal water suppliers, these eventually were resolved, with the help of the NGO Mercy Corps, paving the way for further expansion to other communities.

Bringing It All Together

Sustainable financing for climate change, disaster risk, and the urban poor in cities will need to draw on all available resources, as well as maximize synergies and complementarities. An efficient combination of resources from the instruments described above can leverage public and private sources while ensuring significant co-benefits. Combinations of financial instruments will be needed, with approaches customized to address specific needs, risks, or barriers, while also reducing transaction costs.

Since most international funds for addressing adaptation and mitigation are channeled through national implementing entities, cities have extensive scope to access such funds through national processes (see annex 1), but modalities for more direct access need to be considered. One approach to facilitating access would be allowing cities to access such financing through a more unified "window," which would reduce overhead and administrative complexity. Such an approach could bring together many of the existing resources that are available and draw on some innovative instruments, such as green bonds for cities and results-based financing for basic services. With regard to climate support alone, the World Bank offers more than 30 potential programs, including for capacity building and technical assistance, as well as funding initiatives.

To encourage cities to achieve specified targets, such a program could consider a more standardized approach to benchmarking and monitoring through metrics commonly agreed upon by the international community, such as a city-level GHG index, urban risk assessments, or Local Resilience Action Plans. By meeting specified targets, cities would then be eligible for accessing such financing through the designated window.

In conclusion, this study has pointed to the many challenges for cities and residents around the world as they confront the risks associated with climate change and natural hazards. While the risks have direct and indirect impacts for all urban residents, those at the bottom of the income distribution face the greatest challenges, often on a daily basis. Understanding these risks is an important first step to addressing them, as has been demonstrated in Dar es Salaam, Jakarta, Mexico City, São Paulo, and elsewhere. The study has pointed to broad actions that can respond to the risks identified and help to build resilience for the urban poor. Such actions will require strong commitments from local governments, along with national and international partners. In implementing such actions, benefits will be realized not only by the urban poor, but also by future generations.

Notes

1. http://www.climatefinanceoptions.org.
2. http://web.worldbank.org/WBSITE/EXTERNAL/COUNTRIES/LACEXT/EXTLACP
   ROJECTSRESULTS/0,,contentMDK:227 42596~pagePK:51456561~piPK:51456127~
   theSitePK:3177341,00.html.
3. See Weitz and Franceys (2002), pp. 50–61, for further description of these public-private partnerships, and the full publication for a broader selection of examples.
4. See Weitz and Franceys (2002). See Mehta (1999) for issues related to integrating service provision to the poor into commercially viable projects.

References

Baker and McClain. 2009. "Private Sector Initiatives in Slum Upgrading." Urban Paper No. 8, World Bank, Washington, DC.

Biswas, Smita. 2003. "Housing Is a Productive Asset—Housing Finance for Self-Employed Women in India." *Small Enterprise Development* 14 (1): 49–55.

Economics of Climate Adaptation (ECA) Working Group. 2010. *Shaping Climate-Resilient Development: A Framework for Decision-Making.*

European Environment Agency. 2007. *Climate Change: The Cost of Inaction and the Cost of Adaptation.* Copenhagen.

Franceys, Richard, and Almud Weitz. 2003. "Public-Private Community Partnerships in Infrastructure for the Poor." *Journal of International Development* 15: 1092–94

Freire, M. Forthcoming. "Financing Urban Upgrading." In Metropolitan *Government Finances in Developing Countries*, ed. R. Bahl, J. Linn, and D. Wetzel. Lincoln Institute of Land Policy.

Huhtala, Ari, 2010, Climate Finance for Cities, Mimeo.

International Federation of Red Cross and Red Crescent Societies (IFRC). 2010. *World Disasters Report: Focus on Urban Risk.* Geneva: IFRC.

Mehta, Meera. 1999. "Balancing Commercial Viability with the Needs of the Poor in the Development of Urban Water Supply and Sewerage Projects," *Project Notes* 14. USAID Indo-U.S. Financial Institutions Reform and Expansion Project—Debt Market Component FIRE(D), January. http://www.niua.org/indiaurbaninfo/fire-D/ProjectNo.14.pdf.

Menzies, I., and I. Setiono. 2010. "Output-Based Aid in Indonesia: Improved Access to Water Services for Poor Households in Western Jakarta." GPOBA Approaches Note. Washington, D.C.

Painter, D. 2006, "Scaling up Slum Improvement: Engaging Slum Dwellers and the Private Sector to Finance a Better Future." Paper presented at the World Urban Forum III, June.

Smolka, Martin O., and Adriana de A. Larangeira. 2008. "Informality and Poverty in Latin American Urban Policies." In *The New Global Frontier: Cities, Poverty and Environment in the 21st Century*, ed. George Martine, Gordon McGranahan, Mark Montgomery, and R. Castilla-Fernandez, 99–114. London: IIED/UNFPA and Earthscan Publications.

Velasquez Barrero, Luz Stella. 2010. "La Gestion del Riesgo en el Contexto Ambiental Urbano Local: Un Reto Permanente y Compartido. Caso Manizales, Colombia." Background paper prepared for the 2011 *Global Assessment Report on Disaster Risk Reduction*.

Weitz, Almud, and Richard Franceys, eds. 2002. *Beyond Boundaries: Extending Services to the Urban Poor*. Asian Development Bank, August, 50–61. http://www.adb.org/documents/books/beyond_boundaries/beyond_ boundaries.pdf.

World Bank. 2010a. *Africa's Infrastructure—A Time for Transformation*. Washington, DC: World Bank.

———. 2010b. *Climate Risks and Adaptation in Asian Coastal Megacities: A Synthesis Report*. Washington, DC: World Bank.

———. 2010c. *Making the Most of Public Finance for Climate Action—The World Bank Group at Work*. Development, Climate, and Finance Issues Brief 3. Washington, DC: World Bank.

———. 2010d. *World Bank Urban Strategy*. Washington, DC: World Bank.

———. 2011e. *Climate Change Adaptation and Natural Disaster Preparedness in the Coastal Cities of North Africa.* Washington, DC: World Bank.

World Watch Institute. 2007. *State of the World 2007: Our Urban Future*. New York: Norton.

Annex 1: Literature Review

Over the past two decades, significant research has been carried out on the topics of climate change, disaster risk management, urbanization, and poverty. Although analysis of the inter-linkages among all four of these areas is limited, signs suggest this may be changing. Climate change and disaster risk reduction are increasingly better linked and the impacts of climate change and disasters on the urban poor is gaining prominence. As the frequency and intensity of disasters related to climate change increase, the international development community and policy makers, in particular, are recognizing the importance of identifying the specific vulnerabilities of subgroups within the population to tailor interventions that will help groups cope.

Across the world, the poor disproportionately bear the brunt of changing weather patterns and natural disasters. They lack adaptive capacity to cope with climate change. Urbanization exacerbates these problems. Cities, overburdened with rapidly expanding populations, are grappling with limited infrastructure and funds, unable to provide decent housing and basic health and welfare services to all residents. The urban poor end up more directly exposed to natural hazards as compared to their wealthy counterparts.

Some of the essential foundation documents on the subject of climate change and disasters with some reference to urbanization and poverty (though not necessarily in conjunction with each other) include the Inter-Governmental Panel on Climate Change (IPCC) Assessment Reports, the World Bank's *World Development Report 2010: Development and Climate Change*, the World Watch

Institute's *State of the World: Our Urban Future* (2007) and *Pro-Poor Adaptation to Climate Change in Urban Centers* (Moser et al. 2010).

The IPCC's Fourth Assessment report is a good starting point, since it assesses recent published literature on climate change. While the IPCC report provides the most comprehensive data on climate change, the historic focus of the IPCC has been around the science of climate change. In this regard the IPCC report is an important source of established terminology and climate change definitions, which are followed in this study, especially for confining the concepts of vulnerability, exposure, sensitivity, and adaptive capacity. In its Fourth Assessment Report (IPCC 2007) Working Group II, Chapter 7, titled "Industry, Settlements and Society," deals with issues related to industry, services, and financial and social concerns that raise the vulnerability of human settlements (not only those living in cities) to climate change. The chapter concludes that research on vulnerabilities and adaptation potentials of human systems has lagged behind research on physical environmental systems, ecological impacts and mitigation, uncertainties dominate the subject matter of this chapter. Urbanization and poverty frequently come up in the discussion—as non-climate stresses that amplify the risks that people face from the effect of climate change. The report warns that the poor living in informal settlements such as slums, especially in developing countries, are the most likely to be killed or harmed by extreme weather.

IPCC (2007) Chapter 8, "Human Health," also discusses the impact of climate change on the health of the urban poor. With "high confidence," the IPCC asserts that the urban poor are at greater risk of suffering adverse health impacts related to climate change, along with women, children, and the elderly. It also reminds readers of the Third Assessment Report's (IPCC 2001) conclusion that "an increase in the frequency or intensity of heat waves will increase the risk of mortality and morbidity, principally in older age groups and among the urban poor." The IPCC's Fifth Assessment Report, due in 2011, is expected to deal more extensively with the impact of climate change on urbanization and development. It is unclear, however, to what extent the report will highlight these issues through the lens of the urban poor.

The World Bank's thorough *World Development Report 2010: Development and Climate Change* (WDR 2010) looks at development and climate change from a variety of aspects, including climate change and human vulnerability. This includes a review of adaptation and mitigation priorities in developing countries, impacts of extreme weather, the challenge of coastal cities, and the costs of mitigation and adaptation. The WDR 2010 also addresses the link between climate change and urbanization, along with the associated vulnerability of the urban poor. Several issues are highlighted. Well-planned urbanization can be highly effective in addressing both adaptation and mitigation of climate change, but unplanned urbanization can increase the vulnerability of the urban poor.

Informal settlements are already particularly vulnerable to flooding, often due to clogged drains, land subsidence, heat waves, and increased health risks. The WDR includes much more detailed analysis of climate change risks, extreme events, climate finance, and related issues, but not specifically in the context of urban poverty.

The World Watch Institute's *State of the World: Our Urban Future* (2007) documents good practices on how cities build and manage their infrastructure and service delivery mechanisms to cope with climate change. The report does not focus specifically on the urban poor but many of its case studies on providing clean water and sanitation, transport, energy, and health narrate their stories as well.

One topic receiving a lot of attention in climate-change literature relates to adaptation and its impact on poverty reduction and development. Scholars increasingly acknowledge that adaptation measures that take into account the poor can play a role in reducing poverty and make development truly sustainable. One of most frequently cited works on pro-poor adaptation in cities is by Moser et al. (2008). It examines the role of assets, including "natural, physical, social, financial and human capital" (Mearns and Norton 2010), in increasing the adaptive capacity of the urban poor. Moser describes three reasons why household assets are crucial to helping poor urban dwellers adapt to climate change. For one, city authorities may not be able to provide them with infrastructure or services due to financial limitations. Conversely, many city authorities may be reluctant to work with the poor, especially within informal settlements. And finally, improving the assets of the poor increases the likelihood that they could hold local governments accountable for providing services. Moser et al. (2008) have developed a framework to map asset vulnerability and identify interventions to address the vulnerability of the urban poor. These interventions could be at three levels: household and neighborhood; municipal or city; and regional and national. This framework could be useful in reducing social and urban vulnerability in adapting to climate change, but it has found few takers so far.

Other prominent works relevant for this study—which are not as comprehensive as those discussed above but instead focus on more specific issues—include the World Bank's *Social Dimensions of Climate Change* (Mearns and Norton 2010) and *Adapting to Climate Change in Eastern Europe and Central Asia* (Fay et al. 2010), and publications by the Global Facility for Disaster Risk Reduction and Poverty (Kreimer and Arnold 2000; Kreimer et al. 2003; among others).

Also relevant to this report are the *Global Assessment Report on Disaster Risk Reduction* (ISDR 2009), the United Nations Development Programme's *Human Development Report (2007)*, and *Poverty and Climate Change: Reducing Vulnerability of the Poor through Adaptation* (2009), a collaborative effort between the African Development Bank, Department for International Development,

Organisation for Economic Co-operation and Development, United Nations, and World Bank. A compilation of papers on climate change and urban poverty is available in *Adapting Cities to Climate Change* (Bicknell, Dodman, and Satterthwaite, 2010) published by the International Institute for Environment and Development, an organization that has done a great deal of macro-level work on the intersection of urban vulnerability and climate change. Mehrotra et al. (2010), Sanchez-Rodriguez (2009), and Juneja (2008) provide useful reviews of relevant literature on the climate risks that cities face, adaptation, and the risk linkage between poverty and disasters, respectively.

Linking Climate Change and DRR

Disaster risk reduction (DRR) and climate change adaptation have many overlapping concerns, and are interrelated issues for cities. The impacts of climate change will include increased frequency and severity of natural disasters, so the needs for climate change adaptation in this regard correspond with those of disaster risk reduction (Prasad et al., 2008). Climate change adaptation covers a larger scope than DRR in also accounting for the effects of incremental, gradual changes in climate. Moser et al. (2008) also highlight the need for climate change adaptation to consider not only changes that fall under disaster risk reduction (flooding and other natural disasters) but also important incremental and gradual changes, such as the rise in sea level. As noted above, some authors have noted the differences between climate change adaptation and DRR, but relatively little literature thoroughly acknowledges the synergies of climate change adaptation and DRR. A more careful documentation of these synergies would help maximize the efficacy of both climate change adaptation and DRR projects for the urban poor.

Climate change and disaster risk reduction are more divergent in terms of mitigation. Both climate change and DRR have developed differing meanings for "mitigation." Climate change mitigation refers to reducing GHG emissions, while in DRR literature, mitigation refers to limiting the adverse impacts of natural disasters. Other sources that discuss the differences and similarities between DRR and climate change include Birkmann et al. (2009), WDR (2010), and O'Brien et al. (2006).

Climate Change, DRR, and Urban Poverty

In existing literature, the link between climate change and urban poverty is explored less than between disasters and urban poverty. This, too, is a fairly recent development. In 2000, the World Bank's *Managing Disaster Risk in*

Emerging Economies (Kreimer and Arnold 2000) concluded that a major development imperative was to reduce disasters in order to reduce poverty, since "poverty plays a big role in keeping people vulnerable to disasters." Following this, more documents emphasizing the link between disaster and poverty have been published (DFID's *Disaster Risk Reduction: A Development Concern*, 2004; World Bank's *Hazards of Nature, Risks to Development*, 2006). Yet, analytical literature on the exact links and nature of problems faced by the urban poor due to climate change and disasters is scarce.

There is general consensus, however, that the poor are vulnerable because they lack basic safety and protection from physical harm. Spatial analysis techniques have revealed that the poor in urban areas tend to live in low-income settlements that are highly vulnerable to disasters (Pillai et al. 2010; Hoffman 2009; Lall and Deichmann, 2009). More crucially, the urban poor have limited access to basic services such as drinking water, sanitation, drainage, solid-waste management, transport, food and energy security, and health, among other welfare services.

Service Delivery and the Urban Poor

Lack of access to basic services, such as clean water, sanitation, drainage, and health services, makes the urban poor more vulnerable to climate change and natural disasters. Most published research acknowledges that basic services should be provided to improve the living conditions of the urban poor, and that lack of access to these services increases the vulnerability of the urban poor (for example, Baker 2008). However, there is a major gap in sector-specific analysis of services such as water, drainage, sanitation, energy, roads, transport, and health for the poor living in cities.

Of all basic services, water, sanitation, and drainage have received more attention in the context of climate change adaptation and disasters because of their direct bearing on human health, the second most popular research subject. Inequity in access to clean drinking water, sanitation, and efficient drainage services are reinforced in nearly all publications. For instance, *State of the World: Our Urban Future* (World Watch 2007) reported that the poor in most developing countries are deprived of essential water services, even where there was no water shortage per se.

Most scholars attribute this to poor governance rampant in developing countries. In a study of African towns and cities, Douglas et al. (2008) found that the frequency of flooding had increased—not because of increased rainfall, but inadequate and clogged drainage. Parikh and Parikh (2009) found that most slums in Indore, India, were located along natural paths of water channels and drainages neglected by local authorities. The World Bank's *World Development Report 2004: Making Services Work for Poor People* raised the question of accountability of providers and policy makers in water and sanitation services to the poor living in cities. The report concluded that patronage, "the compact between the politician and provider," renders poor citizens powerless and providers should be made more accountable for their services to the public instead of being shielded by policy makers.

Another area of research receiving attention at the World Bank and the wider research community focuses on providing solutions to water and related service delivery problems in urban areas. Danilenko et al. (2010) provide analytical and strategic guidance to the world regions for incorporating water-related adaptation to climate change in their work programs. Community-driven development interventions are also being proposed. Parkinson and Mark (2005) and Parikh (2009) found that in India, civic authorities successfully established "slum networks" with residents in many informal settlements in order to build drainage channels.

Health services are another area that adaptation planners focus on. With the privatization of health care in many cities across developing countries, access to emergency and basic health care is becoming more inaccessible for the poor (Montgomery 2009). The IPCC (2007) warns, for example, that access to cheap, effective anti-malarials, insecticide-treated bed nets, and indoor spray programs will be important for future trends in malaria. Some major documents that link the vulnerability of the urban poor to poor health services include: IPCC's Fourth Assessment Report Working Group II, Chapter 8, "Human Health" (2007); the World Health Organization's *Protecting Health from Climate Change* (2009); and Kovats and Akhtar (2008).

The rest of the basic services haven't been examined in as much detail. The IPCC's Fourth Assessment Report Working Group III, Chapter 10 (2007), is the most widely cited on solid-waste management (along with Douglas et al. 2008; Wilson 2007; Kebede and Dube 2004). On energy services, some key sources include the IPCC's Fourth Assessment Report Working Group III, Chapter 4, 2007; Fay et al. 2010; Haines et al. 2007; *State of the World: Our Urban Future* (World Watch Institute 2007; World Bank 2006.)

Also, little literature addresses how limited access to roads affects the poor in the context of climate change and DRR. In terms of transport and urban poverty, the key documents include Baker et al. (2005) and the World Bank's *Cities on the Move* (2002). On the subject of climate change and urban transport, the major reports include IPCC's Fourth Assessment Report Working Group III, Chapter 5 (2007); World Bank's *World Development Report 2009*; and the World Business Council for Sustainable Development's *Mobility 2001* (2002) and *Mobility 2030* (2004). At the Urban Research Symposium in 2009, Olvera (2009) presented research on the importance of urban transport for the poor in reducing vulnerability associated with climate change.

Significantly, a lot of the services literature attributes poor service delivery to neglect and poor urban governance (*Global Assessment Report on Disaster Risk Reduction* (ISDR 2009); Sattherthwaite et al. 2007; Lewis and Mioch 2005).

Housing

In most developing countries, the urban poor tend to live in low-cost housing or slum settlements located on the fringes of the city or in environmentally hazardous areas. The World Bank has published major documents on the topic: *Climate Risks and Adaptation in Asian Coastal Mega-Cities* (Pillai et al. 2010); *Safer Homes, Stronger Communities* (Jha 2010); *Density and Disasters* (Lall and Deichmann 2009); *Spatial Analysis of Natural Hazard and Climate Change Risks in Periurban Expansion Areas of Dakar, Senegal* (Hoffman 2009); and *Natural Disaster Hotspots: A Global Risk Analysis* (Dilley et al. 2005). Some other commonly cited works include Moser et al. (2008); Bicknell, Dodman, and Satterthwaite (2009); UN-HABITAT'S *State of the World's Cities* (2008–09); World Watch Institute's *State of the World: Our Urban Future* (2007); Yusuf and Francisco (2009); Nicholls et al. (2007); Peduzzi, Dao, and Herold (2005); Pelling (2003); and Hardoy, Mitlin, and Satterthwaite (2001).

Apart from location, other aspects related to housing have recently gained attention in the context of the urban poor, climate change, and DRR in developing countries: quality (Kenny 2009; Sezen et al. 2002; Ruskulis 2002; Lewis 2003); access to credit markets (Moser et al. 2008); and tenure security (Moser et al. 2008; Lall et al. 2004; Wamsler 2007). This is significant, since most of the existing research addresses developed countries (Bin et al. 2008 and 2004; Kerry Smith et al. 2006; Nakagawa, Saito, and Yamaga 2007; Greenstone and Gallagher 2008).

In 2005, the World Bank's *Natural Disaster Hotspots: A Global Risk Analysis* concluded that global data for assessing disaster risks for urban areas is sufficiently well-developed. Indeed, social scientists have a lot of data (though most of it focuses on coastal cities) that shows that some cities are more hazard-prone than others (Pillai et al. 2010; Lall and Deichmann 2009; Bicknell, Dodman, and Satterthwaite 2009World Bank 2005). UN-HABITAT'S *State of the World's Cities* (2008–09) reports a study by the Centre for Urban Studies, Bangladesh (2005) which shows that slum settlements in Dhaka are already most vulnerable during cyclones and heavy rainfall. Climate change and rising sea levels would make these areas more vulnerable to flooding, but they would also affect the city's non-slum areas. A recent study by the World Bank (Pillai et al. 2010) is unique in that it examines specific areas inhabited by the poor *within* three "hotspot" cities—Ho Chi Minh City, Bangkok, and Manila.

Many studies have also attempted to explain why the poor continue to live in hazard-prone areas despite knowing that they are at risk—reasons being proximity to the workplace and unaffordable local transport networks. The disaster-proneness of their housing is, in turn, reflected in its low pricing and maintenance (Lall, Lundberg, and Shalizi 2008; Bin et al. 2004, 2008).

It would be a mistake, however, to conclude that the poor are helpless victims, unable to fend for themselves. In her study in San Salvador, Wamsler (2006, 2007) found that the slum dwellers she interviewed spent nearly 10 percent of their income on activities, like construction, related to disaster risk reduction. Wamsler concluded that vast differences exist in urban coping strategies that are not fully understood by the development community—which, she says, has so far focused on the rural poor. She also argues that urban coping strategies are more focused on housing construction and land issues than rural coping strategies. This needs to be explored further.

A study that raises important questions for city planners was done by Jollands et al. (2005) in Hamilton City, New Zealand. The study found that the city's infrastructure systems were not very responsive to gradual climate change, such as heat waves and drought. This was because the main potential vulnerability to climate change of the built environment has traditionally been associated with extreme events, such as floods and storms. However, as the large death toll following Europe's 2003 heat wave demonstrated that gradual climate change can be as dangerous and life-threatening as sudden disasters and deserves as much attention.

To conclude, the linkage of housing to climate change and DRR did not receive much attention in until very recently, especially in the context of developing countries. As a result, the published research has major gaps, even on basic details such as how many poor people living in cities face environmental risks as compared to the non-poor living in the same city or as compared to rural populations. A thorough examination of housing issues faced by the urban poor through the lens of climate change and DRR is required to gain knowledge of the specific challenges faced by the poor as a result of changing climate patterns and frequent extreme weather. Such an examination will also help lead to possible solutions to address the development challenges posed by climate change.

Climate Change: Adaptation and Mitigation

Many reports already recognize that climate change *adaptation* is more urgent and fair than mitigation for cities in developing countries. The poor contribute least to greenhouse gas emissions but face the highest risks since they tend to live in low-cost, hazardous areas in cities with little or no access to basic services that could make them more resilient to extreme weather and events like earthquakes and storm surges. Thus adaptation through basic services provided by the government and increasingly public-private partnerships has earned most attention in the context of the urban poor and climate change (Sattherthwaite 2009).

In some cases, the link between adaptation and basic services for the poor is less direct. Instead, as in the case of transport and energy, there are potential co-benefits for the urban poor in *mitigation* work in these sectors. For example, public transit mitigation projects that provide sustainable, low-carbon means of urban transport (if well planned) can significantly improve access for the urban poor. The World Bank is currently supporting climate-friendly urban public transit projects in Mexico, Colombia, Egypt, Morocco, Philippines, Thailand, and Vietnam (World Bank 2010c). For energy, one of the greatest challenges is getting energy services across to all urban residents. Access is defined as areas in the electricity grid extension, with statistics often found to be misleading (*State of the World: Our Urban Future*; World Watch Institute 2007). For instance, about one-third of Africans live in urban areas, and at least one-quarter of city dwellers on the continent do not have access to electricity. Researchers note that renewable energy sources that mitigate climate change can be used to provide energy to the urban poor. Prominent examples of this kind of work include fuel-efficient cook stoves and solar water heaters.

There is a relatively large body of climate change *adaptation* literature related to the urban poor. Many studies have recognized that the poor, and especially the urban poor, are most vulnerable to climate change yet have limited adaptive capacity to take up adaptation. This literature includes *The Cost to Developing Countries of Adapting to Climate Change* (World Bank 2010a); *Climate Risks and Adaptation in Asian Coastal Mega-Cities* (Pillai et al. 2010); *Shaping Climate Resilient Development—A Framework for Decision-making* (ECA 2009); *Adapting Cities to Climate Change* (Bicknell, Dodman, and Satterthwaite 2009); and *Social Dimensions of Climate Change* (Mearns and Norton 2010).

One counterpoint to this view is *Pro-Poor Adaptation to Climate Change in Urban Centers* (World Bank 2010b), which demonstrates that the urban poor are currently and actively adapting to changes in weather, while acknowledging that support for more substantial and long-term protective measures remains much needed.

While adaptation and the urban poor are relatively well researched, mitigation and the urban poor is a topic on which less is available. Most mitigation efforts are focused on large GHG emitters, and the urban poor are among the smallest GHG emitters. There are important issues that relate to the urban poor in mitigation, such as how urban transport mitigation projects will impact and can benefit the poor, as well as energy-efficient housing. (See, for example, *Our Urban Future*; World Watch Institute, 2007). Low-carbon cookstoves are another area where mitigation is particularly important for the urban poor, who often face negative health impacts associated with using cookstoves that emit black carbon. Many projects have investigated low-carbon cookstoves that can reduce GHG emission and improve the health of users over other stoves, yet still cook efficiently. For foundational information on mitigation, the study relies on the comprehensive work of the IPCC report on mitigation and WDR 2010.

Finance

There are many sources of information on climate finance. Among the main studies are the well-known *Stern Report* (2007) on climate finance, which explicitly recognizes that climate change adaptation must reduce the vulnerability of the urban poor, and United Nations Framework Convention on Climate Change report on needed levels of climate finance. The World Bank has also done a study on combining financial instruments for low-carbon development (World Bank 2010c) and a major study on the economics of adaptation to climate change (World Bank 2010a). The latter study consists of two parts: a global overview that estimates adaptation costs at US$75-100 billion per year to adapt to 2^0C of warming by 2050, and country case studies of the costs of adaptation detailed by sector. Two of the sectors with the highest anticipated adaptation costs are infrastructure and water, which are also key issues for the urban poor. The World Bank recently launched a climate finance website offering a comprehensive list of climate funding sources for both adaptation and mitigation, including carbon finance, the Global Environment Fund, CIFs, Special Climate Change Fund, Least Developed Countries Fund, and Adaptation Fund.

Gaps in Existing Literature

As suggested in the review above, there are some major gaps in existing literature on climate change, DRR, and the urban poor. These include the following:

- Lack of detailed quantitative analysis from developing countries that disaggregates urban versus rural and poor versus non-poor.
- Lack of explicit connections between climate change and DRR for the urban poor.
- Limited documentation of practical examples of best practices in climate change adaptation for the urban poor.

- Emphasis of most studies on natural disasters, with less attention on gradual changes in weather induced by climate change, which have a less immediate but more drastic long-term impact on human populations.
- Most analysis on climate impact assessments and cities being focused on coastal cities, neglecting inland cities where, for instance, a heat-island effect, cold waves, and droughts may be more pronounced.
- Limited literature on housing and sector-specific provision of services for the urban poor in the context of climate change and DRR.
- Limited current knowledge on basic services and how they can help reduce the vulnerability of the urban poor, especially in operational terms. Sample topics include how better services can be provided to the poor, given climate change impacts; which sectors require priority interventions; how bottom-up collaborative policy making may be blended with existing scientific know-how; and what financing mechanisms can be drawn on.
- As pointed out by the IPCC (2007), scholars' lack of attention to the uncertainties associated with climate change and its implications for the human populations, let alone the urban poor.

References

African Development Bank, Asian Development Bank, U.K. Department for International Development, DGDev, BMZ, MinBuza, Organisation for Economic Co-operation and Development, United Nations Development Programme, United Nations Environment Programme, and World Bank. 2009. *Poverty and Climate Change: Reducing the Vulnerability of the Poor through Adaptation.*

Baker, Judy. 2008. *Urban Poverty: A Global View.* Washington, DC: World Bank.

———, R. Basu, M. Cropper, S. Lall, and A. Takeuchi. 2005. "Urban Poverty and Transport: The Case of Mumbai." Policy Research Working Paper 3683, World Bank, Washington, DC.

Bicknell, Jane, David Dodman, David Satterthwaite, eds. 2009. *Adapting Cities to Climate Change: Understanding and Addressing the Development Challenges.* London: Earthscan.

Bin, O., J. Brown Kruse, and C.E. Landry. 2008. "Flood Hazards, Insurance Rates, and Amenities: Evidence from the Coastal Housing Market." *Journal of Risk and Insurance* 75 (1): 63–82.

Bin, Okmyung, and Stephen Polasky. 2004. "Effects of Flood Hazards on Property Values: Evidence before and after Hurricane." *Land Economics* 80 (4): 490–500.

Birkmann, et al. 2009. *Addressing the Challenge: Recommendations and Quality Criteria for Linking Disaster Risk Reduction and Adaptation to Climate Change.* DKKV Publications Series 38. Bonn: German Committee for Disaster Reduction.

Centre for Urban Studies, MEASURE Evaluation, and National Institute of Population Research and Training. 2006. *Slums of Urban Bangladesh: Mapping and Census, 2005.* Dhaka: Centre for Urban Studies.

Danilenko, Alexander, Eric Dickson, and Michael Jacobsen. 2010. *Climate Change and Urban Water Utilities: Challenges and Opportunities.* Water Working Notes. Washington, DC: World Bank.

DFID, 2004. *Disaster Risk Reduction: A Development Concern.* London.

Dilley, Maxx, Robert S. Chen, Uwe Deichmann, Art L. Lerner-Lam, and Margaret Arnold. 2005. *Natural Disaster Hotspots: A Global Risk Analysis.* Washington, DC: World Bank/ Columbia University.

Douglas, Ian, Kurshid Alam, Maryanne Maghenda, Yasmin Mcdonnell, Louise Mclean, and Jack Campbell. 2008. "Unjust Waters: Climate Change, Flooding and the Urban Poor in Africa." *Environment and Urbanization* 20 (1): 187–205.

Economics of Climate Adaptation (ECA) Working Group. 2010. *Shaping Climate-Resilient Development: A Framework for Decision-Making.*

Fay, Marianne, Rachel Block, and Jane Ebinger, eds. 2010. *Adapting to Climate Change in Eastern Europe and Central Asia.* Washington DC: World Bank.

Greenstone, M., and J. Gallagher. 2008. "Does Hazardous Waste Matter? Evidence from the Housing Market and the Superfund Program." *Quarterly Journal of Economics* 123 (3): 951–1003.

Haines, et al. 2007. "Policies for Accelerating Access to Clean Energy, Improving Health, Advancing Development, and Mitigating Climate Change." *The Lancet* 370 (6): 1264–1281.

Hardoy, J.G., D. Mitlin, and D. Satterthwaite. 2001. *Environmental Problems in an Urbanizing World.* London: Earthscan.

Hoffman, Christian. 2009. "Spatial Analysis of Natural Hazard and Climate Change Risks in Per-Urban Expansion Areas of Dakar, Senegal." Presented at the World Bank Urban Learning Week 2009.

Intergovernmental Panel on Climate Change (IPCC). 2001. *IPCC Third Assessment Report: Climate Change 2001.*

———. 2007. *IPCC Fourth Assessment Report: Climate Change 2007.*

International Strategy for Disaster Reduction (ISDR). 2009. *Global Assessment Report on Disaster Risk Reduction.* Geneva: UN International Strategy for Disaster Reduction.

Jha, Abhas, with Jennifer Duyne Barenstein, Priscilla M. Phelps, Daniel Pittet, and Stephen Sena. 2010. *Safer Homes, Stronger Communities: A Handbook for Reconstructing After Natural Disasters.* Washington, DC: World Bank Global Facility for Disaster Reduction and Recovery (GFDRR).

Jollands, N., M. Ruth, C. Bernier, and N. Golubiewski. 2005. "Climate's Long-term Impacts on New Zealand Infrastructure—A Hamilton City Case Study." *Ecological Economics in Action.* New Zealand Centre for Ecological Economics, Palmerston North, New Zealand.

Juneja, Shefali. 2008. *Disasters and Poverty: The Risk Nexus. A Review of Literature.* Background Paper for the 2009 ISDR *Global Assessment Report on Disaster Risk Reduction.* United Nations International Strategy for Disaster Reduction Secretariat, Geneva.

Kebede, B., and I. Dube. 2004. *Energy Services for the Urban Poor in Africa: Issues and Policy Implications.* London: Zed Books in Association with the African Energy Policy Research Network.

Kenny, Charles. 2009. "Why Do People Die in Earthquakes? The Costs, Benefits and Institutions of Disaster Risk in Developing Countries." Policy Research Working Paper, World Bank, Washington, DC.

Kerry Smith, V., Jared C. Carbone, Jaren C. Pope, Daniel G. Hallstrom, and Michael E. Darden. 2006. "Adjusting to Natural Disasters." *Journal of Risk and Uncertainty* 33: 37–54.

Kovats, S., and R. Akhtar. 2008. "Climate, Climate Change and Human Health in Asian Cities." *Environment and Urbanization* 20 (1): 165–175.

Kreimer, Alcira, and Arnold, Margeret. 2000. *Managing Disaster Risk in Emerging Economies.* Washington, DC: World Bank.

Kreimer, Alcira, et al., eds. 2003. *Building Safer Cities: The Future of Disaster Risk.* Washington, DC: World Bank.

Lall, S.V., and U. Deichmann. 2009. "Density and Disasters: Economics of Urban Hazard Risk." Policy Research Working Paper 5161, World Bank, Washington, DC.

Lall, Somik, Uwe Deichmann, Mattias Lundberg, and Nazmul Chaudhury. 2004. "Tenure, Diversity, and Commitment: Community Participation for Urban Service Provision, *Journal of Development Studies* 40 (3): 1–26.

Lall, Somik V., Mattias Lundberg, and Zmarak Shalizi. 2008. "Implications of alternate policies on welfare of slum dwellers: Evidence from Pune, India." *Journal of Urban Economics* 63: 56–73.

Lewis, Dan, and Jaana Mioch. 2005. "Urban Vulnerability and Good Governance." *Journal of Contingencies and Crisis Management* 13 (2): 50–53.

Lewis, James. 2003. "Housing Construction in Earthquake-Prone Places: Perspectives, Priorities and Projections for Development." *The Australian Journal of Emergency Management* 18 (2): 35–44.

Mearns, Robin, and Andrew Norton. 2010. *Social Dimensions of Climate Change: Equity and Vulnerability in a Warming World.* Washington DC: World Bank.

Mehrotra, S., Claudia Natenzon, Ademola Omojola, Regina Folorunsho, Joseph Gilbride, and Cynthia Rosenzweig. 2009. "Framework for City Climate Risk Assessment." World Bank Commissioned Research presented at the Fifth Urban Research Symposium, World Bank, Washington DC.

Montgomery, Mark, 2009. "Urban Poverty and Health in Developing Countries." *Population Bulletin* 64(2).

Moser, Caroline, A. Norton, A. Stein, and S. Georgeiva. 2010. "Pro-Poor Climate Change Adaptation in the Urban Centres of Low- and Middle-Income Countries. Case Studies of Vulnerability and Resilience in Kenya and Nicaragua," World Bank, Social Development, Report Number 54947-GLB.

Nakagawa, Masayuki, Makoto Saito, and Hisaka Yamaga. 2007. "Earthquake Risk and Housing Rents: Evidence from the Tokyo Metropolitan Area." *Regional Science and Urban Economics* 37: 87–99.

Nicholls, R.J., C. Hanson, N. Herweijer, S. Patmore, J. Hallegatte, J. Corfee-Morlot, R. Château, and R. Muir-Wood,. 2007. *Ranking Port Cities with High Exposure and Vulnerability to Climate Change: Exposure Estimates.* Environment Working Paper 1. OECD.

O'Brien, G., Phil O'Keefe, and, Joanne Rose, Ben Wisner. 2006. "Climate Change and Disaster Management." *Disasters* 30 (1): 64–80.

Olvera, Lourdes Diaz. 2009. *Climate Change, the Permanence of Mobility, Urban Transport, and Poverty in Sub-Saharan Africa (Changements Climatiques, Permanence de la Mobilite, Transports Urbains et Pauvrete en Afrique Subsaharienne).*

Parikh, H., and P. Parikh. 2009. "Slum Networking–A Paradigm Shift to Transcend Poverty with Water, Environmental Sanitation and Hidden Resources." In *Water and Urban Development Paradigms*, ed. Feyen, Shannon, and Neville. London: Taylor and Francis.

Parkinson, J., and O. Mark. 2005. *Urban Stormwater Management in Developing Countries.* UK: IWA Publishing.

Peduzzi, P., H. Dao, and C. Herold. 2005. "Mapping Disastrous Natural Hazards Using Global Datasets." *Natural Hazards* 35 (2): 265–289.

Pelling, Mark. 2003. *The Vulnerability of Cities: Natural Disasters and Social Resilience.* London: Earthscan.

Prasad, Neeraj, Federica Ranghieri, Fatima Shah, Zoe Trohannis, Earl Kessler and Ravi Sinha. 2009. *Climate Resilient Cities. A Primer on Reducing Vulnerabilities to Disasters.* Washington, DC: World Bank.

Ruskulis, Otto. 2002. "Developing Processes for Improving Disaster Mitigation of the Urban Poor." *Basin News* (Building Advisory Service and Information Network) 23 (June). SKAT St Gallen.

Sanchez-Rodriguez, Roberto. 2009. "Learning to Adapt to Climate Change in Urban Areas: A Review of Recent Contributions." *Current Opinion in Environmental Sustainability.*

Satterthwaite, David. 2009. *Shaping Urban Environment: Cities Matter.* London: International Institute for Environment and Development.

———. Saleemul Huq, Hannah Reid, Mark Pelling and Patricia Romero Lankao. 2007. *Adapting to Climate Change in Urban Areas: The Possibilities and Constraints in Low- and Middle-Income Nations.* London: International Institute for Environment and Development.

Sezen, H., A. Whittaker, K. Elwood, and K. Mosalam. 2002. "Performance of Reinforced Concrete Buildings during the August 17, Kocaeli, Turkey Earthquake, and Seismic Design and Construction Practice in Turkey. *Engineering Structures* 25 (1): 103–114.

Stern, Nicholas. 2007. *The Economics of Climate Change: The Stern Review.* Cambridge, UK: Cambridge University Press.

United Nations Development Programme (UNDP). 2007. *Human Development Report 2007/2008: Fighting Climate Change: Human Solidarity in a Divided World.* New York: UNDP.

UN-HABITAT. 2008. *Harmonious Cities: State of the World's Cities 2008/9.* London/ Sterling, VA: Earthscan Publications Ltd.

Wamsler, Christine. 2006. "Understanding Disasters from a Local Perspective: Insights into Improving Assistance for Social Housing and Settlement Development." *TRIALOG (Journal for Planning and Building in the Third World)* 91 (December), special issue on "Building on Disasters."

———. 2007. "Bridging the Gaps: Stakeholder-Based Strategies for Risk Reduction and Financing for the Urban Poor." *Environment and Urbanization* 19 (1): 115–142.

Wilson, David C. 2007. "Development Drivers for Waste Management." *Waste Management & Research* 25 (3): 198–207

World Bank. 2002. *Cities on the Move. Urban Transport Strategy Review*. Washington, DC: World Bank. http://siteresources.worldbank.org/INTURBANTRANSPORT/ Resources/cities_on_the_move.pdf accessed 13/7/2010.

———. 2004. *World Development Report 2004: Making Services Work for Poor People*. Washington, DC: World Bank.

———. 2005. *Natural Disaster Hotspots: A Global Risk Analysis*. Washington, DC: World Bank.

———. 2006. *Hazards of Nature, Risks to Development*. Washington, DC: World Bank.

———. 2009. *World Development Report 2009: Reshaping Economic Geography*. Washington, DC: World Bank.

———. 2010a. *The Cost to Developing Countries of Adapting to Climate Change*. Washington, DC: World Bank.

———. 2010b. *Pro-Poor Adaptation to Climate Change in Urban Centers: Case Studies of Vulnerability and Resilience in Kenya and Nicaragua*. Washington, DC: World Bank.

———. 2010c. *World Development Report 2010: Climate Change and Development*. Washington, DC: World Bank.

———. 2010d. *Climate Risks and Adaptation in Asian Coastal Mega-Cities: A Synthesis Report*. Washington, DC: World Bank.

World Business Council for Sustainable Development (WBCSD). 2002. *Mobility 2001: World Mobility at the End of the Twentieth Century, and Its Sustainability*. WBCSD. http://www.wbcsd.org/DocRoot/EdJHZvhMSfrbALJqnQvF/english_full_report.pdf.

———. 2004a. *Mobility 2030: Meeting the Challenges to Sustainability. World Bank Urban Transport Transformation Project (UTTP) in Mexico*. http://www.wbcsd.org/web/ publications/mobility/mobility-full.pdf.

World Health Organization (WHO). 2009. *Protecting Health from Climate Change: Global Research Priorities*. Switzerland: WHO.

World Watch Institute. 2007. *State of the World 2007: Our Urban Future*. New York: Norton.

Yusuf, A.A., and H.A. Francisco. 2009. *Climate Change Vulnerability Mapping for South Asia*. Singapore: EEPSEA. http://www.idrc.ca/uploads/user-S/12324196651Mapping_ Report.pdf.

Annex 2: Efforts to Estimate Exposure in Cities

Studies have estimated the magnitude of urban exposure to natural hazards and climate change impacts, yet none to date have integrated exposure of population and of economic assets, as well as the impacts of natural hazards and climate change at the urban scale. While these approaches have their own limitations in rigorously quantifying aggregate vulnerability to climate and natural-hazard impacts given the high degree of complexity and uncertainty, they provide a useful macro-level look at risk and exposure in cities. Below is a brief discussion of five studies, along with key findings, that have attempted such rankings. Each approaches urban risk from a different angle, covering different sets of cities, different types of hazards, different timeframes, and different asset measurements. That being said, all approaches confirm that such risk is increasing and that with the increasing manifestations of climate change, the risk will significantly worsen in the coming decades.

OECD Study on Ranking Port Cities with High Exposure and Vulnerability to Climate Extremes[1]

The Organization for Economic Co-operation and Development (OECD) published an index ranking 136 port cities with populations over 1 million with high exposure to 1-in-100-year, surge-induced floods. The index looks at the exposure of population and assets in 2005 and those predicted in 2070. Future predictions account for population growth, urbanization, ground subsidence, and climatic changes.

The OECD study shows that across all cities, about 40 million people (0.6 percent of the global population or roughly 1 in 10 of the total port city population in the cities considered here) are exposed to a 1-in-100-year coastal flooding. The exposure, as of 2005, is concentrated in a few cities: Mumbai, Guangzhou, Shanghai, Miami, Ho Chi Minh City, Kolkata, Greater New York, Osaka-Kobe, Alexandria, and New Orleans.

The study shows that cities in Asia overwhelmingly have the highest exposure to surge-induced flooding now and in the future. Of the 20 cities with the highest population exposure in 2005, half are in low- and middle-income nations in Asia. Of the total 38.5 million people currently exposed, 65 percent live in Asian cities. Table A2.1 shows the top 20 port cities with exposed populations in 2005. The index predicts that, in the 2070s, 17 out of the 20 cities with the highest population exposure will be in present-day low- and middle-income countries,

TABLE A2.1
Port Cities with Populations over 1 Million Estimated to Have Highest Increased Exposure to Surge-Induced Floods, 2005 to 2070

City	Country	Population 2005 (thousands)	Population exposed 2005 (thousands)	Population exposed 2070 (thousands)	Increase (percent)
Quingdao	China	2,817	88	1,851	2,103
Luanda	Angola	2,766	1	18	1,800
Dhaka	Bangladesh	12,430	844	11,135	1,319
Mogadishu	Somalia	1,320	9	115	1,278
Conakry	Guinea	1,425	41	496	1,210
Chittagong	Bangladesh	4,114	255	2,866	1,124
Ningbo	China	1,810	299	3,305	1,105
Dar es Salaam	Tanzania	2,676	36	351	975
Yangon	Myanmar	4,107	510	4,965	974
Karachi	Pakistan	11,608	49	473	965
Douala	Cameroon	1,761	11	101	918
Lagos	Nigeria	10,886	357	3,229	904
Kulna	Bangladesh	1,495	441	3,641	826
N'ampo	Rep. of Korea	1,102	22	181	823
Port-au-Prince	Haiti	2,129	1	8	800

Source: Nicholls et al. (2008).

and 14 out of the 20 will be in Asia (four in China and two in Bangladesh). Asia's increasing dominance in terms of population and asset exposure is a result of increased urbanization and economic growth during the period, compared with other regions.

When assets are considered across all cities, the current distribution becomes more heavily weighted toward developed countries, as the wealth of the cities becomes important. The total value of assets exposed in 2005 is estimated to be US$3,000 billion, corresponding to around 5 percent of global GDP in 2005 (both measured in U.S. dollars). The top 10 cities in this ranking are Miami, Greater New York, New Orleans, Osaka-Kobe, Tokyo, Amsterdam, Rotterdam, Nagoya, Tampa-St Petersburg, and Virginia Beach. These cities contain 60 percent of the total exposure, but are from only three (wealthy) countries: the United States, Japan, and the Netherlands.

Munich Re's Study on Megacities—Megacities Megarisks

Munich Re Group's NatCat database was used to prepare a natural hazard risk index for 50 of the world's largest (population over 2 million) and most economically important cities (city GDP as a percentage of a country's GDP). The analysis covers 30 large cities in low- and middle-income nations and 20 large cities in high-income nations. This index, which was intended as the basis for discussion, was the first international index for cities to take a multi-hazard perspective including earthquakes, windstorms, floods, volcanic eruption, bush fires, and winter storms.

The index is composed of three variables: exposure to hazards, vulnerability of the built environment, and value of exposed property. Vulnerability is based on an estimation of the vulnerability of the predominant form of residential construction to hazards; the standard of preparedness and safeguards including building regulations; urban planning in respect of specific hazards and flood protection; and building density. The values of exposed property are estimated using the average values per household and the GDP for commerce and industry.

The index is most heavily influenced by values of exposed assets and their degree of vulnerability. Tokyo is, by far, the city at highest risk, followed by San Francisco. Of the 20 highest-risk cities in the index, 17 are in high-income countries, which is to be expected given that the index is trying to gauge the risk for insurers and thus the value of exposed assets. These assets are greater in high-income countries and thus become important in understanding the potential for economic losses in a disaster.

GFDRR—Economics of Disaster Risk Reduction

In this study (Brecht, Deichmann, and Wang 2010), city-specific population projections to 2050 are combined with geographic patterns of hazards representative of the 1975–2007 period. The projected number of people exposed to tropical cyclones and earthquakes in large cities in 2050 more than doubles, rising from 310 million in 2000 to 680 million in 2050 for tropical cyclones, and from 370 million to 870 million for earthquakes. The growing exposure continues to vary by region. By 2050, there will be 246 million city dwellers in cyclone-prone areas in South Asia, but 160 million each in the OECD and East Asian countries. Although East Asia has fewer exposed people, the urban population exposed to cyclones is expected to grow at 2.2 percent a year, similar to South Asia's. Sub-Saharan Africa's exposure growth at 3.5 percent is even higher due to the projected high urbanization rates, reaching 21 million urban dwellers by 2050.

Exposure to earthquakes will likely remain most prominent in East Asia. It is also high in Latin America and the Caribbean, and OECD countries. The fastest growth in exposure is in South Asia (3.5 percent), followed by Sub-Saharan Africa, linked to rapid urbanization in these regions.

Mega-Stress for Mega-Cities: A Climate Vulnerability Ranking of Major Coastal Cities in Asia

The World Wildlife Fund (WWF) assessed the climate change vulnerabilities of 11 large cities in Asia, most of them coastal (WWF 2009). WWF's work focuses on climate vulnerability and adaptive capacity in these cities. The study gave each city a vulnerability score based on the combined rankings of its exposure, sensitivity, and adaptive capacity. Each is rated by a point system; for example, exposure is measured by assigning a point value for (1) frequency of tropical storms, (2) frequency of extreme weather including flood and drought, and (3) potential impact of a 1meter rise in sea level. Based on this point attribution, Dhaka, Jakarta, and Manila are ranked as the most exposed of the 11 cities studied. These same cities are ranked highest on overall vulnerability as well.

WWF's index is unique in that it focuses specifically on climate change in a select number of cities predetermined to be particularly vulnerable. The study uses uniform measurements across the cities to make them comparable; however, the assigned units to rank vulnerability are not easily translatable in the final analysis. It is not clear, for example, why Dhaka has a vulnerability of 9, while Jakarta and Manila have a vulnerability of 8 (on a 10-point scale), or what a one-point difference in vulnerability means. Because the study is limited to only 11 Asian cities, it is also difficult to imagine how these rankings could be used to compare vulnerability with other cities. A further point of interest in this comparison is that the ranking order of the cities is very similar for each of the three factors that are aggregated to measure vulnerability (exposure, sensitivity, adaptive capacity).

Earthquake Disaster Risk Index

The Earthquake Disaster Risk Index (EDRI) was developed by the John A. Blume Earthquake Engineering Center at Stanford University (Davidson and Shah 1997). The index is a composite that accounts for various city characteristics across five components to assess earthquake risk: hazard, exposure, vulnerability, external context, and emergency response, and recovery. Each of these factors uses several data inputs with differing weights. For example, the exposure component is calculated using population, per capita GDP, number of housing units, and urbanized land area. The overall risk formula provides a final risk value between 1 and 100 for each city. In a 10-city sample, the mean risk was 40, with a range between 35 (for St. Louis) and 54 (for Tokyo).

The index increases its robustness by requiring a number of data points for input, but some data can be difficult to access in some cities, such as city per capita GDP or housing vacancy rate. Additionally, while this index allows for intercity risk comparison and potential wise distribution of resources, indexed data are readily available for only 10 cities (Boston, Istanbul, Jakarta, Lima, Manila, Mexico City, San Francisco, Santiago, St. Louis, and Tokyo).

Multi-Hazard City Risk Index (MHCRI)

This is a pilot initiative under the Resilient Cities program in the World Bank's East Asia Region. An initial methodology has been developed and piloted in three cities—Bangkok, Thailand, in collaboration with the Bangkok Metropolitan Administration; Metro Manila, Philippines, in collaboration with the Metropolitan Manila Development Authority; and Ningbo, China, in collaboration with NMBG, Ltd. (World Bank, 2011). The index provides the first methodology to quantify and aggregate risk across a range of 13 hydromet and seismic hazards in a standardized way in order to compare across cities as well as areas (for example, districts) within a city. It aims to provide an aggregate picture of risk to national and city policy makers and planners and guidance on areas of focus for prospective risk management. The index relies on a basic multiplicative risk model that draws on data related to metropolitan elements (population subclasses, building types, and infrastructure sectors); calculates hazard indices for each hazard type (based on frequency, intensity, and area affected); and assesses vulnerabilities (based on 30 parameters related to physical susceptibility, socioeconomic fragility, and institutional and regulatory resilience). While exposure to people and capital stock can be extracted from the model, the primary outputs are risk scores for the city. Risk can be assessed at the citywide or submunicipal scale, for all metropolitan elements or a specific one, for all hazard types or a specific one. The outputs are for two time periods—current (2010) and future (2030), where future scenarios are generated based on high and low hazards (accounting for climate change), and changes to population and built-up area based on government planning and investment documents. The final city scores are still being finalized and the methodology will be further refined in a follow-up phase. In addition, a website is under development that will allow users to select the parameters of interest and generate risk maps accordingly; the site will also allow users to simulate policy changes and resulting implications to the risk maps.

Although the results from the studies reviewed above address urban risk from different angles, they all confirm that such risk is increasing and that with growing climate change the risk will continue to increase significantly in the coming decades. The results provide a call for action in addressing urban risk, and especially in those countries of the developing world that are the least prepared to manage the risk's implications, including financial requirements and organizational challenges (see figure A2.1 in the color section).

Note

1. Nicholls et al. (2007). Also see Hallegatte et al. (2010, 2011).

References

Brecht, H., U. Deichmann, and H. Gun Wang. 2010. "Predicting Future Urban Natural Hazard Exposure." Background note for *Natural Hazards, Unnatural Disasters*.
Davidson, Rachel, and Haresh Shah. 1997. *An Urban Earthquake Disaster Risk Index.* Stanford, California: Stanford University.
Hallegatte, Stéphane, Nicola Ranger, Sumana Bhattacharya, Murthy Bachu, Satya Priya, K. Dhore, Farhat Rafique, P. Mathur, Nicolas Naville, Fanny Henriet, Anand Patwardhan, K. Narayanan, Subimal Ghosh, Subhankar Karmakar, Unmesh Patnaik, Abhijat Abhayankar, Sanjib Pohit, Jan Corfee-Morlot, and Celine Herweijer. 2010. "Flood Risks, Climate Change Impacts and Adaptation Benefits in Mumbai." OECD Environmental Working Paper 27.
Hallegatte, S., N. Ranger, O. Mestre, P. Dumas, J. Corfee-Morlot, C. Herweijer, and R. Muir Wood. 2011. "Assessing Climate Change Impacts, Sea Level Rise and Storm Surge Risk in Port Cities: A Case Study on Copenhagen," *Climatic Change* 104 (1): 113–37.

Munich Re. 2005. *Megacities—Megarisks: Trends and Challenges for Insurance and Risk Management.* Munich Reinsurance Company.

Nicholls, R.J., et al. 2007. *Ranking Port Cities with High Exposure and Vulnerability to Climate Change: Exposure Estimates.* Environment Working Paper 1. OECD.

World Bank. 2011. "Resilient Cities: Multi-Hazard City Risk Index—Methodology Report," East Asia Infrastructure Sector Unit, World Bank, Washington, DC, September.

World Wildlife Federation (WWF). 2009. *Mega-Stress for Mega-Cities: A Climate Vulnerability Ranking of Major Coastal Cities in Asia.* Gland, Switzerland: WWF International.

Annex 3: Learning from Project and Program Experiences: Individuals, Community, and Local Government Partnering to Manage Risk

Introduction

As discussed throughout this study, there are many government and community approaches to building resilient communities. This annex presents some approaches being carried out at a local level, ranging from community strategies, early-warning systems, and local partnerships, to more sophisticated risk-transferring programs.

Traditionally, vulnerable individuals and communities have managed risk through ad hoc coping techniques that draw on their local knowledge of hazards and community resources. Many sources available today discuss ad hoc adaptation to illustrate the strength of social capital; however, many of these coping mechanisms also reflect short-term strategies of individuals or communities that are accustomed to living with risk from recurrent hazards and cannot rely on government protection (Douglas et al. 2008).

While ad hoc adaptation may save lives and assets in the short term, its unregulated nature creates the possibility for maladaptation. Maladaptation happens also when there is a shift in vulnerability from one social group to another, or when future generations' vulnerability is compromised. Per the United Nations Development Programme definition, maladaptation is any action taken in relation to climate change that delivers short-term gains at the cost of creating long-term, higher vulnerability.[1] An example of this can be seen in the unplanned settlements of Dar es Salaam, where common flood-coping strategies include elevating pit latrines and building foundations, which increases street flooding (Kiunsi et al. 2009a). Maladaptation may also include planned development policies that fail to take into account the future effects of climate change.

There are many examples of good practices in addressing the backlogs in infrastructure and service provision for the urban poor in developing countries. For instance, an approach that has resulted in effective identification and mitigation of risks is where city or municipal governments work with the inhabitants of the informal settlements and their community organizations to ensure provision of resilient basic services. This approach is now evident in a wide range of cities, although with differences in the balance between what governments do and what households and community-based organizations do. What these have in common, though, is recognition by local government officials and politicians of the areas where so much more can be achieved if local government supports the investments and capacities that community organizations can bring. There is also recognition of how community investments can be integrated into municipal investments in ways that expand coverage and lower unit costs.

Other examples of good practices come from local government-community organization partnerships initiated by federations of slum/shack dwellers or homeless people. This is perhaps surprising in that federations or other forms of collective organization formed by low-income groups generally seek to influence government by making demands on them, not by offering partnerships (Mitlin 2008). But in 33 nations, women-led grassroots savings groups, and the larger slum/shack/homeless people's federations they form, are engaged in initiatives to upgrade slums and squatter settlements, secure land tenure, develop new housing that low-income households can afford, and improve provision for infrastructure and basic services. These federations have demonstrated a capacity to undertake citywide surveys of informal settlements that include detailed profiles of each settlement and maps. They have also shown their capacity to do detailed enumerations of every household in informal settlements that can then form the information needed for upgrading and infrastructure and service provision. These are both very valuable for any local government wishing to reduce vulnerability and improve conditions in informal settlements.

Individual civil servants or politicians have often catalyzed much improved community-local government relations that led to partnerships in service provision. Yet, the continuity of such partnership in the absence of capable institutions is threatened when politicians' terms ends or they are moved. There is also the constraint on these partnerships from the many community leaders who are not representative or accountable to those they "lead" and who are enmeshed in patron-client relationships with local government. Another challenge is to take a partnership that works well for a particular settlement or district to larger scale—and shifting from projects to citywide processes. It is also difficult for bureaucratic, rule-bound systems and processes to meet the needs and priorities of those in informal settlements working within the informal economy (Mitlin 2008). But the range of successful experiences with community-local government partnerships coming from very different economic and political contexts suggests that the core principles of this approach have wide validity.[2]

In most urban contexts, what community organizations can negotiate from their local government is as important (if not more so) for disaster risk reduction and climate change adaptation than what they can do themselves. So much risk reduction depends on the availability of infrastructure that the residents of informal settlements cannot install themselves. Most urban informal settlements are embedded in a much larger built-up area, and these need a larger system of storm and surface drains into which their own efforts to install, improve, and maintain drainage can fit. They need road and path networks beyond their settlements to allow them to evacuate if needed. They need health care services that can help in risk reduction and disaster response. The willingness of individuals to invest in collective actions for risk reduction in their settlement also depends on how secure they feel from eviction and their tenure (for instance, tenants are usually unwilling to invest in improving the housing they live in). But the contribution of community-level organization and action to disaster risk reduction can also be greatly enhanced where local governments and other key bodies (for instance, civil defense organizations) recognize their role and support them.[3]

Risk management needs to be tailored to the specific needs and resources of each city. Some organizations, cities, and countries are leading risk mitigation. Figure A3.1 lists programs that have innovative elements of good practice, categorized by approach to risk management.

Educate—Good Practices in Knowledge Sharing and Training

For many cities, the first step toward climate and disaster resilience is to educate and raise awareness of natural hazards, vulnerabilities, and institutional capacity. Several programs provide advice to decision makers, such as city technicians and city managers. These programs range in levels of engagement and development, but all have the common goal of aiding local governments to approach the climate challenge, and they recognize that risks are not evenly distributed among

Figure A3.1 Examples of Current Good Practices, by Approach to Risk Management

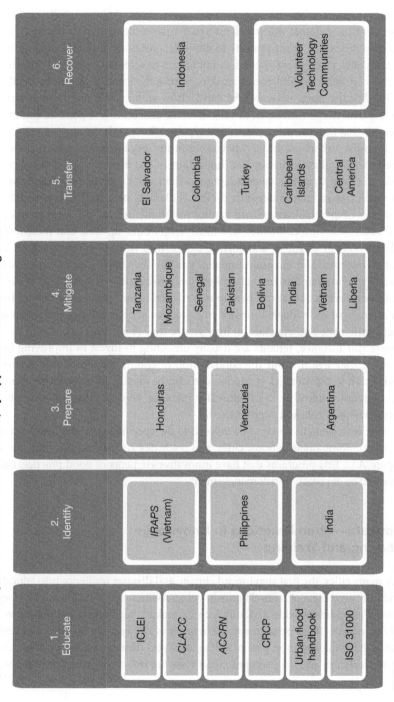

ICLEI: Local Governments for Sustainability; CLACC: Capacity Strengthening of Least Developing Countries for Adaptation to Climate Change network; ACCRN: Asian Cities Climate Change Resilience Network; CRCP: Climate Resilient Cities Primer; ISO31000: International Organization for Standardization.

local populations. Several programs currently under development are mentioned below.

ICLEI—Local Governments for Sustainability

ICLEI USA is working with several North American cities on the Climate Resilient Communities Program. The adaptation program has a five-milestone methodology: (1) conduct a climate resiliency study, (2) set preparedness goals, (3) develop a climate preparedness plan, (4) publish and implement the preparedness plan, and (5) monitor and reevaluate resiliencies. The program is in the early stages, but may expand to the global ICLEI network. A benefit of this program is that it can build on an existing network of cities that have used ICLEI resources to work on mitigation.

Capacity Strengthening of Least Developing Countries for Adaptation to Climate Change Network

The International Institute for Environment and Development (IIED) has helped develop the Capacity Strengthening of Least Developing Countries for Adaptation to Climate Change (CLACC) network, which is composed of international experts working to strengthen organizations in least-developed countries and support their sustainable development initiatives. They are currently operating in 12 African countries and three in South Asia. The CLACC network supports these organizations primarily through publications and capacity-building workshops, meanwhile actively participating in the Conference of Parties (COP) negotiations worldwide. The CLACC methodology focuses on ten lessons for decision makers: engaging in detailed consultations with citizens and community organizations; gathering information on extreme weather impacts; engaging in disaster risk management; facilitating household coping strategies; supporting sustainable livelihoods; ensuring that infrastructure is sensitive to the needs of the poor; supporting slum upgrading; building resilience across sectors (health, tenure, education, etc.); instituting appropriate building standards; and reconsidering planning and zoning regulations.

Asian Cities Climate Change Resilience Network (ACCRN)

This is a Rockefeller Foundation initiative, implemented through the Institute for Social and Environmental Transition (ISET); it focuses on aiding a network of cities to develop climate adaptation plans through engagement with civil society stakeholders. The primary objectives of ACCRN are to demonstrate a range of actions for urban climate adaptation, compile replicable good practices, and help cities implement climate resilient processes. ACCRN is currently working in ten cities: three cities in Vietnam, three in India, two in Indonesia, and two in Thailand. The program is being developed through four phases that began in 2008 with city scoping and selection. Phase 2, currently under way, involves city engagement and capacity building through the Shared Learning Dialogue (SLD) process. SLDs engage community actors and government agencies to explore their current and future vulnerabilities in a transparent and iterative group discussion. The SLD outcome focuses on creating a shared understanding of risk and priorities for action. Phase 3, set to begin this year in Vietnam and India, focuses on implementing urban resilience-building projects, with partial funding from the Rockefeller Foundation. The final ACCRN development phase focuses on program replication in other cities, countries, and sectors. The primary take-away from this activity is how the SLD process engages local civil-society groups to evaluate and create solutions to anticipated climate hazards, enabling marginalized groups to participate as stakeholders.

Climate Resilient Cities Primer

At the World Bank, the East Asia Region has produced the Climate Resilient Cities (CRC) Primer, which is intended as a first step to guiding local governments through the assessment of climate change and disaster risk impacts. The primer presents exercises that focus on identifying "hot spots" for hazard risk and collecting the necessary information to make informed decisions regarding climate action. Next, the primer offers examples of "sound practices" and city profiles to illustrate how other cities are enacting "no-regrets" policies. The CRC Primer has led to Technical Assistance (TA) programs in Vietnam, Indonesia, the Philippines, and China. The primary value of this exercise is that it presents the challenges of climate change and disaster in a format that local governments can use to present complex issues to their constituents.

ISO 31000

In November 2009 the International Organization for Standardization developed ISO 31000—a set of principles and guidelines intended to help a wide variety of organizations in managing risk. ISO 31000 defines risk as the "effect of uncertainty in objectives." Some of the principles of ISO 31000 point toward risk management becoming a value generator for the organization, an integral part of the decision-making and other organizational processes—tailored, transparent, inclusive, systematic, structured, timely, dynamic, iterative, and responsive. The ISO 31000 is a further step in creating a framework for designing, implementing, and maintaining an effective risk management program.

Identify—Good Practices in Risk Identification

As discussed in other chapters, many informal settlements in cities are at high risk from disasters largely due to where they live, deficiencies in providing for infrastructure and services, and the poor quality of housing. For local governments, one of the most difficult tasks is to gather detailed information and maps needed for identifying risk-prone areas, planning upgrading, new house developments, and infrastructure and service provision. Below are a few examples of how much disaster risk reduction is served when low-income groups can work well with local governments (and other actors) in identifying risk (IFRC 2010).

Local Resilience Action Plan (LRAP)—Identifying Local Adaptation Priorities

In Vietnam, the CRC activities in three cities (Dong Hoi, Can Tho, and Hanoi) included the preparation of a workbook outlining the steps local governments can undertake to complete a Local Resilience Action Plan (LRAP). An LRAP, the second step in local resilience planning, comprises four primary inputs and complementary graphic representations. The four inputs include (1) vulnerability assessment; (2) spatial analysis, which is an overlay of maps that identifies geographic "hotspots" at the city level and in specific target areas in the city wider area; (3) inventory of planned capital investments and policy changes to address the hotspots and identification of the gaps that remain; and (4) multistakeholder priority-setting process based on comparison of alternatives in light of limited budgets and abilities to raise external financing. The LRAP identifies short-, medium-, and long-term adaptation priorities for project investment with specific costs, timelines, and responsible actors. Much like the CRC exercises, the LRAP should be completed in a collaborative dialogue between local governments and stakeholders. In the case of Can Tho, recommendations from the LRAP process are currently being integrated into local urbanization planning efforts.

Philippines Partnership between Grass Roots Organizations and Local Governments for Documenting Risk

Identification of communities at risk and documentation of informal settlements for which there is little or no official data is critical in understanding the vulnerability of urban areas (PHPF 2010). The Philippines Homeless People's Federation (PHPF) is an example of how low-income community organizations can partner with local governments to address disaster risk reduction by identifying and documenting communities at risk.[4] PHPF is made up of 161 urban poor community associations and savings groups with more than 70,000 members from 18 cities and 15 municipalities. Federation members work closely with local governments in various initiatives to secure land tenure, build or improve homes and increase economic opportunities. PHPF works in locations impacted by disasters, building capacity at the community level to take action to meet immediate and long-term needs. Drawing from its experience, PHPF developed initiatives for risk management as it identifies at-risk communities in cities and municipalities. Based on this, it supports the design and implementation of risk reduction strategies.

For example, PHPF in partnership with local NGOs has identified and profiled at-risk communities in 12 cities and 10 municipalities located in Luzon, Visayas, and Mindanao, the three island groups in the Philippines. Communities prioritized included informal settlements located under bridges, on cliffs and other landslide-prone areas, along coastal shorelines and riverbanks, in public cemeteries, near open dumpsites, and in flood-prone locations.

Another example of a successful partnership between local and national government, grassroots organizations, and the PHPF took place in the city of Iloilo after the devastation caused by Typhoon Frank in 2008. The city government recognized that the urban poor and their support organizations are partners in the city's development, and provided several opportunities for them to participate in local decision making through representation in technical working groups and multi-sectoral bodies. As a result, the scale and scope of housing delivery, upgrading, post-disaster assistance, and other basic services were much increased because of the resource-sharing from the partnership.

Furthermore, the federation as a member of the Resettlement and Monitoring Task Force has assisted the local government in social preparations and other resettlement-related activities. This includes an information-dissemination campaign among communities living in danger zones (along riverbanks and shorelines, as well as those directly affected by the city's infrastructure projects) who will be transferred to government relocation sites. The city government, through the Iloilo City Urban Poor Affairs Office, assisted in the federation's social mobilization, which includes mapping of high-risk/disaster-affected communities, and identification and prioritization of communities to be given post-disaster assistance (temporary houses and material loan assistance for housing repair).

The effectiveness of partnerships between local governments and grassroots organizations in scaling up disaster risk reduction in the Philippines is sustained by four factors: strong community networks (that can lobby for disaster risk reduction policies that are community-driven and supported and then help implement these); an alternative financial facility (that supports community-driven action, support for insurance for low-income households and loans for reconstruction or rehabilitation and upgrading); technical support (to advise on site selection, land acquisition, housing and settlement designs, zoning based on geo-hazard maps and easy-to-comply building standards); and detailed community-level information systems (including the kinds of community mapping, enumeration, and risk assessment described already).

India: Local Government-Community Organization Partnerships for Vulnerability Mapping and Data Gathering in Cuttack

In the city of Cuttack, India, a citywide survey is currently underway. On the one hand, the city government has stated its commitment to a citywide program for informal settlements. On the other hand, federation groups are developing a GIS system that will prove particularly useful for local government.[5] The mapping process in Cuttack builds on more than two decades of experience in data gathering by the community organizations formed by the inhabitants of informal settlements and other districts—through a partnership between local *Mahila Milan* groups and the local (city or state) slum dweller federations (Appadurai 2001; Patel, D'Cruz, and Burra 2002). What makes this process in Cuttack unusual is that the community-driven data gathering includes preparing digital maps at the city scale for the city authorities. These maps and the data gathered about each informal settlement are being used to negotiate the support needed for upgrading or relocation.

The first step in this mapping is to develop an initial list of informal settlements. Local governments generally have such a list but it needs checking and is often incomplete. The next step is to work with the *Mahila Milan* savings groups and federation members to check the list—which often ends up identifying many more informal settlements. In Cuttack, 77 informal settlements were found that were not on the official list (Agarwal and Sangar 2005; Agarwal 2011). With a list of all informal settlements, visits can be planned to each by *Mahila Milan* representatives and staff from a support NGO. At this meeting with the residents and their community leaders, a profile of the settlement is developed that includes details of who lives there, the nature of their tenure of the land, the buildings, and the extent of provision for infrastructure and services. It also includes questions about extreme weather (and its impacts on them) and other risks they face (or faced in the past). Then this group walks the boundaries of the settlement, marking it with a GPS device (points are marked at every turn, and when the boundary is a straight line, every 5–10 meters). As residents walk with the team doing the mapping, they comment on boundaries and characteristics, which help the visiting team understand the settlement. From this is produced a profile of the settlement and a map of its boundaries (that can be imported into a digital map of Cuttack). Points marked in the GPS device are uploaded onto Google Earth in the office computer. Using the path tool in Google Earth, the federation member connects the points to create boundaries corresponding to each mapped settlement. Slum profile data collected by *Mahila Milan*—usually during mapping—is entered into an Excel spreadsheet and selected data can also be incorporated into the map, attached to the boundary maps.

This process is then repeated for all informal settlements, from which comes an accurate, detailed, disaggregated database. This information can be then aggregated into a citywide map showing the boundaries of all informal settlements and a link to each settlement profile in a GIS system.

The city authorities have been supportive of this mapping, recognizing that this process can help produce the information needed to get central government funding for citywide upgrading. The mapping and data gathered can provide the basis for agreement between city government and the residents of informal settlements on what needs to be done.

For this kind of community-driven approach to mapping and data gathering to be effective, it is important for local governments to see its utility to them. It also depends on a local government capacity to act on this information and for its technical staff and departments or divisions responsible for infrastructure and service provision to be able to work with the resident groups in the informal settlements.

Prepare—Good Practices in Risk Reduction through Early-Warning Systems

In areas where disasters are recurrent, the establishment of early-warning systems and evacuation plans are critical to safeguarding human lives in an emergency. The main objective of early-warning systems is to empower individuals and communities to act in a way that reduces their probability of personal injury or damage to property and critical resources in the threat of hazards. The International Strategy for Disaster Reduction (ISDR) suggests four key elements of people-centered early-warning systems: risk knowledge, monitoring and warning service, dissemination and communication, and response capability (ISDR 2006).

In the case of sudden events, such as tsunamis, flash floods, and landslides, the poor are frequently the last to know of impending danger, and due to a lack of security, they are frequently reticent to abandon their possessions.

Honduras—Promoting Dialogue and Coordinating Responses

There are numerous cases in Latin America where the urban poor have benefited from the establishment of early-warning systems. Hurricane Mitch, which hit Honduras in 1998, is considered the second-deadliest Atlantic hurricane in history.

The many deaths caused by Hurricane Mitch prompted several municipalities in Honduras to establish an inter-municipal association, with the support of GTZ, to promote dialogue on the risks of natural hazards and to coordinate responses. The association known as Mancomunidad de los Municipios del Centro de Atlantida (MAMUCA), the municipalities of La Masica, Arizona, Esparta, San Francisco, and El Porvenir worked together to identify risks, raise awareness, prioritize reconstruction, encourage local decision making in a public forum, and engage in national risk management. This was set up to allow the local governments to work together in preparing for extreme events and to coordinate local response. It included support for participatory diagnoses and participation in local decision making through public meetings (cabildos abiertos) and helped improve evacuation, during rainstorms, through community-based disaster reduction. It also encouraged the formation of local emergency committees (CODELs) integrated with municipal emergency committees to practice early-warning and evacuation drills (Bollin and Mascher 2005). CODELs included representatives from health-care services, the police, the fire department, and the Red Cross.

Honduras has not been the only one in Central America to learn from the experience with Hurricane Mitch. For instance, Cuba, despite being highly exposed to tropical storms, has repeatedly averted disaster through a highly effective system to educate, mobilize, and protect its citizenry. In 2005, this "culture of safety" allowed for the evacuation of 640,000 people from Havana and the path of Hurricane Wilma while the storm surge reached 1 kilometer inland (Simms and Reid 2006). Hurricane Wilma resulted in the loss of one life, a marked difference to the nearly 20,000 Central Americans killed by flooding and landslides associated with Hurricane Mitch in 1998.

Argentina—From Early-Warning Systems to Improvement in Asset Security

Buenos Aires is a low-lying city, and thus faces recurrent flooding from three rivers. While arguably less catastrophic than landslides, the repeated flooding of this area makes it difficult for the urban poor to recover between disasters. In 2004, filmmakers documented flooding in the low-income community of El Zajon, raising awareness within both the community and the government, prompting the installation of an early-warning system (Simms and Reid 2006). The World Bank (2005) has supported several flood-prevention efforts in Argentina under the Urban Flood Prevention and Drainage Project. In its first phase, the project focused on the development of a city risk management program for Buenos Aires, which, among many things, included flood forecasting and early-warning systems. Now in its second phase, the project has expanded to include the six provinces located between the Rio Paraguay and the Rio Parana, the most flood-prone region in Argentina. In addition to early-warning systems, the second phase will improve the asset security of the poor by implementing a housing program for the lowest-income population (World Bank 2006a).

Mitigate—Good Practices in Risk Reduction through Mitigation

In addition to early response, evacuation, and sheltering, community actions may also be more proactive, engaging citizens and governments to work together to build resilience. Disaster mitigation, seen as activities that will reduce the impact of a disaster is generally linked to "good urban service delivery." Good development is not only what governments must do but also what they allow and support at the local level.[6] This is especially the case where local government lacks capacity and funding for needed investments. For disaster risk reduction and climate change adaption, there is a need to look at how people on the ground are taking care of their risks, understanding risk, and developing (household and collective) mechanisms to address risk. It is very difficult to reduce disaster risk without strong local organizations that tailor responses to the specifics of each location and the needs of those most at risk. Similarly, it is difficult to respond effectively to a disaster if the response is centralized and local organizations are not strong and supported.

Flood Management and Urban Planning

Tanzania—Opening up the Dialogue for Larger Government Support

In Dar es Salaam, the African Urban Risk Analysis Network (AURAN) carried out three case studies related to mainstreaming disaster risk management in urban planning practices. Included among them were successes related to the local communities requesting drainage pipes from local governments and community-based organizations building drainage systems. Building upon this, the AURAN project started working on the planned and unplanned settlements of Bonde la Mpunga, where residents have organized themselves to tackle the problem of local flooding (Kiunsi et al. 2009b). The local community established a seven-member Flood Control Committee to address the flooding risk, but its lack of legal mandate made it difficult to solicit funding for local improvements. While the committee did not receive support from the higher levels of government and several of their poorly executed interventions failed to solve the flooding problem, the committee's correspondence with the media opened a dialogue with the municipal government concerning local flooding.

Motivated by this dialogue and recognizing the risks of flooding, the Tanzanian government requested World Bank support in urban upgrading. The World Bank is currently financing loans to the central government for implementing Community Infrastructure Upgrading Programs (CIUP) throughout Dar es Salaam (World Bank 2004a). Targeting unplanned areas in the Ilala, Temeke, and Kinondoni municipalities, communities have selected technical improvements, including roads, drains, and public toilets. CIUP is an extensive program that focuses on improving physical access, complete with the associated surface water drainage and street lighting. The new community infrastructure allows safe access to homes on a regular and emergency basis; roadside and select collector drains dramatically decrease street flooding, and the street lights provide public safety in areas that residents did not previously perceive as safe. Under the first phase of CIUP, 16 sub-wards of Dar es Salaam were upgraded. Covering 453 hectares, the first phase benefited approximately 170,000 residents. Under the second phase of CIUP, which commenced in July 2010, an additional 15 sub-wards will be upgraded. This phase, covering 554 hectares, will benefit an additional 150,000 people; it is scheduled for completion by the end of 2011.[7]

Mozambique—Joint International and Local Effort for Urban Upgrading

In Quelimane City, local communities have partnered with the City Council and international organizations for urban upgrading. Quelimane City has a population of approximately 240,000 and is located in the Zambezi delta, Mozambique (City Council of Quelimane 2006; Cities Alliance 2008; Grimard 2006–2008). It suffers from cyclical floods, due to the combination of a high water table and heavy rain; 80 percent of its population lives in informal housing. Quelimane City, with support from Cities Alliance, embarked on the preparation of an urban upgrading strategy that had a special focus on water and sanitation. The strategy also included interventions in drainage, road network, and waste management. The Improving Water and Sanitation in Quelimane City, Mozambique, program was designed to be the first phase of an urban-upgrading program that, through demonstration effects, increased local capacity, and additional outside funding, could be scaled up across the city.

This program involved organizations working in partnership: UN-HABITAT acted as the implementing agency through its local offices; the project was coordinated with the World Bank's Municipal Development Project, which was already active in Quelimane; other partners included the Danish International

Development Agency (DANIDA), UNICEF, and WaterAid. The City Council of Quelimane provided an in-kind contribution of US$100,000 (by providing office space, equipment, a meeting room, technical and administrative staff, and vehicles). The residential community provided an in-kind contribution of $150,000 (through subsidized manpower, awareness campaigns, operational management teams, and reduced plot size or, in extreme cases, moving to another area because of improvement works). UN-HABITAT, the World Bank, DANIDA, UNICEF, and WaterAid together contributed $440,000 in cash and in kind. Other in-kind contributions totaling $30,000 were secured from a state water supply institution, and from a private-sector firm that made its trucks available during weekends in exchange for paying for only fuel and the driver. This novel and complicated institutional mix presented some challenges of coordination, including between Quelimane institutions themselves—particularly the City Council and community committees. Coordination could not be taken for granted, and it was necessary to establish rules and mechanisms for dialog between them.[8]

Senegal—Combining Efforts between Community Organizations, NGOs, and Local and National Government Agencies in Saint Louis

An example from the city of Saint Louis, Senegal, shows how flooding can be addressed through the combined and coordinated efforts of community-organizations, NGOs, and local and national government agencies. Saint Louis is Senegal's former national capital, with 180,000 inhabitants in 2002. The city is constructed around water, on three islands cut off from each other by the branches of the Senegal River, its tributaries, and the Atlantic Ocean. Some areas of the city are less than 2.5 meters above mean sea level. The city has experienced recurrent flooding since 1990, from the rains and from peak flows in the Senegal River. The rising river level is the product of many factors, including the silting up of the river bed; the disposal of household waste into the river; the reduced area available to floodwater irrigation (as unplanned urbanization means these areas are now occupied by housing); and a shallow water table that rises to the surface when the river swells and drains poorly during the winter season. Flooding generally affects areas inhabited by the lowest-income groups. Many are rural migrants who occupy sites not intended for residential use.

Stagnant rainwater in the flooded areas—less than 10 percent of the population live in homes with sewer connections—combined with a lack of clean water, inadequate drainage, and wastewater and solid-waste management—only 30 percent of households have a regular solid-waste collection service—brings serious health impacts. To these are added the proliferation of disease vectors, such as flies and mosquitoes. Poor hygiene and high levels of overcrowding compound the risks.

The strategy of the Senegalese NGO Enda-Tiers Monde in response to flooding in Saint Louis has been based not on building infrastructure (for instance, some areas are protected by dykes), but on strengthening local governance. Stakeholders have been brought together to discuss the problems they face and exchange views to finding solutions to problems that are beyond their individual skills or capacities. An action plan has been developed and implemented by all stakeholders, managed by a steering committee, which includes information, education, and communication, raising the awareness of the local people. Plays, exhibitions, media broadcasts, teatime "chats," interviews, photographic exhibitions, and open-air conferences have been used for this. Local civil-society organizations (including women's groups, youth associations, *dahiras*—religious groups) all organize in the flood-prone neighborhoods to mitigate the effects of flooding through. Mitigation includes (1) digging paths to evacuate stagnant water, (2) regularly maintaining drainage channels, (3) disinfecting stagnant water, in association with the National Hygiene Department, or (4) placing sandbags to help inhabitants get about within the neighborhood itself.

The authorities also use local labor for some drainage works, and women's groups are involved in awareness raising in order to combat diarrhea and to prevent malaria and other diseases. NGOs work closely with the state's decentralized structures (health and sanitation departments, fire brigade, etc.) to raise awareness and change the population's behavior (Khady 2007; ISDR 2009).

Water Supply and Sanitation

Pakistan—Local Government-Civil Society Partnerships to Provide Sanitation and Drainage in Karachi

There are programs that focus on social asset-building to improve water and sanitation services, making communities more resilient to disaster impacts. The Orangi Pilot Project Research and Training Institute (OPP-RTI) of Pakistan supports slum dwellers and local governments in planning, implementing, and financing basic sanitation (ISDR 2009). For the residents of informal settlements, OPP-RTI helps them to reduce to cost of household sanitary latrines or neighborhood sewers through design modification and the elimination of outside contractors. For governments, OPP-RTI supports them to plan and finance transport and treatment of the sewage from neighborhood collector sewers. Approximately 300 communities have financed, managed, and constructed their own internal sanitation systems, allowing government agencies to effectively channel their resources to larger external infrastructure. This illustrates a particularly important aspect for local government programs—how the design and implementation of piped water, sewers, and drains within informal settlements, which is difficult and expensive for government agencies, can be done far quicker and cheaper by supporting residents to manage it and finance it themselves. These activities have brought major benefits to large sections of the urban poor in Karachi.

Wastewater Management and Energy

Bolivia—Urban Adaptation and Climate Mitigation in Santa Cruz

In addressing climate change, there can be overlap between mitigation and adaptation. For the urban poor, proper wastewater management is critical to reduce contamination and the health problems exacerbated by density. Two World Bank projects respond to the urgent sanitation challenges in Santa Cruz de la Sierra—a city of 1.3 million people in Bolivia, growing at 6 percent each year. Sanitation services are provided by 10 cooperatives—some of which have been recognized as among the best in Latin America—but which give an overall level of sewerage coverage of only 32 percent. This means a high risk of infiltration into the city's main aquifer, which would result in irreversible damage to the city's water supply. Increased coverage of Santa Cruz's sewerage system will also result in avoided costs of developing an entirely new water supply source for the city.

The first project—Bolivia Urban Infrastructure—aimed to improve the access to basic services by the urban poor in Bolivia's major cities, through targeted infrastructure investments and the provision of technical assistance to municipalities in planning, expanding, and sustaining urban services. Part of this project involves the expansion of sewerage coverage in the poor areas of Santa Cruz, by increasing the capacity of four wastewater treatment plants. These plants use a lagoon treatment system, which uses anaerobic bacteria to break down organic matter. Unfortunately, this process produces methane—a powerful greenhouse gas that contributes to climate change.

The second project—Urban Wastewater Methane Gas Capture—involves covering all four large anaerobic treatment lagoons with high-density polyethylene "geomembrane" sheeting, supported by a system of floats and tubes. Those tubes are perforated and are used to capture gas from the lagoons—estimated at more than 44,000 tons of CO_2 per year—which is then transported, via interconnecting pipes, to a flare. The polyethylene covering also raises the temperature of the lagoon, thus optimizing anaerobic digestion, and increasing the throughput of the treatment plant.

This latter project will be funded by an emission-reduction purchase of $2.09 million by the Community Development Carbon Fund (CDCF) and the

Bio Carbon Fund. The CDCF allows industrialized countries to "purchase" emissions reductions from developing countries. That principle is adopted from the Clean Development Mechanism of the Kyoto Protocol, which developed a framework for emissions-reductions purchases until 2012; the CDCF extends that principle beyond 2012. In addition, the CDCF aims to ensure that communities are empowered to play an active role in the delivery of services that help improve their livelihoods and reduce poverty—by identifying, implementing, and monitoring those services. The local cooperative SAGUA-PAC will receive the proceeds from this purchase, and will be responsible for implementing the project, which is estimated to cost $1.48 million to install, and $24,000 a year to operate and maintain.

The project to capture methane leverages the World Bank's considerable experience in financing projects to capture and flare methane gas from landfill sites, and in dealing with the certification of emissions reductions under the Clean Development Mechanism. It is hoped that the Bolivian government will be able to pursue similar projects elsewhere, using the knowledge and skills it will have accrued in Santa Cruz (World Bank 2006b, 2007).

Water Supply and Energy Efficiency

India—Generating Carbon Revenue while Improving Access to Basic Services

Improving basic services for the urban poor can result in co-benefits for climate mitigation and adaptation. In the case of Karnataka, India, emission reductions were achieved while increasing access to water. Karnataka is a state in southern India, with an urban population of approximately 18 million people.[9] That population has grown by 29 percent over the last decade, and continues to grow—creating an urgent need to improve urban services. Ninety-four percent of Karnataka's urban population has some access to water supply, but this access is usually less than four hours a day. The poor service is due mostly to inefficient production and distribution of water, which create high costs and results in absolute shortages.

The government of Karnataka is already engaging in substantial efforts to improve its urban water supply, through investment programs, institutional and financial reforms, and an improved water tariff framework that emphasizes cost recovery. Indeed, the government has foreseen great room for improvement by tackling inefficient energy use, given that electricity represents more than half the operation cost of Karnataka's water supply. Not only does this mean higher operational costs, it also means unnecessary greenhouse gas (GHG) emissions, since the municipal water pumps are powered by fossil-fuel electricity from the national grid.

The Karnataka Municipal Water Energy Efficiency Project represents an effort to reduce emissions and operational costs. The project addresses key inefficiencies in the current system: inefficient and outdated pumping systems, improperly sized pumping systems, poor maintenance, operation at suboptimal loads, and high frictional losses through redundant pumps, pipes, and valves. The system is being improved by installing new and more efficient pumps; properly sizing pumps and components; improving electrical efficiency (for example, through power factors correction and standby transformers); better metering and monitoring; and reducing water leakage in the main pipes into the cities. This project is being implemented in six cities: Belgaum, Gulbarga, Hubli/Dharwad, Mangalore, Bellary, and Mysore. Total energy savings are estimated at more than 16 million KWh. Total emissions reductions are estimated at more than 13,000 tons of CO_2.

Capital investments will be made by a local actor—the Karnataka Urban Infrastructure Development and Finance Corporation (KUIDFC)—and the resulting emissions reductions will be purchased by the Community Development Carbon Fund (CDCF), of which the World Bank is a trustee. The capital investment cost of the project is estimated to be US$4.5 million. The CDCF is expected to purchase approximately 60,000 emissions reduction (ER) units from the project (the final number is to be confirmed after negotiation of an Emission Reduction Purchase Agreement). Depending on the certified emissions reductions price, the gross revenue will amount to between US$600,000 and US$900,000, which will be shared among participating municipalities.

Neighborhood Upgrading

Vietnam—Engaging the Community in Resilient Urban Upgrading

Since 2004, the World Bank has loaned Vietnam more than US$375 million to support its National Urban Upgrading Programs (VUUP), and there is currently a proposal for an additional US$395 million to expand activities to the Mekong Delta Region.[10] The programs aim to improve the effectiveness, accessibility, and sustainability of urban services through priority investments in urban upgrading, environmental improvement, and institutional strengthening at the urban level (World Bank 2004b). Vietnam is one of the most hazard-prone areas in Asia, due to its tropical monsoon location and topography. Typhoons and flooding are the most frequent hazards faced in Vietnam, where populations and economic activities are concentrated along the coastline and in low-lying deltas. In low-income urban areas, such as the Tan Hoa-Lo Gom Canal area of Ho Chi Minh, heavy rains typically inundate homes with a mix of sewage and storm water up to a meter deep. The VUUP focuses on engaging local communities in the critical stages of preparation, design, and implementation while seeking to improve the living conditions of all residents, regardless of their registration status. Using a multi-sector approach, the project aims to provide or rehabilitate infrastructure and housing in low-income areas through capacity building in the local government and through partnerships with communities.

The first major investment, of US$222 million, supports upgrading low-income communities in four cities: Can Tho, Hai Phong, Nam Dinh, and Ho Chi Minh, including the Tan Hoa-Lo Gom Canal area. The project seeks, among other things, to conduct an integrated upgrading of basic infrastructure at the neighborhood level, such as drainage, waste-water collection, electricity and lighting, street-access improvements, and water supply, as well as the provision of social services, such as schools, pre-schools, and health centers in targeted low-income communities.

The lessons learned in this first stage of VUUP activities informed similar projects in the area of Da Nang, the fourth-largest urban area in Vietnam (World Bank 2008b). Among the lessons carried over, the need for active community participation, minimization of relocation and resettlement, and the design of infrastructure to an appropriate technical standard that is still affordable to the communities. The second phase of the project supports the upgrading of tertiary infrastructure, the development of three resettlement sites, microfinance for housing improvement, and improved drainage systems.

The current pipeline proposal to expand the VUUP to the Mekong Delta region would focus on the provinces of Can Tho, My Tho, Kien Giang, Tra Vinh, Dong Thap, and Ca Mau (World Bank 2010). The expected measureable outcomes of the project include improved environmental conditions, improved quality of life, increased access to financing for housing improvements, greater tenure security, and improved capacity at the national level to manage urban systems.

Job Creation

Liberia—Reducing Vulnerability to Natural Disasters while Creating Job Opportunities for the Poor

In 2006, Mercy Corps initiated their Cash-for-Work program in Liberia to promote drainage maintenance. Prior to the initiation of this program, heavy rains would frequently trigger flooding in both urban and rural areas. Cleaning the drains was not a government priority, and the drainage systems had not been properly maintained for decades due to lack of funds and civil war. The one-year program was launched in five counties, generating more than 17,800 days of employment and greatly improving both drainage and the availability of clean water (ISDR 2009). Since 2008, the World Bank has supported the Cash for Work Temporary Employment Project (CfWTEP) in Liberia, through the Liberia Agency for Community Empowerment (LACE). Funding in the form of a US$3 million grant was made available through the Food Price Crisis Response Trust Fund, to provide income support to vulnerable households. Over the course of two years (October 2008–2010) approximately 17,000 workers have been employed to clear drains, sweep streets, repair culverts, and perform other public maintenance (Zampaglione 2008).

Transfer—Recent Practices in Risk Deflection

In the developing world, disasters can suddenly wipe out decades of development gains. Relief, recovery, and reconstruction can be extremely taxing on available resources for both governments and individuals, despite the leveraging of international aid. In some cases, individuals and governments may spread the cost of risk or damages across a population or time by establishing individual insurance or catastrophic risk pools.

El Salvador—Self and Community-based Insurance

In the World Watch Institute's *State of Our World 2007*, Christine Wamsler outlines how self-insurance is much more prevalent than formal insurance in the slums of El Salvador, as most residents are employed in the informal sector and therefore illegible for the national social-security system. Self-insurance coping strategies in El Salvador include having many children, encouraging family members to migrate to the United States to provide remittance income, and stockpiling building materials that can be used or resold. Wamsler estimates that in addition to free help or materials, households spend an average of 9.2 percent of their income on risk reduction. In a more communal context, some Salvadorans choose to contribute to community emergency funds or join religious institutions that traditionally offer post-disaster help. There are, however, cases where slum dwellers employed in the informal sector obtain certificates of employment from entrepreneurs that allow them to pay into the national social-security system.

Colombia—Innovation in Risk Management

In contrast to the preceding scenario, Manizales, Colombia, has arranged for insurance coverage to be extended to the urban poor through municipal tax collection. Any city resident may purchase insurance for their property, and after 30 percent of the insurable buildings participate, the insurance coverage is extended to tax-exempted properties, including properties with cadastral value of 25 monthly salaries or less (estimated at US$3,400). Despite the municipal administration collecting a handling fee of 6 percent, the insurance company has a direct contractual relationship with the individual taxpayer and bears responsibility for the all claims (Fay, Ghesquiere, Solo 2003).

Many of the cities with the strongest programs for reducing disaster risks come from Latin America. The city of Manizales provides an example of a city government committed to partnering with the community for disaster risk reduction. This included involving the population in each district in risk mapping and responses, as well as discussions that brought together all key local stakeholders. The risk mapping of each district identified risk zones and settlements particularly at risk from landslides. The city government then worked with the inhabitants to relocate them to safer sites and convert the land at risk into neighborhood parks with measures to stabilize the slopes (Velasquez 1998). A hundred and twelve women were trained as "guardians of the slopes" to create and maintain slope stabilization in their neighborhood and to report on problems. Environmental observatories have been created in each of the 11 *comunas* into which the city is divided to support public engagement and implementation of the city's environmental plan. The *comunas* monitor progress on environmental conditions, with progress summarized and displayed publicly in a simple set of indicators—the environmental traffic lights (*semaforos ambientales*) (Velasquez Barrero 2010). The city also introduced collective voluntary insurance to allow low-income groups to insure their buildings; the city government has an agreement with an insurance company and allows any city resident to purchase insurance through municipal taxes (Velasquez 1998).

Turkey—Liquidity for Post-Disaster Relief and Reconstruction

At the national level, countries have the opportunity to participate in public insurance, such as catastrophic risk financing. Established before disaster impacts, catastrophic risk financing can provide governments with immediate liquidity for post-disaster relief and reconstruction. The World Bank and the Global Facility for Disaster Risk Reduction (GFDRR) have been helping governments participate in catastrophic risk financing as part of larger disaster risk management (Cummins and Mahul 2008). The World Bank Independent Evaluation Group cites the Turkish Catastrophic Insurance Pool (TCIP) as a successful project, which has tripled the insurance penetration for earthquake coverage in Turkey. Established following the 2000 Marmara earthquake, the TCIP has an annual premium of US$20, despite covering up to $1 billion in damages in a disaster (IEG 2006).

Caribbean Islands—Multi-country Partnership for Risk Financing

For small countries for which a natural disaster could cause damage significantly larger than their national economy, there is the option of sovereign risk financing. The Caribbean Catastrophe Risk Insurance Facility (CCRIF), the first multi-country risk pool in the world, is a regional insurance fund designed to mitigate the financial impact of hurricanes or earthquakes by providing immediate liquidity. There are 16 member nations: Anguilla, Antigua & Barbuda, Bahamas, Barbados, Belize, Bermuda, Cayman Islands, Dominica, Grenada, Haiti, Jamaica, St. Kitts & Nevis, St. Lucia, St. Vincent & the Grenadines, Trinidad & Tobago, and the Turks & Caicos Islands. During its first season of operation, the 2007 hurricane season, one earthquakes triggered payouts for two countries, and the Facility was able to make funds available within two weeks of the event (World Bank 2008a).

Central America—Securing Flexible Funding for Disaster-induced Emergency

Recently, the International Bank for Reconstruction and Development (IBRD) has offered Catastrophe Risk Deferred Drawdown Option, or CAT DDO, as a new product to middle-income country governments with disaster risk-management programs in place. Countries can access the funds if they declare a disaster-induced state of emergency. The maximum amount available is US$500 million, or 0.25 percent of a country's gross domestic product, whichever is smaller. Loan pricing is in line with standard IBRD terms, which include a 0.25 percentage point front-end fee. The funds may be drawn down over a three-year period, which may be renewed up to four times for a total of 15 years. There are currently CAT DDOs under development in the Central American countries of Panama, El Salvador, and Costa Rica.[11]

Recover—Good Practices in Building-Back-Better

After a disaster in which there is widespread destruction of housing and infrastructure, government agencies are often keen to rebuild. Large programs to reconstruct houses after disasters mirror many of the limitations of public housing programs, including a refusal to rebuild on the sites preferred by those they are built for (post-disaster where the survivors previously lived or close by) and the use of distant sites far from survivors' livelihoods. Residents may be frustrated by inappropriate designs and unfamiliar building materials. Costs are often high, as those with the greatest incentive to manage costs (that is, local residents) are not included in decision making; for the same reason, there are frequent concerns with the quality of building materials and construction.[12]

An alternative approach to reconstruction is "owner-driven development." Here, external agencies work with owners to support them in rebuilding their housing, drawing on the successful experiences with upgrading. This helps speed up responsive household-led reconstruction through providing additional resources (cash or building materials) and in some cases technical assistance (in part to improve the ability of houses to build in resilience to local hazards). Costs are kept down as local skilled building workers are used and families help with unskilled labor and, where possible, the use of recovered materials. Yet this approach may also only serve property owners and live tenants unprotected (Lyons 2008; Lyons and Schilderman 2010).

A third approach to reconstruction is for local governments and external agencies to engage community organizations in identifying strategies to support construction and physical improvements. Here, there are very good possibilities for "building-back-better" to remove or greatly reduce disaster risk. A superficial community process will not successfully manage the reconstruction in a way that prevents the benefits from being secured by a few. Locally managed inclusive and representative groups have to be able to manage both finances and construction if they are to be successful in addressing their members' shelter needs. They need to be able to understand the regulatory context and identify the required amendments, and to negotiate with politicians and officials. Here, it is also possible for all those affected to be part of the building-back-better. For instance, in Mandaue, which was destroyed by a fire, the inhabitants were organized (and supported by the Homeless People's Federation of the Philippines) and they re-blocked their settlement and provided for long-term tenants as well as owners (Rayos and Christopher 2010).

Indonesia—Channeling Reconstruction through Community-based Institutions

Somewhat hidden from the world by the ongoing flurry of Aceh tsunami recovery, the 2006 Java earthquake, with a magnitude of 6.3 on the Richter scale, was nevertheless an enormously destructive event. Over 350,000 residential units were lost and 5,760 persons were killed, most from the collapse of non-engineered masonry structures. Using lessons learned from the tsunami experience and resources from the Community-based Settlements Rehabilitation and Reconstruction project in Aceh supported by the World Bank, the Indonesian government was able to response quickly and efficiently. Facilitators were recruited and villages elected boards of trustees, which later were instrumental in organizing community meetings and supervising implementation.

Key activities included (1) identifying beneficiaries and prioritizing the most vulnerable and poorest; (2) establishing community housing groups of 10 to 15 families, and deciding on a coordinator, secretary, and treasurer for each group to be accountable for the use of grants; (3) developing detailed plans to use the construction grants for each group, and preparing group grant applications; (4) opening group bank accounts; and (5) approving plans, disbursement in tranches, and group procurement, construction, and bookkeeping. Training was provided to community members and local workers, as earthquake-resistant construction required consistent construction techniques. Later, the community developed plans to rebuild community infrastructure and facilities, with a particular focus on disaster resilience. Communities conducted self-surveys, prepared thematic maps, analyzed needs and disaster risks, reached consensus on priority programs, and established procedures for operations and maintenance. Grants for infrastructure were also disbursed in tranches through local banks as work progressed.[13]

An adequate understanding of rules and a sense of ownership by the community were essential to ensuring good targeting and plans, accountability, and social control of implementation. The involvement of women increased accountability and enhanced the appropriateness of technical solutions. The role of facilitators is crucial, as they ensure effective communication and adaptability of the program to local situations, as well as compliance with program principles. In all, 6,480 core houses were funded under UPP, and the multi-donor Java Reconstruction Fund funded another 15,153 units using, among other sources, a loan from the World Bank (P103457). This approach to reconstruction became the model for the much larger government-financed rehabilitation and reconstruction program, under which about 200,000 houses were rebuilt in Java.[14]

Volunteer Technology Communities

In 2010 the disaster risk-management communities saw the rise of the "humanitarian technologist": Regular technicians all over the world motivated to collaborate in post-disaster information gathering (GFDRR 2011). Volunteer Technology Communities (VTC) uses flattened, decentralized structures of decision-making and conflict and conflict-resolution mechanisms that were adapted from online communities like Wikipedia and open-source software development projects. For instance, after the Haiti earthquake the World Bank facilitated the mobilization of hundreds of volunteers through the Global Earth Observation—Catastrophe Assessment Network (GEO—CAN), which developed a comprehensive and rigorous damage analysis (GFDRR, 2011). Other promising examples of VTCs include Random Hacks of Kindness (RHoK)—a partnership among Google, Microsoft, Yahoo, NASA, and the World Bank—and Crisis Commons, an international network of professionals drawn together by emergencies like the earthquakes in Chile and Haiti, the oil spill in Louisiana, and the flooding in Pakistan.

Lessons Learned and Recommendations

As climate change and disaster are expected to exacerbate existing inequalities, the most important takeaway from this review is that city managers should not view climate or disaster impacts as independent actions, but rather as impetus to improve the overall living conditions of the poor. Perceived vulnerability, widely considered the primary driver in adaptation planning, reflects the inability of communities or individuals to react to the external forces on their well-being (Satterthwaite et al. 2007). To be proactive rather than reactive, governance practices should aim at providing the basic services, safeguards, and education to the urban poor, supporting their adaptive capacity (Adger et al. 2003). Backlogs in providing infrastructure and services in cities in low- and middle-income nations can be addressed through partnerships between local governments and community organizations. This section has given many examples of partnerships between community organizations formed by the residents of informal settlements and local governments in providing services. This meant a choice by these community organizations to work with government and a choice by government officials and agencies to stop seeing the residents of informal settlements as problems but start seeing their residents' organizations as contributors to good solutions to local and citywide problems.

A growing number of cities around the world have produced climate strategies that focus on mitigation techniques, since adaptation policies are harder to isolate, falling across agency and jurisdictional lines (Roberts 2008). Several cities, however, that do focus on adaptation, and take vulnerability into account, include New York (NYCPCC 2010), London (City of London 2008), Cape Town (City of Cape Town 2006), and Durban (Katich 2009). While much of this annex has highlighted interesting actions on the ground, these are a few of the cities using climate adaptation and disaster risk to reassess government activities—and gaining new perspective in relation to how planning can affect the urban poor. For cities that aim to alleviate climate and disaster risks for the urban poor, the good practices outlined here suggest that improving resilience requires cities to improve services and allow risk to inform future investments and development.

TABLE A3.1
Matrix of Recent Practice Cases

Activity	Country/ region	Area of action	Good practice
Information, knowledge sharing, education and training			
Climate Resilient Communities Program	United States	Planning, assessment	Builds off an existing global mitigation network
Capacity Strengthening of Least Developing Countries for Adaptation to Climate Change (CLACC) Program	Africa and South Asia	Planning, assessment	Network of international experts working to strengthen organizations in least-developed countries and support their sustainable development initiatives
Asian Cities Climate Change Resilience Network (ACCRN)	Asia	Planning, assessment	Shared Learning Dialogue (SLD) engages community actors and government agencies to explore their current and future vulnerabilities in a transparent and iterative group discussion. The SLD outcome focuses on creating a shared understanding of risk and priorities for action.
Climate Resilient Cities (CRC) Primer	East Asia	Planning, assessment	Guidance for local governments for identifying "hot spots"
ISO 31000	World	Framework, standards	Seeks to provide a universally recognized set of standards for organizational risk management
Risk identification			
Local Resilience Action Plan (LRAPs)	Vietnam	Planning, assessment	Guiding local governments through the assessment of climate change and disaster risk impacts and presenting the challenges of climate change and disaster in a format that local governments can use to present complex issues to their constituents
Philippines Homeless People's Federation	Philippines	Planning, assessment, data collection	Identification of at-risk communities and help provide documentation on informal settlements for which there is little or no official data
Vulnerability mapping in Cuttack	India	Data collection	Community-driven data collection and mapping using GIS systems

Risk reduction: preparedness

Project	Country	Theme	Description
Mancomunidad de los Municipios del Centro de Atlantida (MAMUCA)	Honduras	Early-warning systems	Municipalities working together to identify risks, raise awareness, prioritize reconstruction, encourage local decision making in a public forum, and engage in national risk management; establishment of local emergency committees (CODELs) to practice early-warning and evacuation drills
Caracas and Buenos Aires early-warning systems	Venezuela	Early-warning systems	Establishment of early-warning systems to alert the poor living in landslide- and flood-prone areas
Argentina Urban Flood Prevention and Drainage Project	Argentina	Early-warning, forecasting, housing programs	Development of a city risk-management program for Buenos Aires; second phase will improve the asset security of poor

Risk reduction: mitigation

Project	Country	Theme	Description
Community Infrastructure Upgrading Programs (CIUP)	Tanzania	Community engagement in disaster risk reduction (DRR)	CIUP is an extensive program that focuses on improving physical access, as prioritized by the communities themselves.
Improving water and sanitation in Quelimane City, Mozambique	Mozambique	Water, sanitation, transport	Creating partnerships with a broad range of stakeholders to improve water, sanitation, and road networks
Local government strengthening in Senegal	Senegal	Local governance, flood management	Preparing community-driven action plans to mitigate the effects of flooding
Orangi Pilot Project Research and Training Institute (OPP-RTI) of Pakistan	Pakistan	Water, sanitation	Reduce the cost of household sanitary latrines or neighborhood sewers through design modification and the elimination of outside contractors
Bolivia Urban Infrastructure Project and Urban Wastewater Methane Gas Capture Project	Bolivia	Sanitation	Expansion of sewerage coverage in poor areas of Santa Cruz, by increasing the capacity of four wastewater-treatment plants, and collecting methane for CDM purposes

(continued next page)

TABLE A3.1 *continued*

Activity	Country/ region	Area of action	Good practice
Karnataka Municipal Water Energy Efficiency Project	India	Energy, water	Addresses key inefficiencies in the current system: inefficient and outdated pumping systems, improperly sized pumping systems, poor maintenance, operation at suboptimal loads, and high frictional losses through redundant pumps, pipes, and valves
Vietnam National Urban Upgrading Programs (VUUP)	Vietnam	Transportation, disaster risk, sanitation, water	Focuses on engaging local communities in the critical stages of preparation, design, and implementation while seeking to improve the living conditions of all residents
Cash-for-work programs Cash for Work Temporary Employment Project	Liberia	Job creation, sanitation, water	Reducing poverty through job creation to maintain water and sanitation infrastructure
Risk transfer			
Self and community-based insurance	El Salvador	Insurance	Creation of community emergency funds
Manizales insurance for the urban poor	Colombia	Insurance	After 30 percent of the insurable buildings participate, insurance coverage is extended to tax-exempted properties.
Turkish Catastrophic Insurance Pool (TCIP)	Turkey	Catastrophe risk	Prior to a disaster, governments can secure a line of credit for immediate liquidity that can be used for post-disaster relief and reconstruction.
Caribbean Catastrophe Risk Insurance Facility (CCRIF); Turkish Catastrophic Insurance Pool (TCIP)	Caribbean Islands; Turkey	Catastrophe risk	Provide governments with immediate liquidity for post-disaster relief and reconstruction
Catastrophe Risk Deferred Drawdown Option (CAT DDO)	Central America	Catastrophe risk	Countries can access the funds if they declare a disaster-induced state of emergency.
Recover			
Java Reconstruction Fund	Indonesia	Reconstruction	Community-based resettlement and reconstruction in Java
Volunteer Technology Communities (VTCs)	World	Post-disaster assessments	Communities of software developers, engineers, and technology enthusiasts who are using innovative methods and tools to help save lives in the aftermath of natural disasters.

Notes

1. http://www.undp.org/climatechange/adapt/definitions.html#15
2. This approach has also been shown effective in disaster risk reduction and in post-disaster response, as discussed in later sections of this paper.
3. This draws on ISDR, 2011 Global Assessment Report on Disaster Risk Reduction.
4. This is drawn from Rayos and Christopher (2010) and PHPF (2010).
5. This is drawn from Livengood (2011) and from field visits to Cuttack by David Satterthwaite in June and October 2010.
6. This paragraph draws on Archer and Boonyabancha (2010).
7. Personal communication with Barjor Mehta, 2010.
8. Unfortunately an application to the European Union for €1.5 million of funding was not successful, and so it remains uncertain whether the second, scaled-up phase of the program will be pursued.
9. World Bank (2009) and personal communication with Da Zhu (2009).
10. This includes the 2004 Vietnam Urban Upgrading Project and the 2008 Da Nang Priority Infrastructure Investment Project.
11. World Bank. Background note: Catastrophe Risk Deferred Drawdown Option (DDO), or CAT DDO. http://go.worldbank.org/G41ZXJZO30.
12. This section draws heavily on Archer and Boonyabancha (2010).
13. Communication with Sri Probo Sudarmo, World Bank, Indonesia.
14. Communication with Sri Probo Sudarmo, World Bank, Indonesia.

References

Adger, N., S. Huq, K. Brown, D. Conway, and M. Hulme. 2003. "Adaptation to Climate Change in the Developing World." *Progress in Development Studies* 3 (3): 179–195.

Agarwal, Siddarth. 2011. "Health and Inequality in Urban Populations in India." *Environment and Urbanization* 23 (1).

———, and K. Sangar. 2005. "Need for Dedicated Focus on Urban Health Within National Rural Health Mission." *Indian Journal of Public Health* 49 (3): 141–151.

Appadurai, Arjun. 2001. "Deep Democracy: Urban Governmentality and the Horizon of Politics." *Environment and Urbanization* 13 (2): 23–43.

Archer, Diane, and Somsook Boonyabancha. 2010. "Seeing a Disaster as an Opportunity: Harnessing the Energy of Disaster Survivors for Change." Background paper prepared for the 2011 *Global Assessment Report on Disaster Risk Reduction*. Forthcoming in *Environment and Urbanization* 23 (2).

Bollin, C., and F. Mascher. 2005. "'Honduras: Community Based Disaster Risk Management and Inter-Municipal Cooperation,' A Review of Experience Gathered by the Special Inter-Municipal Cooperation." MAMUCA. Eschborn: Deutsche Gesellschaft für Technische Zusammenarbeit.

Cities Alliance. 2008. *Comments on Progress Report, Improving Water and Sanitation in Quelimane City*. P101077.

City Council of Quelimane. 2006. *Improving Water and Sanitation in Quelimane City, Mozambique*.

City of London. 2008. *The London Climate Change Adaptation Strategy*. London: Mayor of London.

City of Cape Town. 2006. *Framework for Adaptation to Climate Change in the City of Cape Town (FAC4T)*. City of Cape Town, Environment Resource Management. Cape Town: University of Cape Town.

Cummins, J.D., and Olivier Mahul. 2008. *Catastrophic Risk Financing in Developing Countries: Principles for Public Intervention*. Washington, DC: World Bank.

Diagne, Khady. 2007. "Governance and Natural Disasters: Addressing Flooding in Saint Louis, Senegal." *Environment and Urbanization* 19 (2): 552–562.

Douglas, Ian, Kurshid Alam, Maryanne Maghenda, Yasmin Mcdonnell, Louise Mclean, and Jack Campbell. 2008. "Unjust Waters: Climate Change, Flooding and the Urban Poor in Africa." *Environment and Urbanization* 20 (1): 187–205.

Fay, Marianne, Francis Ghesquiere, and Tova Solo. 2003. "Natural Disasters and the Urban Poor." En Breve No. 32 (October), World Bank, Washington, DC.

Global Facility for Disaster Reduction and Recovery (GFDRR). 2011. *Volunteer Technology Communities: Open Development*. GFDRR: Washington DC.

Greater London Authority. 2010. *The London Climate Change Adaptation Strategy, Draft Report*. London: Greater London Authority. http://www.london.gov.uk/climatechange/strategy.

Grimard, Alain. 2006–2008. *Grant Progress Report, Improving Water and Sanitation in Quelimane City*. P101077.

Independent Evaluation Group (IEG). 2006. *Hazards of Nature, Risks to Development: An IEG Evaluation of World Bank Assistance for Natural Disasters*. Washington, DC: World Bank Independent Evaluation Group. http://www.worldbank.org/ieg/naturaldisasters/docs/natural_disasters_evaluation.pdf.

International Federation of Red Cross and Red Crescent Societies (IFRC). 2010. *World Disasters Report: Focus on Urban Risk*. Geneva: IFRC.

ISDR. 2006. "ISDR Secretariat Biennial Workplan: 2006–2007." Geneva: UN International Strategy for Disaster Reduction Secretariat.

———. 2009. *Global Assessment Report on Disaster Risk Reduction*. Geneva: UN International Strategy for Disaster Reduction. http://www.preventionweb.net/english/hyogo/gar/report/index.php?id=9413.

Katich, K. 2009. "Urban Climate Resilience: A Global Assessment of City Adaptation Plans." Master's thesis, Massachusetts Institute of Technology. http://dspace.mit.edu/handle/1721.1/49698.

Kiunsi, Robert B., John Lupala, Manoris Meshack, and Robert Kiunsi. 2009a. "Building Disaster-Resilient Communities: Dar es Salaam, Tanzania." In *Disaster Risk Reduction: Cases from Urban Africa*, ed. Pelling and Wisner, 127-146. London: Earthscan.

———. 2009b. *Mainstreaming Disaster Risk Reduction in Urban Planning Practice in Tanzania: AURAN Phase II Project Final Report*. African Urban Risk Analysis Network. http://www.preventionweb.net/files/13524_TANZANIAFINALREPORT27OCT09Mainstrea.pdf.

Livengood, Avery. 2011. "Enabling Participatory Planning with GIS: A Case Study of Settlement Mapping in Cuttack, India." *Environment and Urbanization* 23 (2).

Lyons, Michal. 2008. "Building Back Better: The Large Scale Impact of Small Scale Approaches to Reconstruction." *World Development* 37 (2): 385–398.

———, and Theo Schilderman, eds. 2010. *Building Back Better: Delivering People-centred Housing Reconstruction at Scale.* Practical Action Publishing, Rugby.

Mitlin, Diana. 2008. "With and Beyond the State: Co-production as a Route to Political Influence, Power and Transformation for Grassroots Organizations." *Environment and Urbanization* 20 (2): 339–360.

New York City Panel on Climate Change (NYCPCC). 2010. *Climate Change Adaptation in New York City: Building a Risk Management Response.* Ed. C. Rosenzweig and W. Solecki. Annals of the New York Academy of Sciences, Vol. 1196. Wiley-Blackwell. http://www.nyas.org/Publications/Annals/Detail.aspx?cid=ab9d0f9f-1cb1-4f21-b0c8-7607daa5dfcc

Patel, Sheela, Celine D'Cruz, and Sundar Burra. 2002. "Beyond Evictions in a Global City: People-Managed Resettlement in Mumbai." *Environment and Urbanization* 14 (1): 166–171.

Philippines Homeless People's Federations (PHPF). 2010. "Addressing Vulnerabilities through Support Mechanisms: HPFPI's Ground Experience in Enabling the Poor to Implement Community-rooted Interventions on Disaster Response and Risk Reduction." Background paper prepared for the 2011 *Global Assessment Report on Disaster Risk Reduction.*

Rayos, Co, and Jason Christopher. 2010. "Community-driven Disaster Intervention: The Experience of the Homeless Peoples Federation Philippines." IIED/ACHR/SDI Working Paper, London, International Institute for Environment and Development.

Roberts, D. 2008. "Thinking Globally, Acting Locally: Institutionalizing Climate Change at the Local Level." *Environment and Urbanization* 20 (2): 521–537.

Satterthwaite, David. 2011. How Local Governments Can Work with Communities in the Delivery of Basic Services, processed.

Satterthwaite, D., S. Huq, M. Pelling, H. Reid, and P. Romero-Lankao. 2007. *Building Climate Change Resilience in Urban Areas and Among Urban Populations in Low- and Middle-Income Nations.* Building for Climate Change Resilience, Center for Sustainable Urban Development.

Simms, Andrew, and Hannah Reid. 2006. *Up in Smoke? Latin America and the Caribbean: The Threat from Climate Change to the Environment and Human Development: Third Report from the Working Group on Climate Change and Development.* London: Oxfam.

Velasquez, Luz Stella. 1998. "Agenda 21: A Form of Joint Environmental Management in Manizales, Colombia." *Environment and Urbanization* 10 (2): 9–36.

Velasquez Barrero, Luz Stella. 2010. "La Gestion del Riesgo en el Contexto Ambiental Urbano Local: Un Reto Permanente y Compartido. Caso Manizales, Colombia." Background paper prepared for the 2011 *Global Assessment Report on Disaster Risk Reduction.*

World Bank. 2004a. "Local Government Support Project." Project Appraisal Document P070736, World Bank, Washington, DC.

———. 2004b. "Vietnam Urban Upgrading Project." Project Appraisal Document P070197, World Bank, Washington, DC.

———. 2005. "Argentina Urban Flood Prevention and Drainage Project—Adaptable Program Loan." Project Appraisal Document P088220, World Bank, Washington, DC.

———. 2006a. "Argentina Urban Flood Prevention and Drainage Project—Adaptable Program Loan 2." Project Appraisal Document P093491, World Bank, Washington, DC.

————. 2006b, "Bolivia Urban Infrastructure Project." Project Information Document: Appraisal Stage P083979, World Bank, Washington, DC.

————. 2007. "Bolivia Urban Wastewater Methane Gas Capture Project." Project Information Document: Appraisal Stage P104092, World Bank, Washington, DC.

————. 2008a. *The Caribbean Catastrophe Risk Insurance Initiative: A Review of CCRIF's Operation After Its First Season.* Washington, DC: World Bank.

————. 2008b. "Da Nang Priority Infrastructure Investment Project." Project Appraisal Document, World Bank, Washington, DC.

————. 2009. "Karnataka Municipal Water Energy Efficiency Project." Carbon Finance Assessment Memorandum P100352, World Bank, Washington, DC.

————. 2010. "National Vietnam Urban Upgrading Program—Mekong Delta Region." Project Information Document: Concept Stage, World Bank, Washington, DC.

World Watch Institute. 2007. *State of the World 2007: Our Urban Future.* New York: Norton.

Zampaglione, Giuseppe. 2008. "Liberia Cash for Work Temporary Employment Project." Powerpoint Presentation, World Bank. http://www.google.com/url?sa=t&source=web&cd=9&ved=0CEAQFjAI&url=http%3A%2F%2Fsiteresources.worldbank.org%2FSOCIALPROTECTION%2FResources%2F280558-1138289492561%2F2158434-1228317850075%2F5637583-1228319671628%2FPW_Zampaglione_Liberia.pdf&ei=EGFgTM2mNcH48AaFz_TBDQ&usg=AFQjCNFEWT5-R4n4unDnS5GYoF0z_Ygy9w

Annex 4: Dar es Salaam Case Study

Overview and Key Findings

More than 70 percent of Dar es Salaam's 5 million residents live in informal, unplanned settlements that lack adequate infrastructure and services, and over half of them survive on roughly a dollar per day. With a population growth rate of about 8 percent per year, Dar es Salaam is one of the fastest-growing cities in Sub-Saharan Africa. City and municipal authorities face significant challenges with respect to providing new or even maintaining existing infrastructure and services.

The summary of this case study presents the first comprehensive overview of the intersection between climate change, disaster risk, and the urban poor in Dar es Salaam. It seeks to understand (1) what are the key aspects of the vulnerability of the urban poor in the city; (2) how climate change increases this vulnerability; and (3) which policies and programs can be developed that reduce the vulnerability of the poor, taking both current and expected future climate change into account.

The case study is a joint work among the World Bank, the Institute of Resource Assessment of the University of Dar es Salaam, Ardhi University, the Tanzania Meteorological Agency (TMA), International START Secretariat, and the Dar es Salaam City Council.

The approach used in this case study is based on the Urban Risk Assessment (URA) framework. Accordingly, it includes an assessment of the hazards, socioeconomic vulnerabilities, and institutional aspects related to climate change and disasters in Dar es Salaam.

First, the case study reviews available published information on Dar es Salaam's demographics, access to infrastructure and basic services, and climatic trends and projections. Second, it conducts a household-level socioeconomic survey on populations living in flood-risk areas. The survey is complemented by on-site observations and inspection of surroundings, as well as focus-group discussions with residents. Third, the study interviews relevant institutional representatives. Finally, a flood-modeling exercise is conducted, which maps the potential changes in rainfall regime and sea-level rise and models flooding impacts in those highly vulnerable areas covered in the socioeconomic surveys.

Key Findings of the Study

- Rapid unplanned urbanization in Dar es Salaam has led to flood risk in many informal settlements, with a wide range of associated health and other problems for residents (see figure A4.6 in the color section).
- Disaster risk management has not been addressed and needs to be integrated in all aspects of urban planning in Dar es Salaam.
- The ecological and hydrological role of wetlands is not well understood or incorporated in urban development planning.
- The sustainability of infrastructure development initiatives and their maintenance is poor.

- Coordination among local stakeholders is needed.
- Industries need to be relocated away from residential areas and will require access to a waste-stabilization pond.
- Awareness-raising programs are needed at the community level for improved sanitation practices.

The Government of Dar es Salaam at Work

Despite the number of challenges that Dar es Salaam is facing, the government has been supporting key initiatives in areas such as coastal management, slum upgrading, and greenhouse gas mitigation. For instance, the Kinondoni Integrated Coastal Area Management Project (KICAMP) formulated a comprehensive plan on the management of land and water resources in coastal areas. This project resulted in banning the excavation of sands in critical areas to prevent further beach erosion along the coastal area. Households are being made aware of the value of mangroves and are involved in their protection; combined with heavy protection from KICAMP, this has led to increases in mangroves. The government has also invested recently in sea walls on highly susceptible areas to sea-level rise, storm surges, and coastal erosion such as Kunduchi beach and Bahari beach.

Another example of the government at work is the Community Infrastructural Upgrading Program (CIUP), which improves physical infrastructure such as storm-water drainage networks and strengthens the capacity of communities to better help themselves, especially those living in unplanned settlements.

On the mitigation side, the Dar es Salaam City Council has shown great leadership by closing the Mtoni solid-waste dumpsite and, in collaboration with a private company, created mechanisms for tapping and flaring the gases produced at the dump and recovering costs through clean development.

Key Constraints

Key constraints in dealing effectively with climate change, disaster risk, and the urban poor include:

DATA—The lack of high-resolution digital maps is a limitation for comprehensive risk assessment.

INFORMATION SYSTEMS—Significant increase in revenue generation is needed to ensure both increased service coverage and quality of services, particularly taking into account the additional resilience needed to reduce the risk posed by climate change for the city. Priorities in meeting the challenges include improving information systems (databases) and updating valuation rolls; optimizing the potential of property tax and simplifying the development levy; and developing vigilant collection strategies and more enhanced law-enforcement capacity.

LIMITED CAPACITY—Limited capacity hinders progress in dealing with climate change, natural disasters, and urban poverty reduction. For instance, at the community level, it is important to build capacity on the link between unsanitary waste-disposal practices, stagnant water, unclean drinking water, and disease. At the same time, environmental committees and community-based organizations need to be trained about organized waste collection and its link to reduced vector/insect breeding and disease.

At the local level, research capacity needs to be built to better understand the likely impacts of climate change in the long term for the poor of Dar es Salaam. In the city planning departments, it is important to build a common understanding of the long-term sectoral impacts of climate change for Dar es Salaam.

At the national level, the capacity of the Tanzania Meteorological Agency needs to be improved in weather and climate monitoring, including in more accurately predicting severe weather and extreme climatic events, and in analyzing and interpreting data. Improvements are also needed in disseminating alerts and early warnings.

Finally, links need to be forged and enhanced between climate experts and journalists to ensure effective dissemination of information on climate change.

Main Information Gaps Identified

This case study has been a first step in taking stock of what has already been done in terms of comprehensive risk assessment of informal settlements in Dar es Salaam. An important finding is that laws related to Urban/Town Planning and Settlement need to be reviewed to ensure they deal adequately with vulnerability and risk. It is also important to determine how existing environmental and pro-poor policies and laws can be better enforced.

The case study recommends conducting an in-depth analysis of cost-effective adaptation in light of changing socioeconomic and climatic trends in the city. Furthermore, sectoral case studies with an emphasis on the urban poor should be conducted in order to examine future needs, for a 20- to 30-year timeframe, on drainage, water supply, waste management, housing, and health planning, among others. Such case studies should involve teams of local institutions as well relevant international institutions with advanced technical expertise.

Looking Forward

The case study suggests that the *best starting point* for reducing vulnerability to climate change in the future is to reduce present vulnerability, such as by reducing threats to health by improving city drainage and environmental sanitation. The case study also captures key areas for further collaborative work moving forward:

- Support for public agencies to improve waste collection, drainage, water, and sanitation programs. Although all municipal agencies are required to comply with and implement the National Environmental Policy and the National Environmental Act, often they lack the funding needed to meet the responsibilities entailed, or the supervision capabilities to counter actions that contravene city laws and bylaws.
- Integrate disaster risk management in urban planning. Guidelines for disaster risk reduction should be mainstreamed in the preparation of schemes for general planning, detailed planning, detailed urban renewal, and regularization.
- Support public health programs. Cost-effective mass-treatment programs need to be implemented for Neglected Tropical Diseases (NTDs) and more efforts also need to be put into integrated approaches to control malaria, rather than relying solely on the distribution of nets treated with insecticide. Improvements to drainage systems and their regular maintenance will go a long way toward reducing flooding and consequent ponding and stagnation of water, thereby reducing breeding sites.
- Support Clean Development Mechanism (CDM) activities. Dar es Salaam should seek further CDM support in expanding and scaling up the City Council's existing plans to manage solid waste.
- Support existing successful urban upgrading programs. These have great potential, as they involve communities in identifying problems and solutions

and cover a wide array of physical and institutional measures to improve urban areas.

- Encourage a long-term planning horizon. Adaptation planning for Dar es Salaam's poor residents should address their present urgent needs and those to come, given expected future impacts of climate change.

Case Study Summary

City Profile

Dar es Salaam is located in the eastern part of the Tanzanian mainland at 6°51'S latitude and 39°18'E longitude (see figure A4.1, color section). With an area of 1,350 square kilometers (km²), it occupies 0.19 percent of the Tanzanian mainland, stretching about 100 km between the Mpiji River to the north and beyond the Mzinga River in the south. The Indian Ocean borders it to the east. The beach and shoreline comprise sand dunes and tidal swamps. Coastal plains composed of limestone extend 10 km to the west of the city, 2 to 8 km to the north, and 5 to 8 km to the south. Inland, alluvial plains comprise a series of steep-sided U-shaped valleys. The upland plateau comprises the dissected Pugu Hills, 100 m to 200 m in altitude. Dominated by limestones, sandy clays, coarse sands, and mixed alluvial deposits, the soils of the Dar es Salaam region are not particularly fertile (Dongus, 2000). The city is divided into three ecological zones, namely the upland zone consisting of hilly areas to the west and north of the city, the middle plateau, and the lowlands, which include the Msimbazi Valley, Jangwani, Mtoni, Africana, and Ununio areas.

Built Environment and Basic Service Provision

An estimated 70 percent of Dar es Salaam's population lives in poor, unplanned settlements (World Bank 2002). Residents are usually too poor to pay for services or infrastructure and authorities too resource-constrained to maintain these; thus, health and environmental conditions are generally extremely poor. About half the residents of Dar es Salaam's informal settlements live on an average income of US$1 per day and in constrained circumstances. Many are migrants from other parts of Tanzania in search of better opportunities.

Access to clean water and sanitation are major problems for Dar es Salaam's poor, and contribute to widespread illness, including cholera, malaria, lymphatic filariasis, and diarrhea, particularly during floods, which could be more severe or frequent in the future due to climate change.

Up to about 75 percent of the residents of Dar es Salaam's informal housing settlements are unemployed or under-employed (World Bank 2002), with the

TABLE A4.1
Dar es Salaam Profile

Total city population in 2002	2.5 million Estimated 5 million in 2020
Population growth (% annual)	4.39 (city mayor's statistics, 2006) 8 (World Bank 2002)
Land area (km²)	1,590
Population density (per hectare)	1,500
Country's per capita GDP (US$)	1,300 (2007)
Date of last Urban Master Plan	2010

main source of income for the latter group being through informal activities and micro-enterprise. Employment in Dar es Salaam as a whole declined from 64 percent to 42 percent between 1992 and 2000, and self-employment rose from 29 percent to 43 percent. Poverty for those in self-employment rose from 29 percent to 38 percent over the same period (World Bank 2002).

The city's road network totals about 1,950 km, of which 1,120 km (less than 60 percent) is paved, and is inadequate to satisfy its population density, spatial expansion, and transportation needs. Dar es Salaam hosts about 52 percent of Tanzania's vehicles, and has a traffic density growth rate of over 6.3 percent per year (JICA 1995; Kanyama et al. 2004).

The city's planning agencies have been unable to keep pace with the rapid expansion of the city, largely fueled by migrant growth. Most of the city's population lives in unplanned settlements—many in abject poverty—which are characterized by substandard infrastructure and lack of basic municipal and other services. These communities face transportation constraints, insecure housing, problems accessing clean water, unhygienic sanitation, and lack of awareness on hygienic sanitary practices. Climatic factors, such as heavy rainfall, work in conjunction with this situation to impose additional hardship and increase disease.

Pillar 1—Institutional Assessment

Agencies in Disaster Risk Management and Climate Change Adaptation

Dar es Salaam is managed by the Dar es Salaam City Council and the Municipal Councils of Temeke, Kinondoni, and Ilala. The three municipal authorities are under the Ministry of Regional Administration and local government. Each has individual sets of technical and administrative departments.

The Dar es Salaam City Council (DCC) has a coordinating role and attends to issues that cut across all three municipalities. Its functions are to:

- Coordinate the functions of the three municipal authorities regarding infrastructure.
- Prepare a coherent citywide framework for enhancing sustainable development.
- Promote cooperation between the City Council and the three municipal or local authorities.
- Deal with all matters where there is interdependency among the city's local authorities.
- Support and facilitate the overall functioning and performance of the local authorities.
- Maintain peace, provide security and emergency, fire, and rescue services, ambulance and police.
- Promote major functions relating to protocol and ceremonies.

The municipal councils are responsible for providing basic social services, which include primary education and partly secondary education (especially where the community is involved), primary health care, waste management and cleanliness, district roads, water supply, and monitoring of trade and development, especially informal sector development and management, cooperatives, agriculture and livestock development, forestry, fisheries, recreational parks, and urban planning.

The Tanzania Meteorological Agency (TMA) issues flood warnings for Dar es Salaam. It provides warnings and advisories on extreme rainfall and flooding based on daily weather monitoring. Cloud evolution is monitored through observations and by using satellite pictures. The evolution and pathway of tropical cyclones along the Western Indian Ocean are also monitored on a real-time basis. Warnings and advisories are disseminated to the public as needed, through various stakeholders such as the mass media and the disaster-management department at the prime minister's office. Flood warnings and advisories are given up to a day in advance (24-hour forecast) or at seasonal timescales (up to two months in advance).

Relevant Policies and Legislation

- At national level: National Human Settlements Development policy (2000), National Environmental Policy (1997), Ratification of the UN Framework Convention on Climate Change (UNFCCC) (1996).
- At local level: The Sustainable Dar es Salaam Project and the Strategic Urban Development Plan (SUDP) started in 1992, Community Infrastructural Upgrading Programme (CIUP) started in 2001, and African Urban Risk Analysis Network (AURAN) Project Phases I and II started in 2004.

Ongoing Programs in Disaster Risk Management and Climate Change

- *Rehabilitation of storm water drainage and sewerage system:* City authorities undertook improvements in the city center. However, a new wave of investment has led to construction of new structures in former empty spaces, including the construction of multiple-use buildings that have increased demands for water supply and enlarged high-capacity sewage pipes. The tonnage of solid and liquid waste generated has increased, demanding efficient solid- and liquid-waste management and monitoring services. On occasion, wide and deep storm water drains are appropriated by private homeowners, fenced in as part of their property, and sealed up, which causes waste back-up among poorer neighbors. Laws need to be better enforced and drainage line capacity reassessed. It is important that when this occurs, planners consider the fact that capacity needs are likely to change over the lifetime of the drainage system; the system needs to plan for changing rainfall regimes over the planning horizon, for example, up to 2050.

- *Property formalization in Dar es Salaam:* The government is implementing a project to identify all properties in informal settlements in Dar es Salaam and at the same time issuing land/property licenses or right of occupancy to curb further densification of those areas and to improve security of tenure, which could be used as collateral for economic empowerment (URT 2004 in: Kyessi and Kyessi 2007). This formalization process will be a foundation for the regularization of the slums that will ultimately allow provision of infrastructure including drainage channels for storm water, piped water supply, refuse collection using municipal and private vehicles, sanitation (pit and septic tank emptying services), secure tenure (loans), improved housing conditions, and reduced overcrowding in unplanned settlements.

- *National Adaptation Programme of Action (NAPA):* Tanzania is party to the UN Framework Convention on Climate Change (UNFCCC) and the Kyoto Protocol and has prepared a National Adaptation Programme of Action (NAPA 2007). The capacity for investing in adaptation activities (protecting vulnerable populations, infrastructure, and economies) is still low due to financial constraints (NAPA 2007). However, NAPA will help in integrating adaptation issues in the development process, guiding development to address urgent and immediate needs for adapting to adverse impacts of climate change. Among other objectives, NAPA aims at improving public awareness on the impacts of climate change and on potential adaptation measures that can be adopted. In Dar es Salaam, activities have included planting trees along the beach, roadsides, near houses, and in open spaces.

- *Management of coastal areas:* Dar es Salaam is a coastal city and climate change is expected to exacerbate vulnerability of poor coastal communities through sea-level rise, possibly more intense coastal storms, and increased rainfall variability. Coastal management projects involve beach conservation, including conservation of mangroves and coral reefs, as well as Marine Park protection. Poverty alleviation, such as facilitation of seaweed farming, is also often included. Some of the city's coastal management projects are noted below. In particular, the Kinondoni Integrated Coastal Area Management Project (KICAMP) aims to formulate a comprehensive plan focused on the use of land and water resources in coastal areas. The project has banned the excavation of sands in Kunduchi-Mtongani as a way to prevent further beach erosion along the coastal area. Households are being made aware of the value of mangroves and involved in their protection, and, combined with heavy protection from KICAMP, this has led to an increase in mangroves. Other civil-society organizations involved in conservation, awareness raising, and environmental management included Roots and Shoots, World Vision, URASU (Uchoraji na Ramani na Sanaa Shirikishi Dhidi ya Ukimwi), and the International Organization on Migration, which helped to form environmental management societies in schools, markets, and dispensaries. Schools had already planted trees and botanical gardens in their compounds. Msasani Bonde la Mpunga is also involved in coastal conservation through a partnership with the World Wildlife Fund (WWF), the Wildlife Society for Nature Conservation, the private sector (running tourist hotels and sea boats), the International Union for Conservation of Nature (IUCN), and Tanzania Marine Park authorities.

- *Sustainable coastal communities and ecosystems:* This USAID-funded project (implemented by Rhode Island and Hawaii-Hilo universities) builds adaptive capacity and resilience among vulnerable coastal communities. The program has introduced "raft culture" techniques, where seaweed is grown in deeper water where it is less vulnerable to fluctuations in temperature and salinity, enabling beneficiaries to earn a living throughout the year.
- *Construction of adaptive structures in Dar es Salaam:* A comprehensive beach conservation program has been designed that includes the following components: (1) sea walls have been constructed along the front of the Aga Khan Hospital to prevent further erosion of Sea View Road; (2) sea walls and groins have been constructed along some beaches, which benefits hotels by reducing beach erosion and property damage from waves, and also helps fishing community settlements that live near the sea; and (3) land reclamation is taking place along coastal areas, for example, by covering quarry pits with soil and trees and building houses on these reclaimed areas. The Kunduchi-Salasala quarry area is an example.
- *Other:* The country has strengthened multilateral relations at the international level in order to enhance the ability to cope with climate change and variability for sustainable livelihoods. For example, Tanzania and the Kingdom of

Norway have agreed to partner to combat adverse impacts of climate change. Under this program, Tanzanian scholars are trained on climate change issues (planning and forecasting), and, as short courses on climate change tend to be publicized through newspapers and on television, awareness is raised among the public on climate change impacts, adaptation measures, and mitigation.

Leading Agencies

Currently, there is not a leading agency coordinating the disaster risk management activities at the local level. There is a lack of coordination horizontally among departments and vertically with national policies.

Pro-Poor Services and Infrastructure Local Expenditure

Dar es Salaam's municipal agencies provide infrastructure and socioeconomic services such as health, water, education, solid-waste management, cooperative and community development, roads, development of natural resources, trade and agriculture and livestock, and information and communication technology development. Despite efforts to improve social services for city dwellers, increased migration and unemployment have made services poor and unaffordable. Rapid urbanization in Dar es Salaam is resulting in growing numbers of the population living in unplanned, densely settled squatter areas with little or no access to social services. Despite purported improvements in fiscal position and revenue collection, improved record-keeping, and enhanced accountability, the Dar es Salaam City Council (including its municipalities) still faces considerable challenges in spending on pro-poor services and on improving infrastructure in unplanned and underserved areas. Significant increase in revenue generation is needed to ensure both increased service coverage and quality of services, particularly taking into account the additional resilience needed to reduce the risk posed by climate change for the city. Priorities in meeting the challenges include improving information systems (databases) and updating valuation rolls; optimizing the potential of property tax and simplifying the development levy; and developing vigilant collection strategies and more enhanced law enforcement capacity (City Council, undated Brief DSM V2: 6).

Pillar 2—Hazards Assessment

Past Natural Disasters

Dar es Salaam is already highly vulnerable to climatic variability, which is expected to increase as climate continues to change. The aspect of most frequent concern to Dar es Salaam currently is heavy rainfall. In combination with poor drainage, illegal construction, and other infrastructure problems, heavy rainfall

TABLE A4.2
Natural Hazards

	Yes /No	Date of last major event
Earthquake	N	
Wind storm	N	
River flow	N	2010
Floods, inundations, and waterlogs	Y	
Tsunami	N	
Drought	Y	2006
Volcano	N	
Landslide	Y	
Storm surge	N	
Extreme temperature	Y	

results in flooding that causes major losses and disruptions. For the multitudes of the city's population living in informal settlements, poor sanitation contributes to an additional threat: disease. Diseases commonly occurring in these congested, unsanitary settlements during floods include malaria, cholera, dysentery, and diarrhea. Some other factors that contribute to flooding in these settlements include flat topography, lack of storm-water drainage, blockage of natural drainage systems, building in hazardous areas, and unregulated housing and infrastructure development. Livelihood activities are also adversely affected by both heavy rainfall and drought.

Main Climate Hazards
Temperature trends over the past four to five decades show significant increase. Temperature is projected to increase.

As Figure A4.3 shows, mean annual rainfall has declined in Dar es Salaam over the past five decades (as recorded at the Dar es Salaam Airport station).

Figure A4.4 shows mean and absolute 24-hour maximum rainfall for the period 1971–2009. Mean 24-hour maximum rainfall ranges from over 50 mm in April–May to 10 mm for July–August. The absolute 24-hour maximum rainfall for the time period studied was recorded within the past decade.

Both rainfall amount and intensity are concerns from the point of view of flooding in Dar es Salaam. Intensity has been increasing in the last 15 years, where rainfall intensity has been well above the 38 years' recorded history. This trend is expected to continue with climate change.

An important projected aspect of climate change is an increase in climatic variability, which would result in more frequent and severe floods and droughts in the city. Given that the city's poor are unable to cope adequately with current variability, their situation is likely to worsen in the future, unless steps are taken

Figure A4.2 Trend of Mean Maximum Temperature Anomalies during Warmest Months (December–February) at Dar es Salaam International Airport

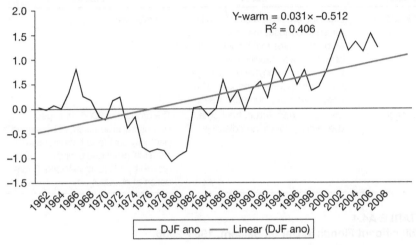

$$Y\text{-warm} = 0.031x - 0.512$$
$$R^2 = 0.406$$

Source: Tanzania Meteorological Agency (2010).

Figure A4.3 Timeseries of Mean Annual Rainfall in Dar es Salaam

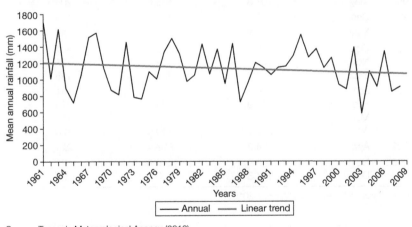

Source: Tanzania Meteorological Agency (2010).

to ensure that urban development and poverty reduction specifically take into account the prospect of changing climatic conditions. Infrastructure development and urban planning, municipal services, and poverty reduction (including safety nets and health services) need not only to better integrate disaster risk management, but also to consider that the trends are changing.

TABLE A4.3
Effects and Losses

Hazard	Effects	Losses
Floods	Drainage channels are blocked by refuse throughout the year as well as by structures that hinder the flow of wastewater, causing houses to be flooded by unhygienic, sewage-based wastewater in houses. Major effects are water-borne diseases.	Not available
Drought	Diseases: malnutrition, trachoma, dysentery, cholera, and diarrhea	The drought of 2006 damaged agricultural production, necessitated electricity cuts (and thus drops in industrial production), and cut GDP growth by 1% (ClimateWorks Foundation et al. 2009)

TABLE A4.4
Significant Floods in Dar es Salaam, 1983–2006

Year	Months	Monthly rainfall Long-term mean (mm)	Actual (mm)	% of long-term mean
1983	May	197.8	405.6	205
1989	Dec.	117.8	175.6	149
1995	May	197.8	374.2	189
1997	Oct.	69.3	250.8	361
	Nov.	125.9	152	121
	Dec.	117.8	231	196
1998	Jan.	76.3	107.3	141
	Feb.	54.9	123.7	225
	Mar.	138.1	155.2	112
	Apr.	254.2	319.9	126
2002	Apr.	254.2	569.4	224
2006	Nov.	125.9	240.9	191
	Dec.	117.8	230.4	196

Source: Tanzania Meteorological Agency (2010).

Projections of Future Climate

A summary of climate baseline data and severity of dry periods for March–May (MAM) and October–December (OND) are presented in the case study. Under the Special Report on Emissions Scenarios (SRES) A2 emissions scenarios, and data representing 14 of the Global Circulation Models used to simulate the 20th century and future global climate, by mid-century, the coarser-resolution global climate models project that this site will become warmer, with more frequent heat waves. They disagree on whether this site

Figure A4.4 Mean and Absolute 24 Hours Maximum Rainfall for Dar es Salaam

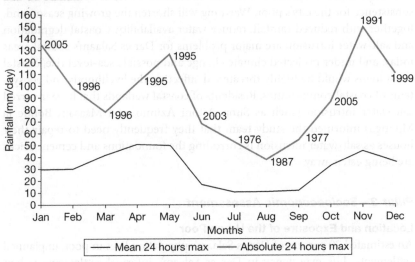

will become wetter or drier. By 2100, mean annual temperature for Tanzania is expected to increase by 1.7°C over the northern coast, including areas around Dar es Salaam. Rainfall intensity is expected to increase. Runoff (precipitation minus evapo-transpiration), a measure of water availability, is projected to increase. The maximum amount of rain that falls in any five-day period (a surrogate for an extreme storm) is expected to increase. The maximum period between rainy days is expected to increase.

Kebede and Nicholls (2010) have analyzed Dar es Salaam's vulnerability to sea-level rise. They estimate that at present 8 percent of the city currently lies in a low-elevation zone below the 10 m contour line, inhabited by over 143,000 people, with associated economic assets estimated (in 2005) at US$168 million.

Magnitude, Distribution, and Probability of Potential Losses

Although future rainfall patterns are uncertain, variability is likely to increase and intensification of heavy rainfall is expected. Thus flooding may become increasingly severe, particularly taken together with socioeconomic projections, unless adaptation measures are implemented. Increases in mean temperature, combined with fewer rainy days per year, could also prolong the length of dry seasons or intensify droughts. Recent extreme climate (for example, the droughts of 2006 and 2008–2009, and the floods of 2009–2010) severely impacted sectors such as transport, energy, and health, with adverse socioeconomic implications. Projected changes in climate will have significant impacts on Tanzania's rain-fed agriculture and food production, and could thus impact urban agriculture in Dar es Salaam, a means of livelihood and subsistence for the city's poor. Warming will shorten the growing season and, together with reduced rainfall, reduce water availability. Coastal degradation and salt-water intrusion are major problems for Dar es Salaam's coastal areas today, and under projected climate change and possible sea-level rise, coastal ecosystems would be highly threatened, affecting the livelihoods and ecosystems of coastal communities. Residents of coastal wetlands that have incurred salt-water intrusion (such as Suna, Mtoni Azimio, and Msasani Bonde la Mpunga) informed the study team that they frequently need to repair their houses as salt-water intrusion is corroding the foundations and cement bricks are being eaten away.

Pillar 3—Socioeconomic Assessment

Location and Exposure of the Urban Poor
An estimated 70 percent of Dar es Salaam's population lives in poor, unplanned settlements. Life expectancy in Dar es Salaam's informal settlements is low,

Figure A4.5 Exposed Population in Dar es Salaam in 2005, 2030, 2050, and 2070 to a 1-in-100-Year Flood under the A1B Mid-range Sea-Level Rise Scenario, No Adaptation

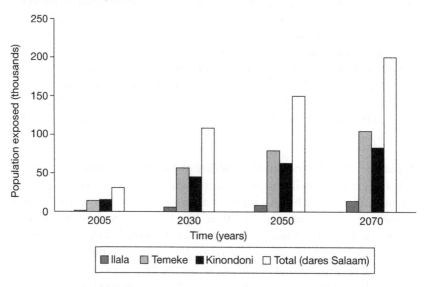

Source: Kebele and Nicholls (2010).

between 44 and 46 years, and infant mortality is high at about 97 deaths per 1,000 live births.

Residents are usually too poor to pay for services or infrastructure and authorities too resource-constrained to maintain these; thus, health and environmental conditions are generally extremely poor. Tanzania's policy toward informal settlements in Dar es Salaam has varied over past decades. In the 1960s, slum clearance was the main approach; slum sites were cleared and buildings with high construction standards were erected on cleared sites (implemented through the National Housing Corporation). This proved unsustainable, however, and was abandoned by the end of the 1960s due to high economic and social costs, and having contributed little to the net housing stock. In the 1970s and 1980s, the government's approach changed, and projects to upgrade squatter areas and to provide services (supported by the World Bank) formed the national strategy for managing the growth of informal settlements. After World Bank funding for these projects ceased, however, the government of Tanzania was unable to continue financing them, and subsequent years saw the growth and emergence of new unplanned settlements as well as deterioration of previously installed infrastructure, due to lack of maintenance.

Reference

World Bank. 2011. *Urban Poverty & Climate Change in Dar es Salaam, Tanzania; A Case Study, processed.*

Annex 5: Jakarta Case Study

Overview and Key Findings

This case study presents the first comprehensive overview of the intersection between climate change, disaster risk, and the urban poor in Jakarta. It discusses city progress in taking stock of policies and programs, both within the Provincial Government (Pemprov) of the Special Capital District (DKI) of Jakarta and with partners. And it discusses progress in understanding the principal hazards in the city and where they are located, as well as some understanding of undocumented citizens in Jakarta and how they are coping with the changes they experience on a day-to-day basis. As part of this effort, there is a longer document assessing risk and a short film that provide the basis for moving toward a comprehensive climate action plan for the city. The Bahasa version of the report will be a useful awareness-raising tool to build capacity among government agencies and other stakeholders on how climate change and natural disasters are and will affect Jakarta.

The World Bank, in close consultation with the Pemprov DKI and other stakeholders and partners, has prepared a case study of Jakarta. Key DKI government agencies, such as the departments responsible for the environment (Badan Pengelola Linkungan Hidup Daerah, BPLHD), planning (Badan Perencanaan Pembangunan Daerah, BAPPEDA), and spatial planning (Biro Tata Ruang) discussed existing city strategies and policies related to climate change. Pemprov DKI also hosted a stakeholder consultation workshop in December 2010, to review and strengthen the findings of this case study through conversations with different city officials and NGOs.

The approach used in this case study is based on the Urban Risk Assessment (URA) framework. Accordingly, it includes an assessment of the hazards, socioeconomic vulnerabilities, and institutional aspects related to climate change and disasters in Jakarta. With a focus on the urban poor, this study considers how poor communities are affected by climate change and natural hazards, examines approaches that have been taken to address these challenges, and identifies priorities and options for further action in Jakarta. This study draws on other reports and resources on disasters and climate change in Jakarta, as well as on interviews and discussions with government officials, local NGOs, and community leaders.

Key Findings of the Study

- Strong and sustained growth in Jakarta's population and economy have resulted in a vast increase in the urbanized area, and concomitant change in land use.
- Jakarta's rapid growth and urbanization have given rise to large-scale infrastructure problems that are mostly well documented and understood by the DKI government and the public.
- Jakarta is now highly vulnerable to the impacts of climate change. The greatest climate- and disaster-related risk facing Jakarta is flooding, which imposes very high human and economic costs on the city.
- Jakarta's poor are productive and integral members of the city's economy, and are also the most vulnerable to flood-related risks.

- The urban poor have important roles to play in addressing Jakarta's vulnerability to climate change and disasters.
- The government of DKI Jakarta has started acting on climate change, but much remains to be done to mainstream climate change across all sectors for the long term.

The Government of Jakarta at Work

DKI is making a concerted effort to develop its climate change strategy and to think more broadly and inclusively about different levels of capacity building and interventions. At the kelurahan level, government officials are starting to take active roles in understanding how climate change is affecting them and what steps they can prioritize in their own actions and local budgets. This is occurring mainly through capacity-building programs of NGOs. The government is also learning how to articulate these issues in terms of spatial interventions. Initially, the main focus of DKI on climate change was about reducing greenhouse gas emissions. The government is now thinking more broadly about adaptation measures like urban greening that address both climate change aspects.

Areas for Improvement

Currently the approach of integrating projects and programs that increase resilience, improve spatial planning, and decrease poverty in one systematized application is new for the DKI government. Both conceptually and in terms of policy creation and social services, the real links between climate change vulnerability and resilience and the urban poor remain weak. The location and required resettlement of the extremely poor communities is a delicate and complicated issue for DKI to manage, but one that is seeing increasing urgency and pressure. Ideas for the development of good climate change projects, ideally those that incorporate mitigation and adaptation, are slow to emerge from inside the DKI government.

Key Constraints

Key constraints in dealing effectively with climate change, disaster risk, and the urban poor include:

DATA—Poor availability and sharing of data for decision-making, from existing studies and new data, is one of the biggest challenges. From the experience of working through the MTF study with DKI Jakarta, data was either extremely scarce, inconsistent, or simply very difficult to access as some agencies were reluctant to release information. Partners of DKI, like other multi- and bilateral organizations, as well as NGOs and private-sector consultants, create their own data sets, but much of this information is not shared or coordinated.

INFRASTRUCTURE AND INVESTMENTS—The macro-infrastructure upgrades that will be required for Jakarta to be considered climate resilient are certainly massive and long term. These upgrades include a huge dike and polder-system called the Jakarta Coastal Sea Defense coupled with land reclamation and improved pumping capacity. This is still in the design stages. The Jatiluruh reservoir just outside of Jakarta's boundaries is the source of much of Jakarta's water. Plans have been under development for some time to expand the capacity of the pipes to increase water supply to Jakarta, and therefore ease the causes of subsidence, but the plans are not yet under way.

COMMUNICATION AND COMMUNITY ENGAGEMENT—The shorter-term micro-level capacity-building exercises and community-led actions are uneven, with some communities better organized than others. Framing the future of Jakarta using the terms "resilience" and "climate change" are new for the government and communities. There is a significant learning curve in terms of thoroughly understanding, then communicating, how climate change affects Jakarta.

Main Information Gaps Identified

In general there is a lack of data. Some of the data available (such as land tenure) may not have been scrutinized and analyzed through the fresh lens of climate change. Updated data gaps include: maps of poverty in the city; subsidence maps and images; socioeconomic and housing data on the very poor; good qualitative definitions of slums and urban settlements; information on land tenure; up-to-date census data; census data on the very poor; immigration and emigration rates; plans for resettlement of vulnerable areas; financing and long-term plans for sea-wall construction; and concrete action plans for working to halt subsidence.

Looking Forward

A few basic principles can guide the way forward for addressing climate change, disaster risk, and urban poverty in Jakarta.

- Climate change adaptation should be not so much an additional challenge to be layered onto existing policies and planning priorities, but rather an opportunity for the DKI government and key partners to gather their focus and priorities for the future.

- Given limited resources, the initial focus should be on addressing existing shortfalls in infrastructure investment and basic services, particularly in drainage, piped water, housing, and transportation.
- Policies and investments should be based on improved information, including quantitative data and an understanding of community actions and adaptive capacities.
- Enhanced collaboration—with the administrations of neighboring provinces, as well as with the local communities as active participants and partners—is crucial to the success of long-term action.
- Capacity building should be emphasized at every level. The shorter-term micro-level capacity building and community-led actions are uneven, some communities being better organized than others. Framing the future of Jakarta using the terms "resilience" and "climate change" are new for the government and communities. There is a significant learning curve in terms of first thoroughly understanding, and then communicating, how climate change affects Jakarta.

Case Study Summary

City Profile

Jakarta is located on the north coast of the island of Java in the Indonesian archipelago in Southeast Asia. It is the country's largest city and its political and economic hub. The city's built environment is characterized by numerous skyscrapers, concentrated in the central business district but also built ad hoc throughout the city, especially in the past 20 years. The rest of Jakarta generally comprises low-lying, densely populated neighborhoods, which are highly diverse in terms of income levels and uses, and many of these neighborhoods are home to varied informal economic activities. The population of Jakarta is considered wealthy relative to neighboring provinces and other islands, and indeed its GDP per capita is more than four times the national average.

Jakarta is located in a deltaic plain crisscrossed by 13 natural rivers and more than 1,400 km of man-made waterways. About 40 percent of the city, mainly the area farthest north near the Java Sea, is below sea level. Jakarta is prone to flooding from water draining through the city from the hills in the south, and also from coastal tidal flooding.

TABLE A5.1
Jakarta Profile

Total city population in 2010	9.6 million
Population growth (% annual)	2.60
Land area (km²)	651
Population density (per km²)	14,465
Country's per capita GDP (US$)	2,329
% of country's population	4
Total number of households	2,325,973
GDP (US$)	10,222
% of country's GDP	20
Total budget (US$)	3.1 billion
Date of last Urban Master Plan	2010

The successful provision and management of services by the provincial government is lagging in most sectors. In spite of a booming economy, much private-sector property development, Jakarta's spatial planning and infrastructure, as well as service provision—transportation, green space, affordable housing, clean water, health care, and education—have not kept pace with demand.

Traffic congestion is a major problem facing the city, with only incremental efforts to relieve congestion through the development of public transportation, most prominently, the TransJakarta Busway. The increasing number of vehicles on the streets of Jakarta is outpacing the development of new roads. Total gridlock in the city is projected to occur as early as 2016 under the transportation Business As Usual scenario.

Lack of piped water is driving large multi-use developments and small residential communities alike to drill wells to access groundwater. This extraction of groundwater is causing areas of Jakarta to sink rapidly, particularly in the north of the city. Along with sea-level rise, land subsidence is one of the greatest challenges facing Jakarta.

The provision of housing for the poor and lower-middle classes continues to be inadequate relative to demand. With consistent in-migration of people into the city, estimated at 250,000 annually, housing is in constant demand, but costs are escalating. Skyrocketing land prices and rampant private-sector development that is under-regulated has resulted in a booming real-estate market that excludes the poor. Large informal settlements have grown over many years along waterways, natural rivers, and reservoirs, contributing to the pollution and clogging of these areas.

There is currently no citywide solid-waste management plan for Jakarta. Waste collection in the city is largely contracted out to private companies, with wealthier areas paying more, and consequently receiving better and more consistent service. In many areas, waste is collected and picked over by a highly efficient but informal waste picker and recycling community.

Pillar 1—Institutional Assessment

Agencies in Disaster Risk Management and Climate Change Adaptation
The key agencies in Jakarta responsible for coordinated efforts on climate change adaptation and disaster risk management are Kantor Asisten Pembangunan dan Lingkungan Hidup (Asbang), Assistant to Secretary for Development and Environment Office; Badan Pengelola Linkungan Hidup Daerah (BPLHD), the environmental agency; Badan Perencanaan Pembangunan Daerah (BAPPEDA), the planning and development agency; Badan Penanggulangan Bencana Daerah (BPBD), the provincial disaster management agency; Satuan Tugas Koordinasi dan Pelaksana (SATKORLAK), the national disaster risk management board; and Biro Tata Ruang, the bureau of spatial planning.

- Assistant to Secretary for Development and Environment Office as a point of coordination for development and environment. Under this office, there are two bureaus that are Spatial Plan (Tata Ruang) and Infrastructure (Sarana dan Prasarana). Biro Tata Ruang is responsible for coordinating the development and management of short-, medium-, and long-term spatial plans for the city. Within the plans are specific laws and articles articulating the incorporation of climate change adaptation and mitigation, as well as the need for disaster risk management. Biro Prasarana dan Sarana is responsible for monitoring the city development. However, the implementation and enforcement of these laws and articles is through BAPPEDA and the Department of Public Works.
- BPLHD is the environmental agency and the key governmental contact for many of the NGOs and other organizations working at the community level. They are involved in programs to abate greenhouse gas emissions in Jakarta, including overseeing the development of a greenhouse gas emissions baseline, to be completed in 2011. BLPHD also manages community-level adaptation initiatives and studies in partnership with NGOs and donor organizations.
- BAPPEDA is the development and management body for Jakarta. It manages large infrastructure projects such as sea-wall construction in north Jakarta, as well as the building of floodgates along the rivers and major infrastructure projects like the East and West Flood Canals. The agency manages, finances,

and monitors the flood infrastructure carried out by Dinas Pekerjaan Umum (DPU), the public-works agency.
• BPBD was established as the citywide agency for disaster risk management only at the end of 2010. Until then, disaster response was handled by SATKORLAK, which is a national association based largely in the fire department and acted as more of a committee since it was not anchored in a particular agency or formalized into government structure. The formal empowerment and role of BPBD has yet to be fully developed, integrated, and made widely public.

Relevant Policies and Legislation
Climate change is integrated to a limited extent in the medium- and long-term city spatial plans, but they relate for the most part to areas of the city experiencing the greatest harm from flooding or other problems. The official language in the plans acknowledges the need for strategies related to climate change as well as plans for disaster mitigation and response, but does not go into specific detail.

Adaptation plans to cope with extreme weather and sea-level rise are piecemeal within the plans and agencies. More generally, the governor of Jakarta has made public commitments in the international arena to reducing the city's greenhouse gas emissions.

The plans and policies of BPBD are not yet known, although a citywide strategy for disaster prevention and response will most likely be developed and managed by this agency. The National Action Plan for Disaster Risk Reduction (NAP-DRR) lists actions for Jakarta specifically, but the actions have been developed by different sectors and ministries. The budget numbers included are the requests by the implementing party and have not been allocated or approved.

Ongoing Programs in Disaster Risk Management and Climate Change
An important step taken by the DKI government was to establish the provincial disaster risk management agency, BPBD. Currently, there is no comprehensive program of disaster risk management or response plan for the city of Jakarta. There are large-scale infrastructure projects, such as the Jakarta Coastal Defense that protects coastal neighborhoods from tidal surges, and the East and West Flood Canals. The Jakarta Coastal Defense has been presented to the Jakarta government as a feasibility study. The East and West Flood Canals are the largest and most ambitious projects for Jakarta in terms of flood management, but the intricate and smaller secondary and tertiary systems are still under-managed and inadequate.

Many of the alert systems work at the community level and are largely self-organized. These are generally warnings from upstream floodgates that water is getting high; the warnings are sent via SMS text message to neighborhood heads so they can warn their communities. It is unknown how many of these small and informal networks are actually in place. It appears that they evolved out of local necessity. Many of the resources for the smaller, community-level projects and programs come from local and international NGOs. Small government agencies at the neighborhood level (RT and RW) are allocated budgets for some infrastructural interventions, but they are not consistent across the city and in many cases kelurahan-level budgets are not entirely spent every fiscal year due in part to complicated and lengthy approval mechanisms by the provincial government, or a lack of capacity at the local level to carry out physical interventions. This is a national trend and not specific to Jakarta.

Policy Shortcomings

Formalization, publication, and awareness-raising are still sorely lacking in the areas of climate change and disaster risk management in Jakarta, both inside many government agencies and in the public realm. In many ways the Jakarta government is only beginning to comprehensively measure and understand the city's key vulnerabilities—as well as its strengths and resources—to become climate-resilient and to anticipate potential disasters. There is also a lack of coordination between the agencies described above, and very little enforcement of well-meaning laws to create a safer and more secure built environment. BNPB (Badan Nasional Penanggulangan Bencana) was developed as the national coordinating and monitoring agency in 2008, with an operating budget for disaster response of about IDR 4 trillion (US$464 million). However, more is currently needed for upgrades and implementation as reported in the National Action Plan for Disaster Risk Reduction (NAP-DRR). (See complete case study for list of items submitted for financing by various agencies for Jakarta.)

Lead Agency for Disaster Risk Management

Until recently, a national ad hoc agency (SATKORLAK) anchored in the fire department and was responsible for disaster response, but was doing little anticipatory planning. Jakarta did not have a dedicated working group or agency. At the end of 2010, BPBD was established for the province of Jakarta. As it is a new agency, the role it will play in developing disaster mitigation plans or allocating funding for the city's kota or kelurahan remains unclear.

Mainstreaming Risk Reduction

In order to mainstream risk reduction, the government is incorporating those activities and projects into the long-term spatial plans, the most recent of which is Jakarta's plan for 2010–2030. NGOs and other donor organizations are playing important roles currently to aid communities and community-level governments to educate and prepare individual citizens, families, and community leaders to prepare for damaging events such as floods from extreme rainfall or from rises in tides. However, these actions are piecemeal across the city and it is mostly poor communities that are targeted by these organizations.

Expenditure on Pro-Poor Programs and Climate Adaptation

The 2011 city budget for Jakarta is slightly more than US$3 billion. Indonesia has a countrywide program to alleviate poverty (Program Nasional Pemberdayaan Masyarakat (PNPM)—Mandiri or the National Program for Community Empowerment[1]) that has had success in other urban areas, but has not adequately reached extremely poor parts of Jakarta. Many of the activities to reduce poverty are disbursed throughout various services and departments, such as community empowerment, health, family planning, and social services.

Table A5.2 shows the most relevant spending on climate change adaptation—larger-scale initiatives related to infrastructure.

Pillar 2—Hazards Assessment

Past Natural Disasters

The largest floods in Jakarta's history took place in 2002 and 2007. Jakarta's floods are notorious, and the resulting stalling of traffic, lost productivity, and property

TABLE A5.2
Infrastructure Investments per Year DKI

	Annual budget, 2009	Annual budget, 2010
Flood control		
East flood canal	$93,132,994	$60,350,180
Drainage and river dredging	$10,803,427	$11,424,314
Dam, polder, and catchment area development	$620,887	$40,605,985
Pollution containment		
Open green space development	$15,909,599	$77,238,296
Climate change adaptation		
Sea wall	$2,235,192	$5,587,980

TABLE A5.3
Institutional Mapping of Disaster Risk Management Functions

Risk assessment	Technical (planning, management, maintenance)	Risk reduction early warning and response	Public awareness
DNPI Climate change technical studies and coordination of mitigation activities	BNPD National disaster risk reduction plans and policies and NAP-DRR (2010)	RT and RW Localized early-warning systems for floods via SMS	BPLHD Climate change events and programs like car-free days
BPBD Disaster risk management and reduction plans, management, and training	BPBD Local disaster management and response plan for Jakarta (to come)	DKI Department of Public Works (PU) Coordination of early-warning system with other provinces (water management)	DNPI Conferences and publications
BAPPENAS Inter-agency coordination for infrastructure plans	BAPPEDA Infrastructure and planning projects; maintenance with PU and other agencies	SATKORLAK Emergency response	BIRO TATA RUANG Publication of 20-year spatial plan available to public
P2B Risk mapping for earthquakes			

damage costs the city more than US$400 million per year. By 2002, more than a quarter of Jakarta's area was affected. The most disastrous flood to date, in February 2007, cost 57 lives, displaced more than 422,300 people, and destroyed 1,500 homes, damaging countless others. Total losses to property and infrastructure were estimated at US$695 million.[2] However, flooding of that magnitude is relatively infrequent and is not necessarily the principal issue for Jakarta; flooding occurs regularly throughout the year, stalling traffic, damaging houses, and gravely attenuating the flow of business at all levels of society. Even with just a moderate amount of rain, vehicular mobility in the city is critically impaired, often for hours.

The NAP-DRR cites parts of Jakarta as vulnerable to three hazards. However, for DKI Jakarta, the analysis does not go beyond the level of the kota, so it is hard to know how the risk affects different areas of the municipalities and their diverse populations.

Table A5.4
Natural Hazards

	Yes/No	Date of last major event
Earthquake	Y	September 2009 and periodic
Wind storm	N	
River flow	Y	Regularly, extreme during rainy season
Floods, inundations, and waterlogs	Y	October 2010
Tsunami	N	
Drought	N	
Volcano	N	
Landslide	N	
Storm surge	Y	January 2008 and recurring
Extreme temperature	Y	Increasing on a yearly basis

TABLE A5.5
Jakarta's Kota in National Ranking of Kabupaten or Regencies at High Risk for Various Disasters

Earthquake (out of 151 listed)		Drought (out of 182 listed)		Flood (out of 174 listed)	
80	West Jakarta	8	North Jakarta	2	North Jakarta
95	North Jakarta	9	East Jakarta	3	West Jakarta
122	East Jakarta	10	Central Jakarta		
137	South Jakarta	11	West Jakarta		
		37	South Jakarta		

Main Climate Hazards

The main hazards for Jakarta relate to water management and flood control. Extreme weather causes overloading of the existing drainage system, while sea-level rise coupled with land subsidence is making Jakarta increasingly vulnerable to tidal floods due to its coastal location (figure A5.4). Jakarta has also experienced earthquakes (although minor, but as recently as 2009) and should be prepared for other unprecedented geological events and tsunamis.

Areas at High Risk of Disasters and Climate Impacts

Given the sea-level rise and subsidence that have been modeled for North Jakarta, some industrial and residential areas and ports will be submerged in the next 100 years. Most of Jakarta's remaining industries are located in the north, as are its historic and active ports, which are key for Java's fishing economy. The airport

TABLE A5.6
Main Climate Hazards

Hazard	Effects	Losses
Earthquake	Until now small, with very little physical damage.	Until now, no great material or life loss from earthquakes.
River flow	Disruption of business, damage to property, power outages, groundwater pollution, and distribution of solid waste through high and fast water flow.	Property damage, business damage, tainting of ground water, loss of life, and spread of disease and refuse.
Floods, inundations	Depending on severity can affect traffic circulation, business activity, damage to property, power outages, displacement, and spread of disease.	Loss of property and businesses, spread of illness and loss of life, and loss of access to clean water.
Storm surge	Locally known as rob, extreme tidal floods from the sea have become more serious in the past few years in the coastal areas of the city. Sea water intrusion into aquifers.	Seawater intrusion into drinking water, damage to property including boats, and halt of industry and mobility.
Extreme temperature	As a result of both urbanization and loss of green space, increases in ground temperature and resulting instances of dengue.	Loss of life due to dengue, usually within very poor communities.

and other major roads, as well as Kota Tua, the 17th century remnants of the first Dutch settlement, will also be affected (figure A5.5).

Other Sources of Information on Potential Impacts of Disasters

- Jakarta Coastal Defense Strategy (JCDS): Recommendation and study by an international consortium to build a 60 km sea defense along the coast to prevent damage from both land subsidence and sea-level rise. The consortium is funded by the city of Rotterdam and is still only at the stage of a feasibility study.[3]
- Jakarta Urgent Flood Mitigation Project (JUFMP): A study and dredging plan by the World Bank and DKI Jakarta, which included the "Jakarta Flood Hazard Mapping Framework," which does not include cost analysis but provides the infrastructure framework required. The complete financial study is available at DKI and the World Bank.[4]
- The Jakarta Building Control and Monitoring Office (Penataan dan Pengawasan Bangunan: P2B): The office is developing a risk map for Jakarta within micro-zones of 150 m^2 each, which analyzes buildings and soil conditions within each. This initiative relates specifically to earthquakes and building quality. The map is not yet complete.[5]

Pillar 3—Socioeconomic Assessment

All of Jakarta is considered at high risk to disaster, since very few areas of the city are immune to recurrent floods. However, the most vulnerable areas of the city are along the coast, since they are susceptible to the effects not only of tidal flooding from the sea, but also of floods from the rivers and canals that are discharged into the Jakarta Bay (see figure A5.3 in the color section). These communities in the northern areas are also experiencing the greatest land subsidence. The poorest people in Jakarta are generally those squatting on empty land along riverbanks and canals. It is estimated that they comprise about 3.5 percent of the urban population.

Location of the Urban Poor

The level of exposure of very poor communities in Jakarta to both climate and natural hazards is extremely high. This is due in part to many of the poorest communities have settled illegally in areas close to sources of water: along major drainage and water management areas and along the coast. This renders them vulnerable to flooding from increased rain, as well as extreme hydrological events and tidal anomalies and floods from the sea.

Characteristics of Informal Settlements

The poorest communities in Jakarta live in self-constructed settlements, usually on land without formal legal title, and working in informal jobs. In some instances, illegal and undocumented land leasing and landlord-tenant contracting is practiced. Jakarta has a long history of these informal settlements. In many of these areas, some individuals and families have lived in what could be considered as "slums" for decades, so well-established social networks and cultural identities of place in Jakarta run extremely deep. While the numbers for Jakarta may be slightly lower, and remain hard to accurately measure, up to 68 percent of Indonesians across the country make their living through informal means (ILO 2010). In most areas of Jakarta, the residents of informal settlements work as maids, janitors, security guards, and parking attendants, and also run small local businesses such as food stalls and small retail kiosks. In coastal settlements, the fishermen are key to providing larger companies with supplies of fish to sell across the city.

Examples of Good Practice

Jakarta has yet to develop a comprehensive plan to address extreme poverty in the city, especially in terms of involuntary relocation, housing provision, and economic development of very poor communities. Indonesia has policies to alleviate poverty like conditional cash transfers and other mechanisms, but many

TABLE A5.7
Social Assessment

City population below poverty line (%)	3.60
Social inequality (Gini index) in 2002 (UN Habitat)	0.32
Unemployment (% of total labor force)	11.05
Areal size of informal settlements as a percent of city area	Unknown
City population living in slums (%)	5
Human Development Index (2009)	77.36
Predominant housing material	*For the very poor, assorted salvaged materials; for self-builders, concrete blocks and brick.*

of these policies do not reach the poorest, particularly those in informal settlements. Many of the very poor subsist on jobs and small businesses that are part of Jakarta's vast informal economy. Integrating climate change adaptation and education into plans for social services and community awareness is new for the Jakarta government. It has only been in 2011 that DKI Jakarta has been engaging with local NGOs and other organizations and funders to develop and understand community resilience specifically toward risk management related to climate change. PNPM (Program Nasional Pemberdayaan Masyarakat) is a 10-year government program to reduce poverty funded in part by the World Bank, a program that will incorporate disaster risk reduction activities into their established community empowerment and capacity building; the addition US$15 million, funded over 5 years, is through a grant from the Global Facility for Disaster Reduction and Recovery, starting in 2011. However, only one or two of Jakarta's kelurahan may be eligible for this program.

Constraints and Opportunities
Very little quantified, centralized information is available about the most vulnerable communities in Jakarta, the urban poor and informal settlements. However, the highly visible climate-vulnerable locations of these communities allow for easy identification of specific locations for interventions in spatial planning and social programming (like in North Jakarta and along many of the rivers). The creation and organization of data about the urban poor in Jakarta, and specifically about their livelihoods and economic contribution to Jakarta, is key. Another asset in terms of community information dissemination and preparedness is the already-fairly decentralized local government structures of the RW and RT, with budget and administrative allocation down to a minute level in the city. With this

strong system already in place, it is relatively simple to scale up or replicate good community-level programs across the city.

GHG Emissions Inventory

A GHG emissions inventory for Jakarta is currently under development in partnership with BPLHD, DNPI, and the NGO group Swisscontact.

Notes

1. For more information, see www.pnpm-mandiri.org.
2. *Why Are There Floods In Jakarta? Flood Control by the Government of the Province of Jakarta*, PT Mirah Sakethi, 2010.
3. http://www.beritajakarta.com/2008/en/newsview.aspx?idwil=0&id=17983.
4. http://web.worldbank.org/external/projects/main?pagePK=64283627&piPK=73230& theSitePK=40941&menuPK=228424&Projectid=P111034.
5. http://www.thejakartaglobe.com/opinion/editorial-mapping-out-path-to-a-quake-ready-jakarta/432586.

Reference

World Bank. 2011. *Jakarta: Urban Challenges in a Changing Climate*. Jakarta: World Bank.

Annex 6: Mexico City Case Study

Overview and Key Findings

The Mexico City case study under the Mayor's Task Force brings together new and existing knowledge for dealing with climate change, disaster risk, and the urban poor. Results from this case study are contributing to the definition of the Mexico City Climate Change Adaptation Program to be implemented in 2012. The objectives of the Mexico City case study were to (1) establish the historic pattern and trends of hydro meteorological events in the Metropolitan Area of Mexico City (MAMC) and assess its spatial distribution and socioeconomic impacts; (2) model climate change impacts in the MAMC; (3) develop indicators of risk and vulnerability; and (4) present institutional and policy recommendations to respond to the challenges posed by climate change, natural disasters, and urban poverty.

The case study was prepared in collaboration between the World Bank and the government of Mexico City. As part of this effort, a complete document in Spanish, "Pobreza Urbana y Cambio Climático para la Ciudad de Mexico," and a short film are available for wider dissemination.

The approach used in this case study is based on the Urban Risk Assessment (URA) framework. Accordingly, it includes an assessment of the hazards, socioeconomic vulnerabilities, and institutional aspects related to climate change and disasters in Mexico City. This case study provides valuable geo-referenced information regarding location of increased risk to landslides as a result of extreme rain, and identifies areas where increased heat-island effect is expected.

Institutionally, this case study has served to identify shortcomings in the current operational framework for climate change and disaster risk management, respectively.

Key Findings of the Study

In dealing with climate change, disaster risk, and the urban poor, the key challenge for Mexico City is to define actions that will facilitate the streamlining of adaptation measures within a context of limited institutional coordination and cooperation across the 50 geopolitical and administrative units that make up the Metropolitan Area.

The Vulnerability of the Poor to Climate Change and Natural Hazards

Vulnerable groups in terms of population include about 7 million people (or 42 percent of population of the Mexico City Metropolitan Area) and about 1.5 million dwellings (see figure A6.5 in the color section). Most of the vulnerable population in high-risk zones lives in locations with slopes over 15 degrees (about 1 million people). This places them at risk of landslides as a result of extreme precipitation. The total population that lives in high-risk zones represents about 40 percent of the vulnerable population.

The Government of Mexico City at Work

The government of Mexico City has taken an active role in initiating climate change programs and the city is the first in Latin America to launch a local climate change strategy. The Mexico City Climate Action Program (MCCAP) consists of two complementary objectives: mitigation and adaptation.

Furthermore, the government has established the distinguished Virtual Center on Climate Change for Mexico City (CVCCCM). The CVCCCM contributes to increased and improved knowledge on the impact of climate change in the metropolitan area, and contributes the formulation and implementation of public policies. The CVCCCM operates in partnership with the Institute of Science and Technology of the Federal District and in conjunction with the Centre for Atmospheric Sciences of the National Autonomous University of Mexico (UNAM).

Mexico City has shown significant leadership in bringing together the climate change and disaster risk agendas, and has established the Inter-institutional Climate Change Commission of Mexico City, which is in charge of coordinating and evaluating the Mexico City Climate Change Action Program. Although it is premature to confirm or refute whether the measures proposed in this program will be mainstreamed into urban management practices, the wide participation and the higher-level commitment suggest solid first steps.

Key Constraints

Key constraints in dealing effectively with climate change, disaster risk, and the urban poor include:

INSTITUTIONAL COORDINATION—Despite significant progress in establishing an interinstitutional commission, the main challenge continues to be coordination and cooperation. Even though the program is designed to cut across institutional boundaries, limited ownership by the participants might hinder its success.

COMMON DATA PLATFORMS—Currently multiple agencies are taking actions but with limited communication or information exchange among concerned agencies. Furthermore, each agency has its own information platform, which hinders data sharing. This signals a strong need to develop a single common interface that all government agencies can use for data storage and use.

LIMITED BUDGET ALLOCATION—Although the execution of the MCCAP has an estimated cost of approximately US$5 billion, most of which is budgeted for mitigation, there has been limited transfer of money. The only instrument that could specifically provide resources for the action plan is the Environmental Public Fund, while the remaining identified actions would have to be financed through each respective agency's annual budgets.

Looking Forward

A few basic principles can guide the way forward for addressing climate change, disaster risk, and urban poverty in Mexico:

- The consolidation of an institutional framework able to drive the medium- and long-term challenges posed by climate change and natural disasters is instrumental for protecting the most vulnerable. This framework must specify clearly each agency's role while fostering synergies and collaboration.
- A common language (for example, technical terms and concepts), as well as a common strategic direction for assessing challenges and progress toward adaptation and resilience, is critical for mainstreaming this agenda in metropolitan governance.
- The strategies for climate action plans should explicitly include reducing and mitigating the impacts of meteorological events to the most vulnerable.
- Community-based social prevention is an important component of disaster prevention
- Further work is necessary to unlock barriers in the development of the early-warning system.

Case Study Summary

City Profile

Figure A6.1 Administrative Map of Mexico City Metropolitan Area

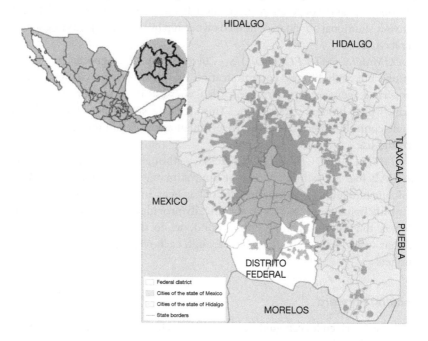

The Mexico City Metropolitan Area (MCMA) is one of the largest urban agglomerations in the world. Located in a closed basin of 9,600 km², the MCMA spreads over a surface of 4,250 km² at 2,240 meters above sea level. The MCMA has a metropolitan population estimated at 21.2 million, concentrates 18 percent of the country's population, and generates 35 percent of Mexico's gross domestic product on a surface equivalent to less than 0.3 percent of the national territory. Approximately 8.8 million people, or 42 percent of the metropolitan population, live in the city proper (Mexico City or the Federal District). The MCMA comprises the 16 boroughs of Mexico City and 34 municipalities of the State of Mexico, for a total of 50 geopolitical and administrative units that must coordinate among themselves in terms of urban planning, public services, and overall city management.

The MCMA has been growing constantly since the 1930s both physically and demographically. The pace of geographic and population growth, however, has been distinct. Physical and demographic growth reached its peak in the 1960s, and until the 1990s the physical expansion (urban sprawl) formed a continuous urbanized area with gross population density decreasing over time, and spatially increasing with distance from the historical city center. Since 1990 growth has been characterized by leapfrog expansion, and urban spatial continuity was broken. Current land use now bears limited contiguity to previously urbanized areas. For example, in 2000 the neighboring municipalities located in the State of Mexico represented 52 percent of the population and grew at an annual rate of 2.4 percent on average, while the 16 boroughs of Mexico City had a population growth rate of 0.3 percent annually.

The MCMA is characterized by seismic risk and with no natural drainage for runoff from the surrounding mountains; it is also vulnerable to flooding, particularly in the western part. The metropolitan area is affected by severe storms, heat waves, and droughts. The size of the population in the MCMA complicates the possible impacts of these events, as the infrastructure and public services are stretched thin. As a national economic engine, Mexico City's geophysical characteristics and presence of risk of multiple natural hazards underscores the need for the city to implement activities and programs that will increase its physical and social resilience. To take a recent example, the economic impact of the 2009 A (H1N1) influenza epidemic amounted to 0.4 percent of GDP (40 billion pesos).

Figure A6.2 Urban Expansion of Mexico City Metropolitan Areas, 1950–2005

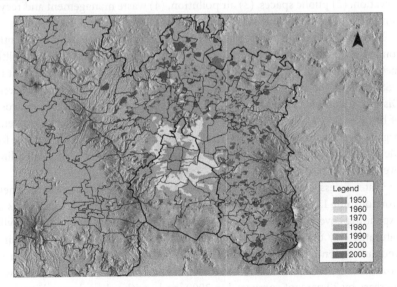

TABLE A6.1
Mexico City Profile

Total city population in 2010 federal district	8.8 million (INEGI 2010)
Total metropolitan area population in 2010	21.2 million
Population growth (% annual)	3.05 (CONAPO 2010)
Land area, federal district (km²)	1,485
Land area, metropolitan area (km²)	4,250
Population density (per km²)	5,958
Country's per capita GDP (US$)	9,243 (2010 estimate)
Country's population (federal district) (%)	7.87
Total number of households	2,388,534 (INEGI 2010)
Dwelling density (per hectare)	23.9 (SEDESEOL)
Avg. household income US$ (2008)	53,295
GDP per capita US$ (2008)	14,382
Country's GDP (%)	21.8
Total budget (US$)	11.7 billion
Date of last Urban Master Plan	n/a

The Built Environment and Basic Service Provision

Mexico City was the first city in Latin America to introduce a strategy for local climate action that has been designed to reduce overall greenhouse gas emissions by 7 million metric tons from its inception by Mayor Marcelo Ebrard in 2008–2012. The climate action program is part of a 15-year plan in which Mexico City is investing US$1 billion a year (approximately 9 percent of the yearly budget). The Green Plan (Plan Verde) has seven pillars: (1) land conservation, (2) public spaces, (3) air pollution, (4) waste management and recycling, (5) water supply and sanitation, (6) transportation, and (7) mobility.

Mexico City has the largest metro system in Latin America, which currently comprises 200 km of subway lines. It is currently being expanded with a twelfth metro line stretching 25 km, due to be finished in 2012—with an investment of US$2 billion. The Metro, which does not extend outside the limits of the Federal District, is complemented by a suburban rail system and an extensive network of bus routes. Mexico City's first Bus Rapid Transit line, the Metrobus system, began operation in June 2005. The city has begun construction of a third line for Metrobus that will run from the city's northwest to the central-south, extending over 16 km with 31 stations.

Water access is a complex problem for Mexico City, which has a supply network of some 13,000 km of primary and secondary pipelines. Beyond issues of expanding coverage and continuity of water services, the city rests on heavily saturated clay that has been collapsing and causing areas of the city to sink and subsequently endure more frequent flooding due to over-extraction of groundwater. Forecasts to 2015 estimate that rates of water consumption will increase by 20 percent compared to 2000 levels, with urban demand reaching

62 m³ per second. Mexico City's climate action program therefore includes measures to invest in water infrastructure, for example, the rehabilitation of the city's sewerage system as part of a program of hydraulic works.

Regarding land conservation, 59 percent of the total land area of Mexico City is designated a conservation area, with the city's remaining forested areas located in the southern boroughs. These areas are under threat from illegal development, logging, and fires, which impact regional rain patterns. At present the city's generation of garbage is increasing at a rate of 5 percent a year and the current insufficient rates of its collection have created "clandestine" fields. Bordo Poniente, one of the world's largest landfill sites, receives 12,500 tons of waste every day. In response, Mexico City has initiated a recycling program and is encouraging its citizens to separate trash.

Pillar 1—Institutional Assessment

Given the institutional and political complexities of the Mexico City Metropolitan Area, the Mexico City Climate Action Program (MCCAP) 2008–2012 requires a high level of coordination among multiple agencies and civil society. The MCCAP was developed as part of both the Green Plan and the Environmental Agenda of Mexico City. The Green Plan extends to 15 years, laying out strategies and actions of sustainable development for Mexico City. The Environmental Agenda of Mexico City is a 5-year plan that defines the city's environmental policy. At the same time, both the Green Plan and the Environmental Agenda are part of one of the pillars of Mexico City's Development Program.

The main objectives of the MCCAP are twofold: (1) reduce carbon dioxide emissions by 7 million tons (or equivalent) in the period 2008–2012 and (2) develop a Climate Change Adaptation Program for the Federal District and begin its implementation by 2012. To achieve these objectives, the government uses various policy instruments, including direct investment from Mexico City, regulation, economic incentives, voluntary carbon markets, and education and information campaigns.

The Inter-institutional Climate Change Commission of Mexico City is in charge of coordinating and evaluating the MCCAP. This commission includes representatives from all the administrative units of the Federal District. In addition, three deputies from the district's Legislative Assembly are invited to attend each session. Among its specific responsibilities are to design, encourage, and coordinate policies to mitigate climate change effects in Mexico City; to evaluate, approve, and disseminate related projects; to develop financial strategies that generate revenue; and to coordinate actions and policies with other programs linked to the MCCAP. To facilitate coordination and provide support to the MCCAP, the Legislative Assembly of Mexico City is working on a proposal for a climate change law (not yet entered into force as of March 2011).

Although the execution of the MCCAP has an estimated cost of approximately US$5 billion, most of which is budgeted for mitigation, there has been little transfer of money. The only instrument that could specifically provide resources for the MCCAP is the Environmental Public Fund, while the remaining identified actions would have to be financed through each agency's annual budgets.

The main challenge of the MCCAP is the lack of institutional coordination and cooperation. Even though the program was designed to cut across institutional boundaries, there is lack of ownership and it is mostly considered a program of the secretary of environment. Currently multiple agencies are taking actions but with limited communication or information exchange among concerned agencies. Further exacerbating the open exchange of data is that each agency has its own information platform. This signals a strong need to develop a single common interface that all government agencies can use for data storage and use.

Climate Change Adaptation and Disaster Response

The MCCAP's program of adaptation consists of short- and long-term actions that aim to reduce risks to the population and economy of Mexico City by taking the potential impacts of climate change into account. The lines of action regarding adaptation are: (1) identifying key threats and performing a vulnerability analysis, (2) mainstreaming adaptation to enhance existing capabilities in Mexico City's government, and (3) implementing adaptation.

There are multiple agencies involved in responding to extreme hydro-meteorological events, including: The Water System of Mexico City, the Civil Protection Agency, the Public Safety Agency, the Health Department, the Social Development Agency, the Social Assistance Institute, and the Urban Development and Housing Agency. Their main tasks follow.

TABLE A6.2
Institutional Responsibilities Relating to Climate and Disasters

Institution	Headed by/level	Major function
Water system of Mexico City	Secretary of environment	Responsible for public services related to water supply, drainage, sewerage, and water treatment. They also coordinate and operate the "Storm Unit" during high-precipitation emergencies in 90 previously identified high-risk locations, with the participation of the Civil Protection Agency, the Public Safety Agency, and the Fire Department.
Civil Protection Agency	Secretary of interior	Responsible for coordinating prevention and response to natural disasters, mainly floods and earthquakes, using a "Risk Atlas" that has more than 100 maps depicting multiple hazards. In terms of flooding, they have

(continued next page)

TABLE A6.2 *continued*

Institution	Headed by/level	Major function
		identified critical locations based on past events, but these are not necessarily the same maps used by the Water System of Mexico City. Importantly, this agency has focused mainly on prevention, response, and capacity building for seismic disasters. They defined and are implementing the Crisis and Immediate Response Action Plan.
Public Safety Agency	Operates in coordination with the water system of Mexico City and the Civil Protection Agency	Intervenes when natural disasters occur.
Health Department	In emergencies, coordinates with the Civil Protection Agency	Responsible for periodic monitoring of epidemic prevention and response (including AH1N1 and dengue). In addition to medical attention, it organizes vaccination campaigns.
Social Development Agency		Provides support and responds to emergencies related to heat and cold waves and floods. In addition to operating public dining locations, the agency establishes shelters with food and provides psychological assistance.
Social Assistance Institute		Responsible for general social assistance (including psychological support) for the Federal District, but also during emergencies. Through one of its programs, it operates a hotline to support homeless people. It also supports families affected by disasters and operates 11 centers for social assistance.
Urban Development and Housing Agency		Responsible for medium- and long-term prevention of disasters through urban planning. It is involved in issues related to irregular terrains in high-risk locations. It has plans to develop an information system for Mexico City that will include geographic and urban development indicators.

Ongoing Programs and Projects Related to Disaster Risk Management or Climate Change Adaptation

Programs for climate change adaptation focus on early-warning systems and medium-term response:

- Programs on early-warning systems and upstream prevention include the implementation of a hydro-meteorological monitoring and forecasting system for Mexico Valley, an epidemiological monitoring system, and a remote identification and monitoring system for fires. In addition, initiatives are in place for management of hillside risk, the protection of native vegetation to reduce erosion, and the establishment of processes to help vulnerable populations.

• Regarding medium-term response, Mexico City is running projects on water and land conservation, land management for agricultural rural areas, reforestation with more resilient species, and green roofing in urban areas. Table A6.3 shows the goals and key results of the main projects to adapt to climate change in the context of the Climate Action Program for Mexico City.

• For emergency response in case of landslides or flooding, the most relevant agencies are the Department of Civil Protection, Fire and Health, complemented by Brigades of the Ministry of Social Development, to provide shelter, hot food, and psychological help to those affected, as well as the Ministry of Public Security to control access and prevent vandalism. As a permanent activity, there are homeless shelters and soup kitchens and attention to patients with severe respiratory or dehydration.

TABLE A6.3
Status of Main Projects to Adapt to Climate Change

Program/responsible agency	Goals	Results
Urban Hillsides Program—Environmental Agency	By 2012, identify 33 hillsides and develop and disseminate their management programs	As of 2009, nine hillsides identified and seven programs developed
Dengue Monitoring—Health Department	Determine mortality rate due to dengue	Annual studies made to identify the presence of the virus, risky areas mapped, and household surveys made
Monitoring and prevention of health effects due to extreme weather—Health Department	Avoid mortality and mitigate risks and health effects of exposure to extreme temperatures	Information campaigns conducted, serum kits distributed, and chlorine in water closely monitored
Epidemiological and health monitoring of climate change—Health Department	Monitor chlorine in water, water supply systems, sanitary monitoring of food production and distribution, among others	In 2010, over 36,000 water samples and 125 food samples taken for analysis. Over 1,900 visits to establishments to evaluate sanitary conditions
Support to vulnerable populations during winter season—Social Assistance Institute	Provide support and social assistance to vulnerable people	In 2010, over 200,000 warm dinners and 15,000 blankets distributed. Also, over 6,000 medical consultations provided, among other services
Risk Atlas of Mexico City—Civil Protection Agency	Develop an integrated information system shared by all administrative units	Efforts ongoing

(continued next page)

TABLE A6.3 *continued*

Program/responsible agency	Goals	Results
Preventive program for hydro-meteorological risks—Civil Protection Agency	Prevention, mitigation, and response to emergencies due to hydro-meteorological events	260 informational reports disseminated, often daily during the week
Storm Unit Program—Water System of Mexico City	Response to negative effects of precipitation during the rainy season	Between 2008 and 2010, over 6,000 cases were attended and resolved
Reduction of extreme precipitation impacts in "El Arenal"—Government Secretariat	Mitigate negative impact of extreme precipitation in 14 areas	Food, drinks, blankets, and cleaning products distributed. Equipment installed to speed up the drainage, and sewers cleaned
Sustainable housing in the Federal District—Housing Institute of the Federal District	Incorporate green technologies into new housing	Solar water heaters, energy efficiency lamps, and water treatment by re-utilization, among others, incorporated in over 5,000 new dwellings

Source: Leon et al. (2010).

Shortcomings in Current Disaster Risk Management or Climate Change Adaptation Management

Disaster risk in Mexico City is handled in a reactive manner with limited preventative measures in place. Implementation of the early-warning system, envisioned as one of the priority adaptation measures included in the MCCAP, has been delayed due to administrative issues. In addition, there is an evident need to improve the sharing of information among the relevant government agencies, taking as an example the Risk Atlas (elaborated by the secretary of civil protection), to which not all agencies have access.

Leading Activities to Coordinate Agency Risk Management

The secretary of civil protection is in charge of risk management in Mexico City, although many other agencies are also involved.

Pillar 2—Hazards Assessment

Natural Disaster History

The Mexico Valley is exposed to increases in extreme temperatures, which with expanding urbanization has contributed to a significant heat-island effect for Mexico City. Projections reveal that the mean temperature is expected to increase by 2–3°C toward the end of the 21st century, and extreme precipitation is also expected to increase. Characteristically rising temperatures are accompanied by

TABLE A6.4
Natural Hazards

	Yes /No	Date of last major event
Earthquake	Y	1985
Wind storm	Y	2010
River flow	N	
Floods, inundations, and waterlogs	Y	2010
Tsunami	N	
Drought	Y	2011
Volcano	N	
Landslide	Y	
Storm surge	N	
Extreme temperature	Y	

an increase in extreme rain, consequently placing Mexico City at heightened risk of flooding and landslides, particularly in the western part of the city.

Current Trends and Projections

TEMPERATURE—The temperature in the Mexico Valley reflects its geography, where warmer temperatures are concentrated in the lower elevations and cooler temperatures in the elevated areas. Nevertheless, with time, the temperature in the Mexico Valley has changed due to urbanization, constituting one of the clearest examples of a heat-island effect in the world. The highest values are observed in the northeast, where the average maximum reaches 30°C. The area with main maximum temperatures over 24°C increased considerably between 2000 and 2007, and the minimum temperature increased by 2°C and 3°C in the north and northeast, respectively, in the same period. While temperature increase in the western part of Mexico City has been lower, the frequency and duration of heat waves in the area are increasing. For example, the number of heat waves of three or more days with 30°C or higher increased from 2 in 1877–1887 to 16 in 1991–2000 in the west of the Federal District (Jáuregui 2000). Simulation exercises for temperature in January show that temperature in the northeast, which is the region that has grown fastest, increased 2°C. Although this temperature rise may in part be the effect of urbanization, some atmospheric conditions may also have had an impact, and this order of magnitude is in line with those expected this century by models simulating global warming.

To further understand temperature increases associated with urbanization, an analysis was undertaken of temperature trends in areas with rapid urbanization against those in regions that are close to highly vegetated areas. For Mexico City, the trend in the minimum temperature in regions with rapid urbanization between 1963 and 2000 is an increase of about 0.7°C per decade, while for regions close to vegetated areas the associated increase was about 0.1°C per decade.

Another way to evaluate the effects of extreme events is to analyze the 90th percentile of the maximum temperature using a projection from the Earth Simulator. For 2015–2039, the northeast region will have temperatures around 30°C for at least 10 percent of the year, as shown in figure A6.3.

PRECIPITATION—Precipitation projections for Mexico City seem to be consistent with the general projection made by the Intergovernmental Panel on Climate Change (IPCC) in 2007, which states that precipitation will increase in regions with high precipitation and decrease in regions with low precipitation. Particularly, the intensity and quantity of extreme precipitation is expected to increase in the west of the city, and decrease in the east. In the Mexico Valley the highest precipitation occurs between mid-May and early October, with the western region receiving the most precipitation in August. On average, annual precipitation is between 700 and 900 mm (±30 percent). The highest intensity usually occurs during the afternoon and early evening. The western region presents upward trends for daily precipitation and episodes over 20 mm/hour over the past 100 years. During September and October, more than 30 mm/hour of rain may occur, which, based on a review of landslides, is the critical threshold for landslides of saturated land. Projected increases in extreme precipitation in terms of the intensity and duration are shown in figure A6.4. In the west of Mexico City, these increases constitute a significant hazard for vulnerable populations located on hillsides. Additionally, projected increases in extreme precipitation add to the risk of flooding in the west of Mexico City and the southern areas of the Federal District.

WATER RUNOFF—Climate change projections indicate that with increasing temperature, evapotranspiration increases at the expense of infiltration and runoff. For many urban areas, including the MCMA, changes in land use also affect this ratio, whereby as urbanization increases, less water is naturally absorbed into the ground and more runoff occurs. Assuming 100 mm of rainfall and using information about land and vegetation types, the approximate amount of water runoff was calculated for Mexico Valley.[1] The findings show a noticeable increase in runoff in

Figure A6.3 90th Percentile of Maximum Temperature, in Celsius, in 1979–2003 (left) and 2015–2039 (right)

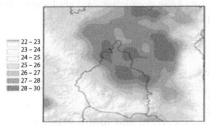
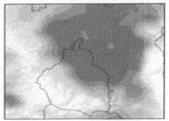

22 – 23
23 – 24
24 – 25
25 – 26
26 – 27
27 – 28
28 – 30

Source: Leon et al. (2010).

Figure A6.4 95th Percentile of Precipitation (mm/day) in 1979–2003 (left) and 2015–39 (right)

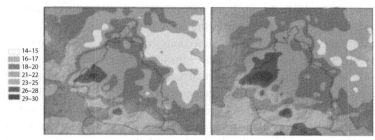

14–15
16–17
18–20
21–22
23–25
26–28
29–30

Source: Leon et al. (2010).

2000 when compared with 1980. The increased precipitation and resulting runoff increases flood risk in the city, particularly given the existing drainage system.

Pillar 3—Socioeconomic Assessment

Location of the Urban Poor

Vulnerable groups were identified and mapped in terms of population and housing characteristics by doing a cluster analysis with data from the 2000 official census.[2] In terms of population, vulnerable groups include areas with high concentration of people over 18 years without secondary education, people that moved in the past 5 years, and people with low income. As shown in table A6.5, this group includes about 7 million people (or 42 percent of the population of the Mexico City Metropolitan Area) and about 1.5 million dwellings.

In terms of housing, vulnerable groups are concentrated in areas characterized by use of precarious construction materials in walls and ceilings, those without access to basic services, and where formal property ownership and rights are limited. This group includes about 5 million people (or 30 percent of the population) and about 1 million dwellings. The location of these groups is shown by figure A6.5, in the color section. The most vulnerable in terms of both population and housing represent about 27 percent of the population and are located in the peripheral area of the MCMA, mostly to the north and east.[3]

Exposure of the Urban Poor

The information on vulnerable groups was overlaid with information on extreme precipitation and temperature, and locations with steep slopes. Maps similar to figure A6.5 were created to observe the location of these groups with respect to high-risk zones: current and future extreme precipitation and vulnerable housing; vulnerable population and housing located

TABLE A6.5
Vulnerability Matrix in Terms of Population and Housing

		Population	
		Low vulnerability	High vulnerability
Housing	Low vulnerability	2,609 PSUs* 9,516,901 people 2,329,416 dwellings 54.8% of population	514 PSUs 2,639,058 people 584,547 dwellings 15.2% of population
	High vulnerability	164 PSUs 577,583 people 128,831 dwellings 3.3% of population	1,354 PSUs 4,635,298 people 964,144 dwellings 26.7% of population

*Primary sampling units.

Source: Leon et al. (2010).

TABLE A6.6
Social Assessment

City population below poverty line (%)	59.4
Social inequality (Gini index) in 2002 (UN Habitat)	0.43 (2008) CIA factbook
Unemployment (% of total labor force)	6.3
Areal size of informal settlements as a percent of city area	n/a
City population living in slums (%)	22
Children completing primary and secondary education: survival rate	57.4 (Mexico City)
Human Development Index (2009)	75
Predominant housing material	For the very poor, assorted salvaged materials; for self-builders, concrete blocks and brick

in zones with high risk of extreme precipitation; vulnerable population and housing located in zones with slopes over 15 degrees; vulnerable population and housing located in zones with risk of heat waves; and vulnerable population and housing located in zones with risk of extreme precipitation and slopes over 15 degrees.

Figure A7.4, in the color section, shows the distribution of population and housing for each event. Most of the vulnerable population in high-risk zones lives in locations with slopes over 15 degrees (about 1 million people). The total population that lives in high-risk zones represents about 40 percent of the vulnerable population and about 41 percent of the vulnerable dwellings. Importantly, about 60 percent of the vulnerable population and dwellings are not located in high-risk zones.

TABLE A6.7
Distribution of Vulnerable Groups Located in High-Risk Zones

Event	PSUs[1]	%	Population	%	Housing	%
I. Extreme precipitation	48	3.55	179,019	3.86	38,909	4.06
II. Slopes over 15 degrees	288	21.27	1,004,586	21.67	208,546	21.63
III. Heat waves	117	8.64	367,450	7.93	76,771	7.96
I + II	59	4.36	251,118	5.42	53,455	5.54
I + III	1	0.07	39	0.00	10	0
II + III	23	1.70	62,449	1.35	13,175	1.37
I + II + III	0	0.00	0	0.00	0	0.00
Vulnerable in high-risk zones	536	39.59	1,864,661	40.23	390,866	40.54
Total vulnerable	1354	100	4,635,298	100	964,144	100

Source: Leon et al. (2010).

[1]PSU refer to primary sampling units defined in the context of the 2000 census.

ECONOMIC COSTS OF CLIMATE CHANGE—Another important aspect of the socioeconomic assessment was the analysis of the economic costs of climate change in terms of GDP for the Federal District. This analysis incorporated four scenarios. The base scenario, named A2, does not include climate change impacts and assumes 1.99 percent of annual GDP growth, 1.81 percent of annual GDP per capita growth, and 18 percent of population growth for 2100. The other three scenarios correspond to different goals on reduction of greenhouse gas emissions considered in international negotiations (that is, 550, 450, and 350 parts per million, or ppm). The analysis incorporated three discount rates (0 percent, 1 percent, and 4 percent); however, based on the literature on the costs of climate change, the authors recommend using 0 percent to draw conclusions. Table A6.8 shows costs for each scenario in terms of GDP reduction and additional number of poor people by 2100 for the Federal District, using a 0 percent discount rate. Shown is the average value, as well as the 95 percent confidence interval in parentheses.

Under the status quo scenario (A2), it is expected that the GDP will be reduced 19 times on average. These results are not too different from those under the 550 ppm scenario. However, if the 350 ppm scenario is realized, the benefits could reach 32 times the current GDP (in terms of avoided losses). Also under the A2 scenario, the number of poor is projected to increase to over 1 million (or about 10 percent of population in 2100), although the average increase is expected to be 450,000. The analysis also pointed out that economic losses are not distributed equally among administrative units. Those that will lose the most are those that are currently worse off. In other terms, if the temperature increases by 2°C, Mexico City could lose up to 7 percent of its GDP and get 150,000 additional poor annually.

TABLE A6.8
Costs in Terms of GDP and Additional Poor

Scenario	GDP reduction by 2100, no. of times	Additional number of poor people by 2100, in thousands
A2	19.10 (5.22, 45.79)	441 (98,1281)
550 ppm	17.35 (4.52, 43.04)	392 (81,1176)
450 ppm	10.77 (3.15, 24.38)	213 (51,560)
350 ppm	6.50 (2.03, 13.70)	104 (26,249)

Source: Leon et al. (2010).

Notes

1. Runoff calculation was undertaken using the curve number method, developed by the USDA Natural Resources Conservation Service.
2. The census data are coded, for all variables, in primary sampling units (PSUs) or territorial units, called by the Mexican official census institution basic geo-statistic areas (AGEBs, Areas Geoestadísticas Básicas).
3. In addition to those living in low-income neighborhoods, Mexico City also has a sizable homeless population, which is particularly vulnerable to extreme events. Importantly, this segment of the population is not accounted for in the city's calculations of urban poverty, as such information relates to those who possess a dwelling.

Reference

Leon, C., V. Magaña, B. Graizbord, R. González, A. Damian, and F. Estrada. 2010. "Pobreza Urbana y Cambio Climático para La Ciudad de México." Unpublished, Mayor's Task Force Study, Mexico City.

Annex 7: São Paulo Case Study

Overview and Key Findings

In São Paulo, the largest city in Latin America, almost 11.5 million people live in 1.5 km². More than 40 percent of the population lives in peripheral areas that concentrate a vast proportion of the city's poor and socially vulnerable citizens. São Paulo is already experiencing some consequences of a changing climate: more frequent heavy rains, higher temperatures, and decreased air humidity. An estimated 900,000 houses in the peripheral areas are considered at risk—some located in slopes and floodable areas—and will be the most affected by climate change.

In this context, this case study presents the first comprehensive revision of policies and programs at the intersection of climate change, disaster risk, and the urban poor in São Paulo. The case study has been prepared by the World Bank, in close consultation with the São Paulo Housing Secretariat and the Green and Environment Secretariat. These two secretariats have contributed with their expertise in working with slums and informal settlements, as well as working in disaster risk management and climate change adaptation.

The approach used in this case study is based on the Urban Risk Assessment (URA) framework. Accordingly, it includes an assessment of the hazards, socioeconomic vulnerabilities, and institutional aspects related to climate change and disaster risk management in São Paulo. Extensive data collection and stakeholder consultation was carried out as part of this study. In particular, two highly vulnerable communities in São Paulo were consulted and analyzed more in depth.

With a focus on the urban poor, this study considers how poor communities are affected by climate change and natural hazards, examines approaches that have been taken to address these challenges, and identifies priorities and options for further action in São Paulo. This study draws on other existing reports and resources on disaster risk management and climate change, as well as on interviews and discussions with key stakeholders.

Key Findings of the Study

Independent studies predict that in the absence of significant policy changes, by the end of the century urban occupation in São Paulo will be twice the current one and 11 percent of the future occupied areas could be located in areas at risk for landslide. This will increase the risks of floods and landslides, impacting disproportionally the poorest.

Although this scenario will occur only in the absence of significant changes in the spatial distribution and socioeconomic characteristics of the city, it does highlight the importance of dealing with climate change and disaster risk with a focus on the urban poor.

The Mayor's Task Force in the city of São Paulo found that:

- The vulnerable groups who occupy areas at risk will have difficulty coping with unpredictable and extreme weather. Slum dwellers (currently more than 890,000 households) lack the resources necessary to adapt rapidly to the changing circumstances.
- Slums face the most hazardous conditions; more than 5 percent of slum areas are highly or very highly exposed to landslides and are highly prone to be affected by destructive events in the next 12 months.
- While the location of certain settlements in areas of flood plain or wetlands does not necessarily indicate flood hazards, it is an indirect estimate of areas potentially more exposed to such events. The incidence of precarious and informal settlements in these areas shows how intensive their occupation has been. About 20 percent of the slums and informal urbanized centers are located in flood plains. About 13 percent of the allotments and informal settlements are located in flood plains and flood hazard areas.
- In the slums, virtually all families live in poverty or extreme poverty. In addition, a great number of the basic services that the people depend upon suffer negative impacts with the severe weather. For instance, the public transportation system in São Paulo is not fully equipped to handle floods and overflows.
- The sanitation system has some deficits (6 percent of houses do not have proper sewage collection and 25 percent of the effluent is not treated).

- Energy service is irregular and the systems suffer with the storms, which lead to electricity shortage in houses and streets, creating an unsafe feeling among the inhabitants.

The Government of São Paulo at Work

The city of São Paulo has been a pioneer in monitoring greenhouse gases at the city level. As part of the C40 group, São Paulo has committed to prepare a GHG emissions inventory, adopt a future reduction target on GHG emissions, create a local action plan in a participatory process, implement climate policies and measures, and monitor and verify results.

In 2005 São Paulo launched its first inventory. Furthermore, in 2007, the City Assembly passed a law that required new houses and buildings assembled with more than four bathrooms to adopt a solar-panel heating system. In 2009 the City Assembly approved the City Climate Law to ensure the city´s contribution to stabilizing GHG in the atmosphere in accordance with UNFCCC principles.

The City Climate Law set a reduction target of 30 percent in GHG emissions against the baseline 2005 emission levels. Additional targets should be defined each two years. The law establishes a number of commitments for the city to follow by sector. From 2005 to 2010, the city already has cut its emissions by 20 percent, largely due to implementing biogas power plants on two large landfills.

A Special Fund for the Environment and Sustainable Development was created in 2001 with the purpose of financially supporting projects that aim to improve the sustainable use of natural resources; control, monitor, protect, and recuperate the environment; and initiate environmental education. Currently, the fund does not have budget revenue from the municipal government of São Paulo, instead its revenue coming from various resources (R$8 million) that are directed to 15 projects from NGOs chosen through tenders; and Carbon Credits Auctions (R$33 million + 37 million), the amount originated from CDM projects implemented at the Bandeirantes Landfill and São João Landfill. The fund has been used to support the creation of a database on GHG emissions, publication of an inventory of anthropic emissions every five years, and actions for climate change mitigation, including incentives for the private sector and research institutions.

Areas for Improvement

Some of the recommended areas for work out of the Mayor's Task Force include:

- Housing—Increase the regularization and improvement of slums and irregular allotments and relocate families from risky areas.
- Health—Increase the number of people served in health services and increase its qualities.
- Transportation—Increase the coverage of bus, trains, and subway routes, improve bus stops and terminals, renovate electric bus system and cars, enable public transport, decrease traffic rates, and increase traffic safety.

- Education—Improve public system, decrease evasion rates, especially for the medium (or secondary) education; increase the number of public nurseries (insufficient to meet the growing demand).
- Water supply—Increase the water quality and protect water basins.
- Sewage—Increase system coverage and avoid illegal disposal of sewage into water courses.
- Waste management—Increase inspection of illegal dumping places, decrease waste generation, and increase recycling.
- Cleaning—Improve cleaning coverage for culverts and streets.
- Drainage—Clean and dredge the river bottoms, clean and increase the existing drainage underground channels, and build more "pools" ("piscinões") around the city.
- Looking forward—Mainstream climate change, climate variability, and disaster risk reduction in planning land use. This should strengthen the municipality's own medium-term planning, enabling them to prepare for (among other things) the hosting of Global Expo in 2020.

Looking Forward

Overall, this study highlights some of the challenges a metropolis like São Paulo is facing regarding present and future climate change and disaster risk scenarios, especially when dealing with an ever-increasing socially vulnerable population. The document also shares the lessons already learned by the city when addressing this subject. In the short and medium term in addressing climate change, disaster risk and urban poverty, key areas for reform include:

- Coordinate and integrate information databases among the different city secretariats. As of now the city faces a multiplicity of information produced and used by different agencies. The unification of information could lead to shared programs.
- Extend public disclosure of information and public participation in the design and implementation of climate projects to ensure stakeholders are involved.
- Incorporate climate change policies into city administration in order to guarantee continuity.
- Enhance mapping capacity to better inform resilience in decision making.
- Improve inequality in adaptive capacity across the city through capacity-building programs for stakeholders, practitioners, city managers, and decision makers. Structured learning resources and the exchange of experiences with other cities can be applied to increase the understanding of the linkages between climate change and disaster risk management and the urban poor in different levels.

Case Study Summary

City Profile

Figure A7.1 Administrative Map of São Paulo

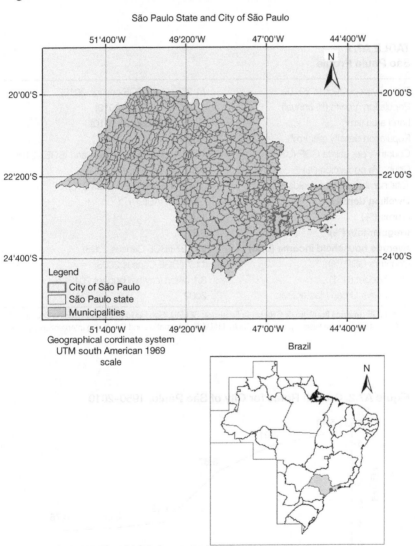

São Paulo State and City of São Paulo

Legend
- City of São Paulo
- São Paulo state
- Municipalities

Geographical cordinate system
UTM south American 1969
scale

Brazil

The population growth rate in São Paulo is decreasing (in 2010 it was only 0.76 percent compared to 1.16 percent in 1990). The difference between the numbers of people in the city between day and night could reach 2 million people. Nevertheless, the population rate in the periphery is increasing (growing from 4.9 million to 5.5 million from 1991 to 2000), representing 30 percent

TABLE A7.1
São Paulo Profile

Total city population in 2010	11.25 million (IBGE census 2010)
Population growth (% annual)	0.75 (SEADE 2000/2010)
Land area (km²)	1,523 (IBGE census 2010)
Population density (per km²)	7,388
Country's per capita GDP (US$)	10,960 (Brazil central bank and IBGE 2010)
Country's population (%)	5.89 (IBGE Census 2010)
Total number of households	3,576,864 (IBGE Census 2010)
Dwelling density	(SEHAB/HABISP)
Slums (%)	1.6
Irregular lots (%)	6.32
Average household income (US$)	891.37 (IBGE Census 2008)
Country's GDP (%)	11.7 (IBGE Census 2008)
Total budget (US$)	3.1 billion (city hall budget 2010)
Date of last Urban Master Plan	2002

Note: IBGE: Instituto Brasileiro de Geografia e Estatística; SEHAB: Sao Paulo Municipal Housing Secretariat; SEADE: State Data Analysis System Sao Paulo; HABISP: Information and Prioritizing Intervention System

Figure A7.2 Growth Rates for City of São Paulo, 1950–2010

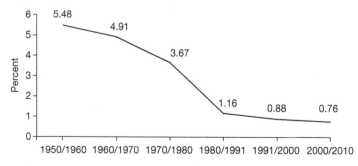

Source: HABISP.

Figure A7.3 São Paulo City Social Vulnerability Index, IPVS

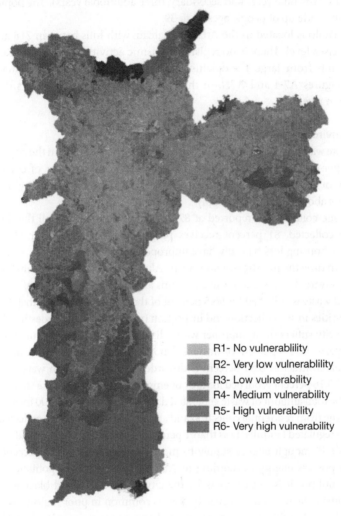

R1- No vulnerablility
R2- Very low vulnerablility
R3- Low vulnerability
R4- Medium vulnerability
R5- High vulnerability
R6- Very high vulnerability

Source: HABISP.

of the urban expansion. The periphery concentrates the majority of the poorer inhabitants (the average household income is half the average for the city and the per capita household income is up to three times lower than the city rate).

Life expectancy in São Paulo is 71 years. The mortality rate is 6.53 for each thousand and the child mortality rate is 15.83 for each thousand. The city has 4.89 percent illiteracy among youth above 15 years old. Almost 47 percent of the population above 25 has less than eight years of formal education (primary education lasts nine years and secondary, three additional years). The population is mainly made up of people ages 25 to 59.

São Paulo is located in the Atlantic Plateau, with hills between 718 and 720 m above sea level. There is no registered seismic activity in São Paulo. Regional hills climb from large floodplains through fluvial terraces into interfluvial areas. Figures A7.4 and A7.9, in the color section, shows the city's declivity and main rivers.

Built Environment and Basic Services

Adequate water supply is provided to 98.6 percent of the houses in the city (almost 65 m³ per inhabitant/year), though the increase in the number of consumers, scarcity of new water resources, and decrease in basin water quality increases concerns about future water supply.[1]

Sewage collection is reported at 87.2 percent (2006). From all the domestic sewage collected, 81 percent receives proper treatment. However, slums and irregular housing lots typically have improper sanitation conditions and sewage is thrown directly into streams and rivers. Almost 48 percent of the inhabitants of the city's water basin wetlands live in slums and irregular settlements.

Solid waste is collected for 96.5 percent of the houses. In spite of that, there are irregularities in site collection and inspection (more than 300 clandestine dumps), and the city suffers from improper waste-disposal clogging and polluting culverts and waterways: 2.6 percent of waste is deposited in containers and removed by a City Hall contractor; 0.64 percent is discarded in the land or in waterways; and another 0.16 percent is burned in yards or empty lands. City Hall data shows that, in 2010, the total amount of waste generated daily by the city was 17,000 tons—10,000 tons come from residential collection and almost 100 percent of the collected waste went to regulated landfills. Less than 1 percent of this waste was recycled.[2]

There is enough energy supply to meet city demands (99.99 percent of the houses possess energy), according to AES Eletropaulo Metropolitana S.A. (an energy utility). It is not unusual for the city to have localized blackouts, especially during heavy rains. Electricity theft is common in poor regions of the city. The industrial, residential, and commercial sectors are more or less equal in their energy consumption (17 percent of the national consumption is equivalent to 35.3 million megawatt/hours).

The city's traffic is extremely heavy, with more than 7 million vehicles. The subway system (managed by the state) is connected to the rail system (also managed by the state), through a CPTM (Train Management Agency). An average of 2.1 million passengers a day are transported through 89 stations, 260.8 km, and 63.5 km of subway tracks. Approximately 15,000 buses circulate through 1,335 routes and 28 terminals. Every three years it is estimated that the number of bus trips increases by 1 million (CPTM, Metro and SPTrans 2010). The design

Figure A7.5 Greenhouse Gas Emissions from Electric Energy Use by Sector in São Paulo

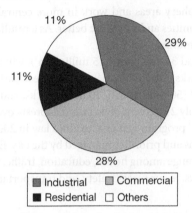

Source: São Paulo GHG's inventory.

Figure A7.6 Transport Use in São Paulo

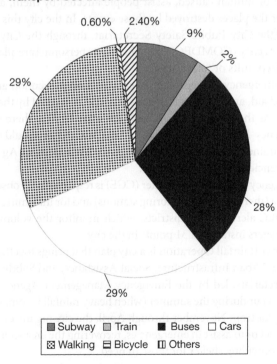

Source: Research Origin and Destination 2007.

and number of routes is considered insufficient to adequately serve the entire population. The situation is even worse for the poor, since a great number of them live in the periphery areas and work in more centralized neighborhoods where the job opportunities and wages are better. As a result, they spend hours in public transport commuting.

In 2005, the city had 34 city parks (15 million m³), which increased substantially in 2008 to 48 parks (24 million m³) and 17 linear parks.[3] The SVMA plans for 100 parks by 2012 (50 million m³), 20 linear parks, and 5 natural parks. São Paulo had, in 2009, only 21 percent of its original forest coverage.[4]

The "Agenda 2012" program was enacted into law in 2008 and prescribes the transparency of actions and priorities managed by the city. Each region of the city has its targets, which range among health, education, traffic, water quality, sewage piping, quality of parks, leisure areas, safety, and transportation.[5]

Pillar 1—Institutional Assessment

Agencies in Disaster Risk Management and Climate Change Adaptation

The Emergency Management Agency acts on the federal, state, and municipal levels. Its goal is to plan actions to prevent and minimize effects of disasters, either natural or human caused, assist people affected by them, and rehabilitate or recover the places destroyed by those events. In the city this responsibility rests with the City Public Safety Secretariat, through the City Emergency Management Agency (COMDEC). Nonetheless, its personnel are allocated to the 31 decentralized units or "subdistricts."

The City Emergency Management Agency acts on prevention and recovery, assistance and aid, and on search and rescue, and is assisted by the Firefighter Department. At the communities located in areas of risk, there should be a Local Emergency Management Group, or NUDEC. They should be made up of volunteers trained by the National Emergency Management Agency to help during emergencies and risky situations.

The Emergency Management Center (CGE) is responsible for observing meteorological data (there are 180 monitoring stations) and for informing COMDEC. Then COMDEC alerts the subdistricts, which monitor the volume of rainfall using pluviometers installed at 31 points in the city.

The Summer Rainfall Operation is a city plan that brings together the Housing, Transport, Urban Infrastructure, Social Assistance, and Subdistricts Coordination Secretariats, led by the Emergency Management Agency, and targets disasters that occur during the summer (when heavy rainfall is common). Whenever necessary or from November through April, the city organizes initiatives to prevent disasters or to assist in emergencies, recovering the area after the flood or landslide and providing shelter for those in need.

When a heavy rainfall approaches, CGE issues an alarm to COMDEC, as well as to the traffic authorities (CET), the Health Secretariat (SMS), Green and Environment Secretariat (SVMA), and Housing Secretariat (SEHAB). Each subdistrict must then activate the process using the Emergency Management Agency agents allocated to the region, following a standard operational procedure. The initiatives include prevention (evacuating houses in at-risk areas), search and rescue of people in floods or landslides, and restoration of affected areas.

After the flood or landslide, the firefighters rescue possible victims. Water and sanitation authorities fix broken water pipes and energy agents check the electricity posts. Social assistants verify housing conditions and, if necessary, direct people to temporary shelters while SEHAB arranges for "rent allowance" or allocate housing for the needy. The City Health Secretariat, through its Health Vigilance Coordination (COVISA), trains its environmental agents to inform—both before and after the heavy rains—the vulnerable communities about endemic diseases spread by water (such as leptospirosis), their symptoms, and the need for medical treatment. The basic health units (UBS) receive folders and posters to distribute to the population on how to avoid leptospirosis and the proper treatment. COVISA also alerts each region of the city about its specific risk of leptospirosis, aiming to prepare the health professionals for the emergence and spread of the disease.

Examples of Disaster-Related Program or Relevant Decrees
The Summer Rainfall Operation is an existing plan from the city that brings together the Housing, Transport, Urban Infrastructure, Social Assistance, and Subdistricts Coordination Secretariats, led by the Emergency Management Agency.

Decree 47.534/2006 reorganizes the city system of the Emergency Management Agency. There are other laws at administrative levels that regulate the Emergency Management Agency and the operation procedures.[6]

There is no information on the maintenance and testing of the procedures. From an ordinary citizen's point of view, those alarms are neither timely nor efficient, since they require constant monitoring through the CGE´s website. In at-risk areas, this is even less likely to occur, since the rate of viewing the Internet in general in the city in 2003 was 25 percent. There is no data available on expenditures on disaster risk management or adaptation programs.

Shortcomings in Disaster Risk Management and Climate Change Adaptation Management
The interviews and research indicate that the Emergency Management Agency has a shortage of agents in the at-risk communities, for distributing and teaching the use of the plastic pluviometers (PET) and water-level rulers. CGE also needs resources to train emergency management local agents about informing the population of the risks of heavy rain. The Health Secretariat has a shortage

of medical personnel and adequate facilities to assist citizens with lepstospirosis or climate-related diseases. A direct and efficient channel with the community in at-risk areas must be created to alert people in emergencies. The same needs to be done for the general population. Overall, prevention measures in at-risk communities should be strengthened.

Estimated Levels of Spending on Pro-Poor Services and Infrastructure

The City Emergency Management Agency works on disaster management activities. Interviewees noted that the agency lacks resources to carry out its projects, develop new initiatives, train and support communities based on units or groups, properly service the population in emergencies, and develop means of preventive maintenance.

At the beginning of 2011, the mayor of São Paulo and the governor of São Paulo jointly launched a US$5 million initiative to fight floods in the city. It included cleaning the Tietê River; acquisition of pumps to move water from the Pinheiros River to the Billings water reservoir; a system of underground channels to dredge the Tietê River; and the creation of the Varzeas Tietê River Linear Park (with plans to remove 5,000 families that should not be living at the edges of the river).

Pillar 2—Hazards Assessment

Past Natural Disasters

There is no publicly available systematization of climate hazards or measurement of potential impacts and losses. This is a substantial gap in information that the city needs to address.

A prominent city newspaper provides information on recent rainfall events:

- November 2009–March2010. Heavy rainfall accounted for 78 deaths and 20.000 homeless. Jardim Romano (a poor neighborhood) was flooded for more than two months.
- October 2009. Tietê and Pinheiros's rivers overflowed and there were 86 flooding points in the city.
- February 2008. In the neighborhood of Mooca in the east of the city, the water height reached 2 meters. Firefighters were called 53 times to rescue stranded people. Train passengers were trapped in the railway cars for more than six hours (due to lack of power caused by the rain).
- November 2006. The city experienced 230 flooding points (doubling the number for the same month the previous year).
- May 2004. The heaviest rainfall in years (140 mm in a single day) caused 120 flooding points in the city; small rivers flooded. One person disappeared in a flooded area.

TABLE A7.2
Institutional Mapping of Disaster Risk Management Functions

| | Risk reduction | | |
Risk assessment	Technical (planning, management, maintenance)	Early-warning and response	Public awareness
Civil defense	Civil defense • Agents and NUDECs	CGE • 18 meteorological stations	CGE • Website

TABLE A7.3
Natural Hazards

	Yes/No	Date of last major event
Earthquake	N	N/A
Wind storm	N	N/A
River flow	Y	2009
Floods, inundations, and waterlogs	Y	2011
Tsunami	N	N/A
Drought	N	N/A
Volcano	N	N/A
Landslide	Y	2011
Storm surge	Y	2010
Extreme temperature	N/A	N/A

TABLE A7.4
Hazards, Effects, and Losses

Hazards	Effects	Losses
Heavy rainfall—more than 30 mm/day	Landslides Floods Stream overflow River overflow Leptospirosis and water-transmitted diseases	Lives Houses and material, resident property, cars Health conditions
Extreme heavy rain—more than 100 mm/day	Landslides Floods Stream overflow River overflow Leptospirosis and water-transmitted diseases	Lives Houses and material, resident property, cars Health conditions
Air dryness	Health problems (mainly respiratory)	Health conditions

Source: Institute of Research and Technology 2009.

Main Climate Hazards

According to the Institute of Research and Technology (Instituto Nacional de Pesquisas Espaciais, or INPE 2009), São Paulo is composed of a variety of surfaces with different temperatures, forming a mosaic of urban climate. There are heat islands, thermal inversion areas, pollution bubbles, and local differences in the wind patterns. Therefore, it is impossible to plan a single initiative or define

Figure A7.7 Days with Intense Rainfall per Decade

Source: IAG/USP, Analysis by INPE 2010.

Figure A7.8 Number of Flooding Points Registered by CGE in São Paulo per Year, 2004–2011

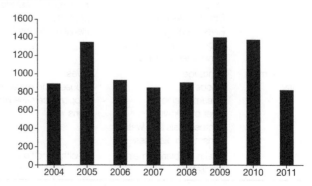

Source: CGE and Mauricio Maia blog, 2011, http://alagamentos.topical.com.br/pontos.

a precise quantity of rain or degree of heat that could cause tragedies. Each area has its specific soil, drainage, occupation, and permeability conditions and, as a result, a different threshold to be met.

That said, INPE produced table A7.5, which shows the amount of heavy rainfall in São Paulo per decade, from 1933 to 2000, indicating an increase in the number of days of heavy rainfall—with more than 100 mm of precipitation in just one or two days.

INPE confirms that rainfall above 10 mm per day is considered heavy, but is not potentially dangerous. More than 30 mm per day of rainfall can cause serious floods, and more than 50 mm can be even riskier for the city (before the 1950s, rainfall above to 50 mm per day was nonexistent, but currently this occurs two to five times every year).

Summary of Climate Projections from the Regional Eta-CPTEC (Centro de Previsão de Tempo e Estudos Climáticos) Model for São Paulo

For INPE, the main climate risk scenarios for São Paulo are:

- Floods—This risk scenario is characterized by the overflow of river water onto the adjacent lowlands, when the plains along the main watercourses of the Alto Tietê Basin become flooded. Despite investments to increase flow capacity of the main waterways, floods continue to occur due to urban growth and the natural dynamics of floods and existing interventions in waterways.
- Heavy floods—Rugged conditions allow for heavy floods, that is, high water volume and speed. Flooding of this nature may destroy buildings and other urban infrastructure, cause other material damage, and endanger the lives of residents living near rivers.
- Flash floods, with high potential for drag—Public policies for channeling streams and constructing roads in valleys cause flash flooding along the streets, where surface water concentrates (which also occurs in suburban areas, without paving). This process is characterized by the power of accumulated surface water and the high destructive power of drag. These conditions expose people and housing to high risk. The greatest probability of loss of life is found in the periphery regions, and loss of goods in consolidated central neighborhoods. Rainwater runoff concentrated along watercourses or on public roads is responsible for most deaths in floods, when people are dragged by the water.
- Occasional flooding—Occasional flooding (accumulations of shallow water that rarely penetrate the interior of the buildings and affect most public roads) occur widely in various parts of the city, primarily because of deficiencies in the drainage system. Occasional floods are temporary inconveniences for pedestrians and vehicles.
- Trash thrown into water courses—Some 6,000 households throw waste directly into waterways in the metropolitan region of São Paulo. The garbage

TABLE A7.5
Climate Projection for Metropolitan São Paulo

	Present observed	Present simulated	2030–2040	Conf.	2050–2060	Conf.	2080–2090	Conf.
Temperature	↑	↑	↑	High	↑	High	↑	High
Warm nights	↑	↑	↑	High	↑	High	↑	High
Cold nights	↓	↓	↓	High	↓	High	↓	High
Warm days	↑	↑	↑	High	↑	High	↑	High
Cold days	↓	↓	↓	Average	↓	High	↓	High
Heat waves	Unobserved	↑	↑	Average	↑	Average	↑	High
Total rain	↑	↑	↑	High	↑	High	↑	High
Intense precipitation	↑	↑	↑	Average	↑	Average	↑	High
Precipitation > 95th	↑	↑	↑	Average	↑	Average	↑	High
Precipitation days > 10 mm	↑	↑	↑	Average	↑	Average	↑	High
Precipitation days > 20 mm	↓	↑	↑	Average	↑	Average	↑	Average
Consecutives dry days	↓	↑	↓	Average	↑	Average	↑	High

Source: INPE/CEPTEC.

▶ Increase   ◀ Decrease

contributes to siltation and clogging of these waterways, and can be carried by runoff, captured by the river, and taken to lower slopes, where the waste is deposited. The detention reservoirs of Tietê River are located in these lower slopes and can be damaged by the debris.

- Landslides on slopes—The slope regions are generally subject to informal settlements and prone to landslides, which can cause serious accidents and deaths of residents.
- More severe rainfall—There is a clear correlation between more severe rainfall (greater than 100 mm) and more rugged terrains. The climate analysis by INPE indicates that severe rainfall will occur more in areas of the city that are at risk of landslides and flooding, increasing the vulnerability of the inhabitants.

Exposure to Hazards

The Technological Research Institute (Instituto de Pesquisas Tecnológicas, or IPT) was commissioned by the city to map the geotechnical hazardous areas in São Paulo in order to identify sector vulnerabilities to landslides and stream washouts in areas of precarious urban settlements. In this study, a hazardous area is defined as one likely to be hit by natural or human-induced conditions that cause adverse effects. People living in such zones are exposed to physical harm and are prone to material losses. Typically, in Brazilian cities, these areas correspond to low-income housing units (precarious informal settlements).

The factors found essential for analyzing hazards include the type of process expected, the likelihood of the process occurring, the vulnerability of the urban settlements, and the potential for damage.

The analysis included morphological and morphometric features of the terrain; geological materials and profile of the alteration; geological structures; evidence of geological movements; ground coverage; and conditions associated with wastewater, rainwater, and subsurface water. As a result, a hazard zone for landslides and stream washouts has been defined for vulnerable urban settlements. The methodology used to map the zone included the following activities:

- Oblique low-height helicopter aerial photography.
- Field work to examine the features and limits of hazardous terrains in previously identified hazards zones.
- Assessment of the likelihood of destructive processes.
- Assessment of potential consequences due to dwelling vulnerability.
- Estimate of hazard level per sector.
- Recommendations for hazard-control initiatives.
- Data input into a geo-referenced database, integrated with the Housing Secretariat's (SEHAB) HABISP System.

Table A7.6
Incidence of Hazardous Areas in Informal Settlements in São Paulo

	Urbanized centers	Settlements/allotments	Slums
Landslide risk (%) (IPT 2010)	10.43	3.90	14.79
Washout risk (%) (IPT 2010)	2.44	0.68	5.38

Source: HABISP–SEHAB; IPT 2010.

Displayed below are the hazardous areas mapped in the informal, vulnerable settlements. Slums have the highest rate of landslides and washouts. About 20 percent of the land where slums are settled is subject to geotechnical hazards. Slums in São Paulo represent roughly 76,000 households exposed to hazards. There are 407 highly hazardous areas located in 26 subdistricts.

Figure A7.9, in the color section, shows geotechnical hazard areas overlapping data on steepness. As expected, critical areas are closely associated with high steepness. Such areas are more likely in the peripheral zone of the city (northern, eastern, and southern suburbs). The most critical areas are precisely where the most precarious settlements are located. Lack of access to a formal land market by the poorest families generates the conditions for these combined factors of social and environmental vulnerability.

In addition to identifying hazardous areas, the IPT also ranked them in four levels of criticality. A qualitative hazard analysis has been made on the data obtained from field observation, integrating the analysis parameters into a hazard assessment record card, with the support of aerial imagery. The degrees of hazard are displayed in table A7.7.

A cross analysis of hazardous areas ranked by their critical level and informal settlements, as shown in table A7.8, concludes that slums face the most hazardous conditions. In total, more than 5 percent of slum areas are highly or very highly exposed; these areas are highly vulnerable to destructive events in the next 12 months.

This conclusion stresses the urgency of taking preventative measures. Furthermore, such hazards can be leveraged by prospective climate conditions, potentially increasing the degree of hazard level in areas currently ranked as low or medium risk.

It is worth stressing that IPT's map does not take into account floods and water logging. While floods are not as lethal as mudslides and landslides, they represent the most frequent hazards to which the population is exposed. These events result in great material damage and may have secondary effects on health by increasing the likelihood of spreading waterborne diseases such as leptospirosis. People living near streams or rivers—especially children and the elderly,

TABLE A7.7
Degrees of Landslide Hazard

Class of hazard	Description of hazard
R1—low	Potentially low degree of geological and geotechnical predisposing factors (steepness, type of terrain, etc.) and of intervention in the sector for developing landslides and washouts. There is no evidence of instability in slopes and drainage banks. It is the least critical condition. If the status remains unchanged, no destructive events are expected over one year.
R2—medium	Potentially medium degree of geological and geotechnical predisposing factors (steepness, type of terrain, etc.) and of intervention in the sector for developing landslides and washouts. There is some evidence of instability (yet incipient) in slopes and drainage banks. If the status remains unchanged, there is little probability of destructive events during long, strong episodes of rain over one year.
R3—high	Potentially high degree of geological and geotechnical predisposing factors (steepness, type of terrain, etc.) and of intervention in the sector for developing landslides and washouts. There is significant evidence of instability (ground cracks, sag of embankments, etc.). If the status remains unchanged, destructive events may be expected during long, strong episodes of rain over one year.
R4—very high	Potentially very high degree of geological and geotechnical predisposing factors (steepness, type of terrain, etc.) and of intervention in the sector for developing landslides and washouts. There is strong evidence of instability, supported by numerous accounts of hazardous conditions (ground cracks, sag of embankments, , walls cracking in houses or retaining walls, tilted trees or poles, slide scars, erosion features, dwellings built near stream banks, etc.). It is the most critical condition. If the status remains unchanged, destructive events are highly probable during long, strong episodes of rain over one year.

TABLE A7.8
Cross-Referencing Data: Areas Ranked by Their Critical Level and Types of Settlements in São Paulo

	Low hazard	Medium hazard	High hazard	Very high hazard
Slums (%)	2.92	11.90	4.11	1.40
Settlements/allotments (%)	0.65	2.93	0.97	0.43
Urbanized centers (%)	4.59	7.62	0.56	0.09

Source: HABISP–SEHAB; IPT 2010.

TABLE A7.9
Social Assessment

City population below poverty line (%)	5.6 in 2000. Atlas DH
Social inequality (Gini index) in 2002 (UN-Habitat)	0.543 metropolitan area (PNAD 2006)
Unemployment (%)	12.3 in 2009 (SEADE)
Areal size of informal settlements (% of city area)	7.92 in 2010 (HABISP)
City population living in slums (%)	0.48
Households without registered legal titles (%)	7.9
Children completing primary and secondary education: survival rate (%)	Abandon rate for primary, 1.3; and for secondary, 5.4
Human Development Index (2009)	0.841 in 2000 (IBGE)
Predominant housing material	Brick

who are the most vulnerable—are also exposed to direct risks such as drowning and physical injury in highly destructive landslides.

Pillar 3—Socioeconomic Assessment

Population Exposure to Hazards

The most significant climate hazards for São Paulo are floods and landslides. Flooding points have not been fully mapped by the city, only floodable points on streets; these are related to traffic problems, as shown in figure A7.10.

When dealing with landslides, the city commissioned IPT to map and rank the critical spots. A qualitative hazard analysis has been made on the data obtained from field observation, integrating the analysis parameters into a hazard-assessment report card, with the support of aerial imagery.

A map overlapping social vulnerability (mapped through the IPVS index) and climate vulnerability (using IPT and INPE data) was produced.

The following layers were included in the database to produce the map:

- Informal/precarious settlements in São Paulo (2010): Obtained from HABISP-SEHAB (Housing Secretariat) containing the official demarcation of each settlement organized by slums, urbanized slums, and informal settlements. Information about the quantity of houses, infrastructure, and average income level available.
- Geotechnical risk areas (2010): Obtained from HABISP-SEHAB, a study from the Technological Research Institute (IPT) from the state of São Paulo, the data consists of the areas mapped by the IPT using in-place verification,

Figure A7.10 Main Flooding Points of Streets

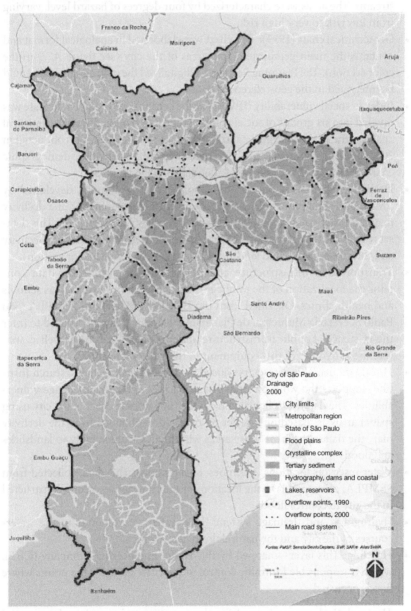

City of São Paulo
Drainage
2000

— City limits
— Metropolitan region
— State of São Paulo
Flood plains
Crystalline complex
Tertiary sediment
Hydrography, dams and coastal
■ Lakes, reservoirs
•• Overflow points, 1990
••• Overflow points, 2000
— Main road system

Source: SVMA, Environmental Atlas, 2000.

which presents geotechnical risk for landslides and undermining among water streams. The areas were characterized by four degrees of hazard level, varying from low risk to very high risk.

- Geotechnical chart (1999): This chart was elaborated in analogical format and contains the main geomorphologic areas of the city (see figure A7.9 in the color section). The Planning Secretariat digitalized the map and the data could be integrated in the geo-referenced dataset.
- Index of social vulnerability (IPVS), per the census (2000). São Paulo State was divided into six groups of social vulnerability. Based on multivariate statistical analysis, the IPVS uses the data from the last population census, conducted in 2000. The calculation of the IPVS uses two types of information: demographic characteristics and socioeconomic condition of the families;
- Declivity map: Based on the topographic chart of the city developed by EMPLASA (Empresa Paulista de Planejamento Metropolitano), the declivity map is a raster dataset containing classes of declivity for each pixel. This dataset reveals the topography of the city, indicating those areas with high declivity and thus more inclined to landslides (see figure A7.4 in the color section).
- Transportation infrastructure and public infrastructure: This data contains the localization of the public infrastructure of the city, such as schools and health clinics. Obtained from the HABISP-SEHAB and SEMPLA (São Paulo Secretaria Municipal de Planejamento), this dataset was used to infer the existence of public infrastructure under geotechnical risk as well as analyze the proximity of this equipment to the vulnerable areas.
- HAND model: This dataset, produced by the National Spatial Research Institute, supports the work on Brazilian megacities and climate-change vulnerabilities. The data was calculated from the topographic chart of the city using spatial analysis. Based on a raster representation obtained from the declivity map, the dataset informs those areas with highest vulnerability to landslides and floods.
- Water reservoir locations (piscinões, or big pools): This data, collected from SEMPLA, corresponds to the locations of the 16 water reservoirs constructed in the city to control floods.
- Hydrograph and drainage system: This system corresponds to the watercourses of the city and the natural drainage system.
- Flooding: This layer—mapped by the Traffic Engineering Company (CET), which is responsible for traffic control in the city—contains the points where floods occurred.

The analytical approach used for the mapping task was based on spatial analysis techniques in the Geographical Information System (GIS). All the layers were compiled in an integrated geo-referenced database. The calculations

were based on overlays applied over the reference layers of informal settlements, slums, and urbanized slums. It was then possible to calculate the relative
incidence in terms of area of geotechnical risk of flooding. It was also possible
to calculate the relative incidence of the Social Vulnerability Index in each of
the reference layers.

Calculating both incidences, social vulnerability and geotechnical risk, led to
comparisons between all the informal, precarious settlements in the city. The
results of the geographical analysis operation were tabulated and organized by
themes of vulnerability and hazards. The most vulnerable settlements were those
that present the higher percentage of areas within highest geotechnical risk and
social vulnerability. Finally, thematic maps were generated showing the layers included in the database, allowing visualization of the critical areas all over
the city.

Location of the Urban Poor

Most precarious settlements are located in more peripheral areas of the city. Such
areas concentrate environmentally vulnerable situations and are the most poorly
served by basic services and urban infrastructure. The analysis indicates that
there is a strong overlap between the locations of high-risk areas and the informal
settlements throughout the city. Shown in figure A7.11 is the location of precarious housing (slums, irregular lots, and urbanized slums).

Slum Characteristics

The distribution of the census in the city by groups of social vulnerability clearly
discloses the socioeconomic macro-segregation pattern that places the central
area. In particular, the distribution shows the southwest quarter of the city as the
region with the lowest levels of social vulnerability, as opposed to the peripheral
zone, where the highest levels of social vulnerability are recorded. These more
critical situations can be found in the southern, northern, and eastern periphery
of the city. Not by accident, most of São Paulo's precarious settlements are set up
in these peripheral areas.

According to the city, in 2010 approximately 890,000 precarious dwellings were in the city. Over 85 percent of these households are located in slums
and irregular settlements, spread across all regions of the city. Displayed in
table A7.10 is the distribution of households per type and location in the large
administrative regions of the city.

Slums record the highest proportion of children and youth up to 19 years old
(41.7 percent), which is consistent with the presence of younger heads for households and a greater number of children. As for household income, most families
earn less than three times the minimum wage.[7] Although many of the heads of

Figure A7.11 Spatial Distribution of Precarious Settlements in City

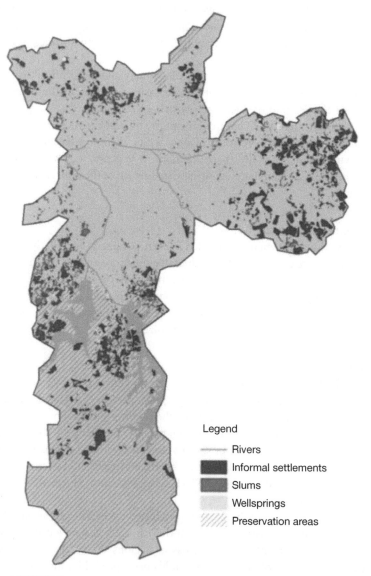

Legend

─── Rivers

■ Informal settlements

■ Slums

░ Wellsprings

▨ Preservation areas

Source: HABISP 2010.

household are employed in the formal labor market, low levels of education hinder access to better work opportunities. About two-thirds of the heads of household have not completed primary education (SEADE Foundation 2008).

These areas still lack access to urban infrastructure and services supply, as shown in table A7.11. There are significant deficits in public lighting, paving,

TABLE A7.10
Houses by Type of Precarious Settlements and Administrative Regions of City Housing Secretariat

	Wellsprings1	North1	South1	Southeast1	East1	Center1	Diffuse2	Total
Slum1	54,886	65,696	117,793	64,980	67,072	10,724	0	381,151
Informal settlement (1)	100,031	60,769	44,953	22,739	154,552	0	0	383,044
Urbanized center (1)	11,193		1,973	1,051	2,640	262	0	24,522
Tenement (cortiços) (2) (3)						11,086	69,303	80,389
Irregular housing complex (1)	669	7,403	4,657	2,533	3,056	1,659	0	20,702
Total	166,779	141,996	169,376	91,303	227,320	23,731	69,303	889,808

Source: (1) HABISP, February 2010; (2) obtained from SEADE Foundation survey; (3) the total amount of tenement houses is an estimation by the SEADE Foundation.

TABLE A7.11
Access to Urban Services and Infrastructure in Precarious Settlements in São Paulo

	Urban Infrastructure			Waste Collection			Sanitation	
	Access to public lighting	Paving	Walkways and culverts	Door-to-door collection	Curb container collection	Other	No access	With access
Households in slums (%)	68.30	67.10	55.70	64.90	20.70	14.40	52.30	47.70
Households in residence centers (%)	86.30	91.10	80.80	67.90	13.50	18.60	8.20	91.80
Households in allotments (%)	92.30	81.50	81.20	91.50	3.40	5.10	20.20	79.80
Total (%)	**81.90**	**75.70**	**70.40**	**79.50**	**11.10**	**9.50**	**33.30**	**66.70**

Source: Fundação Seade; Secretaria Municipal de Habitação, SEHAB; Pesquisa Socioeconômica em Favelas e Loteamentos no Município de São Paulo, 2007.

and urban drainage in slums, urbanized centers, and allotments. Waste disposal and collection are not available to all households, often because collecting vehicles have no space to circulate. The most critical problem, however, concerns the sanitation network. The severity of this situation is mostly evident within the slums, where more than half of the households have no access

TABLE A7.12
Number of Precarious Inhabitants per Level of Poverty

	Poverty		
	Indigent	Poor	
Families in slums (%)	31.90	66.60	98.50
Families in residence centers (%)	33.60	66.40	100.00
Families in settlements (%)	26.10	53.30	79.40
Total (%)	**28.90**	**59.40**	**88.30**

Source: SEADE Foundation; SEHAB/HABISP (São Paulo City Housing Information System) São Paulo Slum and Allotments Socioeconomic Research, 2007.

to sewerage facilities, thus greatly exacerbating environmental problems and exposing inhabitants to disease and health hazards.

A poverty ranking based on the World Bank's poverty threshold criteria reveals the gravity of the situation for the families living in those settlements, as shown in table A7.12.[8] In the slums and urbanized centers, virtually all families live in poverty or extreme poverty. There is a slight improvement in housing settlements with regard to this indicator; yet about 80 percent of the families in that setting live in poverty or extreme poverty. This finding reinforces the importance of public services supply and policies for those whose ability to fulfill basic needs is extremely low, exposing them to even more critical levels of social vulnerability.

The situations of social vulnerability disclosed by the data are often associated with exposure to geotechnical and flooding resulting from occupying land unsuitable for housing. Moreover, in most cases the dwellings are self-built over long periods. Thus, low technical quality of dwellings associated with occupying areas unsuitable for housing brings about hazards, often involving imminent risk. Characteristic of these areas are steep slopes and unstable land and flood zones during rainfall periods.

Climate Smart Practices
The Várzeas do Tietê Park, a project of the state government, in partnership with São Paulo, will be 75 km, the largest linear park in the world. There are about 7,000 households that will have to be removed. The resettlement will be done in the same region, with the construction of new housing units in a partnership between the City Housing Secretariat (SEHAB), Housing and Urban Development Agency (CDHU), and Metropolitan Housing Company of São Paulo (COHAB). The park will cover São Paulo and seven other cities, benefiting an estimated 2 million people. In addition to the 7,000 households removed in São Paulo, 2,000 more will be removed in other cities. The Várzeas do Tietê Park will have a total area of approximately 10,000 hectares, with significant environmental

gains, because it is considered essential for preserving the river and sanitizing the areas that affect the margins. The project should be completed in 2016. The project will restore and preserve the environmental function of wetlands, provide flood control, and create options for leisure, tourism, and culture. In the project, Via Parque will be built, a track with a 23 km extension with car and bike paths and a lot of space for walking. The Tietê River, including its tributaries, lakes, and ponds, will be restored, as well as riparian and native vegetation. Special areas for leisure, courts, arenas, cafeterias, and administrative spaces will also be built.

Key Lessons in Addressing Poverty in a Climate-Smart Way
The study points to recommended actions, which are listed below:

- Allocate personnel from the Emergency Management Agency to each vulnerable community, working as the Local Emergency Management Group, or NUDEC. The personnel should be made up of volunteers, trained by the National Emergency Management Agency, to help in emergencies and risky situations. This would allow preparation for emergencies and quicker and more effective response. The same would apply to health agents.
- Extend mapping and systematization of the city's entire flooding areas— including all housing regions—and use this data to prioritize initiatives.
- Improve measures to enable public transportation and the use of cleaner fuels.
- Implement an emergency transport plan for heavy rainfall, using buses with bi-articulated engines and special corridors for those vehicles to transit.
- Implement an efficient alert system for the entire population when there is heavy rainfall, with all government entities working rapidly with a direct channel of communication to the communities in the areas impacted by the heavy rain.
- Extend studies to analyze and enable change in the city's growth pattern and land-use patterns to concentrate housing and job opportunities in specified regions. Providing adequate facilities, such as hospitals, schools, places for leisure and sports, and other facilities, would avoid long daily commutes and decrease the traffic and greenhouse gas emissions (such as São Francisco Global, described in "Opportunities"). Another approach is to promote the occupation of other degraded places downtown (such as Nova Luz), which already have infrastructure but which are undervalued and contain dilapidated buildings.
- Promote an integrated policy to manage waste issues in the city. Not only should the policy take care of public cleaning, but also deal with waste reduction, inform the population about sustainable consumption, and enable recycling.

- Extend measures for supervision and adequate disposal of waste, as well as improve the periods between cleanings of streets and culverts.
- Extend enforcement of the Municipal Climate Law obligating buildings with high concentrations or circulation of people (such as malls, large residential condos, or commercial buildings) to install recycling centers.
- Extend procedures related to environmental inspection, and epidemiological and entomological control in selected locations, aiming at the quick discovery of biological effects caused by climate change and potential treatments.
- Extend initiatives to restore all permanent conservation areas, especially those located in floodplains, in order to avoid or minimize risks caused by extreme climate.
- Extend the law that obligates new corporate projects to maintain a permeable area in order to absorb water.
- Extend energy-efficiency measures throughout the city.
- Find funding for public projects and NGO climate safety activities.
- Extend awareness of the Municipal Climate Law to public agents, that is, the law must become part of the daily routine of planning and executing policies in all related government agencies.
- Integrate and extend climate change policy, bringing together several organizations and public players. The Climate Change Economy Committee begins this movement, but its role needs to be reinforced.
- Promote increased citizen participation and planning on climate initiatives, including organized demands for new policies. In order to do that, society needs to be informed about the issue and their role in it.
- The climate policies must be incorporated into the city's management. The policies should be implemented regardless of changes in mayors in a new election or a change of secretary in the middle of the term.

Constraints Identified by the Consulted Communities

- Lack of an efficient public transport system, which would improve accessibility to other parts of the city and reduce walking distances.
- Lack of quality and coverage of piped water and a sewer system, which currently could rupture during heavy rainfall and infiltrate houses and reach rivers and streams.
- Lack of means to prevent electricity theft through makeshift connections, resulting in a high cost of energy and posing a risk during heavy rain.
- Lack of channeled streams, which could prevent the death of people who may fall during heavy rains.
- Lack of retaining walls on hillsides at risk.

- Lack of quality of garbage collection and inspection of illegal dumps.
- Lack of adequate cleaning of streams and culverts.

Opportunities
The City Housing Secretariat—SEHAB—provides the Housing Information System—HABISP:
This information provides a comprehensive overview and update of planning and environmental conditions in the settlements of the city. The information allows people to define priorities for intervention, as well as assist in developing city policies and integrated plans with other agencies. These include: SABESP, São Paulo State Sanitation Utility; SVMA, City Green and Environment Secretariat; SME, City Education Secretariat; CDHU, Housing and Urban Development Agency; and Caixa Econômica Federal (the Federal Bank). The HABISP information system is a tool that is easy to use, as well as being interactive and readily accessible via the Internet (www.habisp.inf.br). HABISP promotes increased citizen participation—it provides an opportunity for data disclosure and is an important resource for the population, providing information about policies and plans under development.

Opportunities to promote adaptation strategies:
Existence of a comprehensive legal framework: The legal framework for the city to deal with the impact of climate change already exists. The Municipal Climate Law sets the foundation for the necessary measures related to energy, transport, land use, health, construction, and waste management to be performed by the city, other government entities, and private players. A reduction target was established and public disclosure of the results is expected. Nevertheless, future regulation is needed on some issues, such as payment for environmental services and subnational cooperation.

Mapping of areas where landslides occur: The areas at risk for landslides are already identified and geo-referenced by the municipality, allowing the prioritization of prevention. The same is needed for all flooding areas beyond the locations already mapped. This data would be most useful if shared among secretaries for planning. If strong preventive projects are implemented, the risks will be lower and less will need to be spent on emergency action.

Existence of the beginning of a unified approach to climate issues and policies: The EcoEconomy and Climate Committee were created to unite the city entities around the subject, and also bring together state and national players, citizen organizations, and government agencies. The 2009 Decree 50.866/2009 inaugurated the committee's works. The forum aims to propose, stimulate, and follow the adoption of plans, programs, and actions that help satisfy the city policy. It also intends to support actions to mitigate greenhouse gas emissions, promote adaptation strategies, create seminars and campaigns, and promote the adoption of social and environmental criteria in the city's purchases of products and services. Members of the committee can help in identifying technology trends linked to climate change and offer feedback on eventual amendments to the Municipal Climate Law. The structure exists and meetings take place regularly; there is still need to strengthen community capacity to propose and implement projects.

São Francisco Global Urban Plan, by SEHAB: The plan creates guidelines to integrate the 50,000 inhabitants of the third-largest slum on the east side of São Paulo into the formal city, by extending social housing, the construction of a hospital, school, community center, and services center, which will also serve as a commercial center and income generator. It also includes extending the transport system and improving roadways. With paved streets and nearby trees, the ease of access to public transportation, town inhabitants will use a car less in everyday tasks. The objective is that the town will stop being a "bedroom city" and will provide the products and services essential for every-day day living in central city locations. Plans for new housing will maximize the conservation of the remaining green areas and water springs in the new town. Together with SVMA, a park will be created, at an old dump, measuring 367,000 thousand m².

Ecofrota Program: At the beginning of 2011 the city initiated a program that provides for the use of 20 percent biodiesel in public transport throughout the city. The initiative aims to reduce the emissions of particulate matter by 22 percent, carbon monoxide by 13 percent, and hydrocarbons by 10 percent, and reaches the annual goal of reducing fossil fuels by 15 percent, as provided in the Municipal Climate Law. This states that the entire public transportation system in the city should operate on renewable fuels by 2018. The project will identify any public transport fueled with cleaner fuels, including biodiesel, ethanol, hybrid, and electric.

City hall to renew the transport fleet: SP Trans has been renewing its bus fleet, which services the city, substituting the old vehicles with more advanced modern models. Of the 15,000 buses in the city, 9,684 (65 percent) have already been replaced, lowering the average age of the vehicles in use to four and a half years. In addition, just by adding larger buses between 2006 and 2010, the fleet capacity increased 21 percent and the number of transported passengers grew by 11 percent.

Solar systems to heat the water: The City Assembly approved Law 14459/07 requiring that from that date forward all new residential or commercial buildings should be prepared to use a solar-based system to heat the water used by its inhabitants. The new houses and buildings assembled with more than four bathrooms must adopt a solar-panel heating system. Some commercial buildings, such as private clubs, gyms, hotels and motels, schools, hospitals, clinics, and industrial laundromats also must install the solar panels. The system should meet at least 40 percent of the annual energy needs of the toilet water and water for pools that the building may require.

Sustainable Building Project: Developed by PMSP/SEHAB, this project has been initiated in a part of Heliópolis, a large slum in the southeast of the city with almost 130,000 residents. Over the last few years this area has been undergoing urbanization and improvement: houses are now made mainly of bricks instead of scarce wood.

Carbon credits: Carbon credits are being used to develop social and environmental projects in areas near the plants, such as linear parks, public squares, eco-points installation, and a center being built to hold wild animals and to house birds. For example, the Bamburral slum (570 families living next to the Bandeirante waste site) is the first slum to be urbanized with funds from carbon credits. The community urbanization provides infrastructure, stream channeling, and construction of four clusters of houses that will receive 260 families that live in at-risk areas. The construction of a deck over the creek is also planned in order to facilitate the movement of residents, as well as a linear park with areas for sports and leisure.

Linear parks: The Várzeas do Tietê Park, at 75 km, will be the largest linear park in the world. There are about 7,000 households that will have to be removed. The resettlement will be done in the same region, with the construction of new housing units in a partnership between the City Housing Secretariat (SEHAB), Housing and Urban Development Agency (CDHU), and Metropolitan Housing Company of São Paulo (COHAB). Várzeas do Tietê Park will have significant environmental gains, because it is considered essential for preserving the river and the sanitation of the areas that affect the margins, restoring and conserving the environmental function of wetlands, and providing flood control. Riparian and native vegetation will also be restored.

Operation Clean Stream: This operation is a joint initiative with the state government of São Paulo to recover and treat streams throughout the city. The first phase was initiated in 2007 and ended in 2009. More than 800,000 people benefited from cleaning 42 streams and piping 500 liters per second of sewage. The program deals with the remediation of the water and improvement of the sanitation in informal homes, benefiting 1,637 inhabitants. The program will continue with the cleanup of 40 more streams up to 2012. During operations, the city is responsible for maintaining stream margins and layers, and removing houses that may prevent the passage of the sanitation piping system.

Headwaters Program, by SEHAB: The program aims to service all vulnerable settlements located in protection areas such as Guarapiranga and Billings dams in order to restore drinkable water quality. The program partners among the three parts of the government and focuses on using the sub-basin as an integrated planning unit of government initiatives. The city's master plan allows the construction of new vertical housing projects for 4,000 people at the margins of the drinking water reservoirs of Guarapiranga and Billings (the first supplies water to 1.2 million inhabitants, and the second to 3.8 million). Billings currently has 12 km² of its water mirror occupied by informal settlements and receives 400 tons of waste every day. Guarapiranga has 1.3 million illegal residents in its margins.

Social Partnership Program: The City Housing, Social Welfare and Social Development of Public Policies in São Paulo has the objective of providing access for low-income people to the formal rental allowance market. They are subsidized by the fixed monthly amount of $300.00, with no adjustments for 30 months. Eligibility into the program requires income of 1 to 3 minimum wages, enabling access by vulnerable groups, including: the homeless in special social protection networks; families from areas expropriated by São Paulo, displaced due to floods or fires; and residents in at-risk areas. The social work is based on a development program that systematically monitors eligible families, providing social and economic development initiatives to restore social rights, especially decent housing.

Urban Carbon Footprint

According to a 2005 study,[9] the city's main source of emission comes from energy use, especially from transport (11,986 tons of carbon dioxide equivalent CO_2e).

Solid-waste disposal is the second-most important source (2,696 tons of CO_2e). Liquid effluents (7 tons of CO_2e), Land Use Change and Forestry (51 tons of CO_2e), and agricultural activities (1 ton of CO_2e) are not relevant sources in terms of city emissions.

In terms of energy, the use of fossil fuels in transport is the most critical issue for the city, since the fleet is made up of more than 7 million vehicles (growing each year) and the traffic is heavy (the average peak in traffic varies between 80 and 111 km in 2010, and the medium speed rate was of 16 km per hour in 2008).[10]

Although most recent models of cars are "flex"—using both ethanol and gasoline—most private and public fleets run on fossil fuel, especially gasoline and diesel (52 percent of the fossil fuel emissions come from gasoline, 45 percent from diesel, and 3 percent from natural gas). The law prescribed reducing the city's greenhouse gas emissions by 30 percent, compared with 2005 emissions. Additional targets should be defined every two years.

Initiatives such as the use of more energy-efficient street and traffic lighting and the establishment of infrastructure and incentives to promote the use of low-carbon vehicles are being offered, but specialists agree that the city needs to face the problem of planning land use in order to promote shorter commutes between home and work.

Notes

1. IBGE Census 2000 and City Hall website 2006.
2. City Hall website 2006.
3. Linear park is an area around an important reservoir or drinking water basin, where a structure is implemented to protect the environment and at the same time provide the nearby population with leisure or sports activities.
4. City Hall site/environment section.
5. http://www.agenda2012.com.br/oprograma.
6. http://www.prefeitura.sp.gov.br/cidade/secretarias/seguranca_urbana/defesa_civil/legislacao/pops__2009/index.php?p=7929.
7. The minimum wage established by 2011 is around US$325.00 per month.
8. As the threshold for indigency and poverty, the value of R$280.40 (updated in September 2007) was used, based on the POF (Family Budget Study) undertaken by IBGE in 1987. Indigents are considered those with total family income per capita below R$140.20 and, poverty stricken, those who earn up to R$280.40.
9. São Paulo's GHG's inventory, http://ww2.prefeitura.sp.gov.br/arquivos/secretarias/meio_ambiente/Sintesedoinventario.pdf.
10. São Paulo's GHG's inventory, http://ww2.prefeitura.sp.gov.br/arquivos/secretarias/meio_ambiente/Sintesedoinventario.pdf

Reference

World Bank and Diagonal Ltd. 2011. *Climate Change, Disaster Risk Management and the Urban Poor: São Paulo, processed.*

Figure A1.1 Population and Megacities in Low-Elevation Coastal Zone (LECZ) Threatened by Sea-Level Rise and Storm Surges

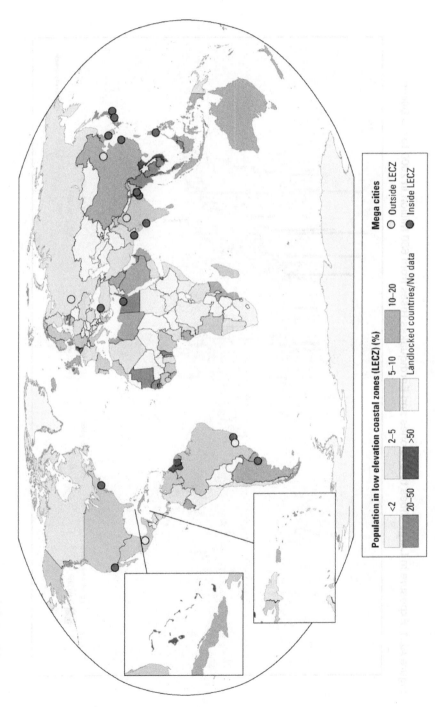

Source: United Nations (2008), as reported in the World Development Report 2010, World Bank.

Figure A2.1 Exposure in Large Cities to Cyclones and Earthquakes Rises from 680 Million in 2000 to 1.5 Billion

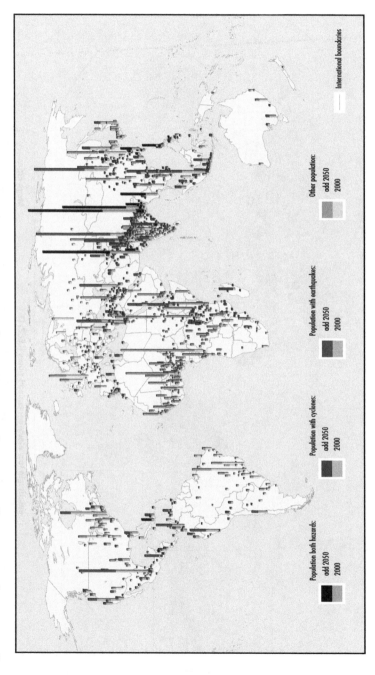

Figure A4.1 Administrative Map of Dar es Salaam

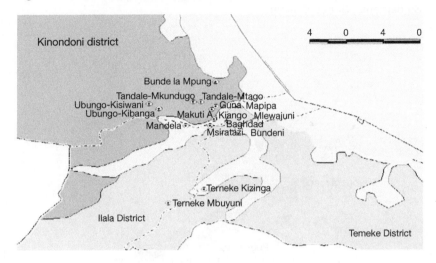

Figure A5.3 Impact of Sea-level Rise on North Jakarta with Business as Usual

Blue = inundation due to sea
level rise at 1cm/yr
(ITB 2007)

Figure A4.6 Map of Flood Hazard Zone Overlaid on Urban Poor Settlements, Dar es Salaam

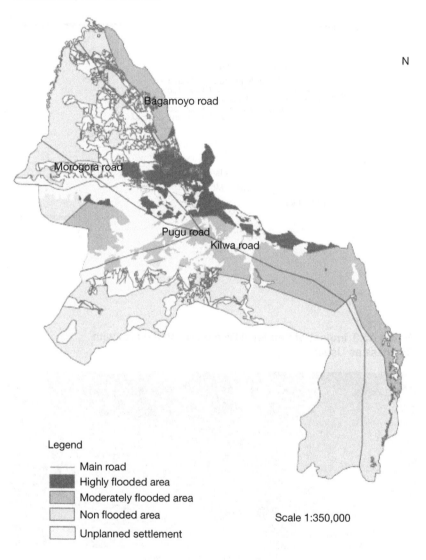

N

Legend

— Main road
█ Highly flooded area
▒ Moderately flooded area
☐ Non flooded area
☐ Unplanned settlement

Scale 1:350,000

Source: Ardhi University (2010).

IBRD 30971

Figure A5.1 Administrative Map of Jakarta

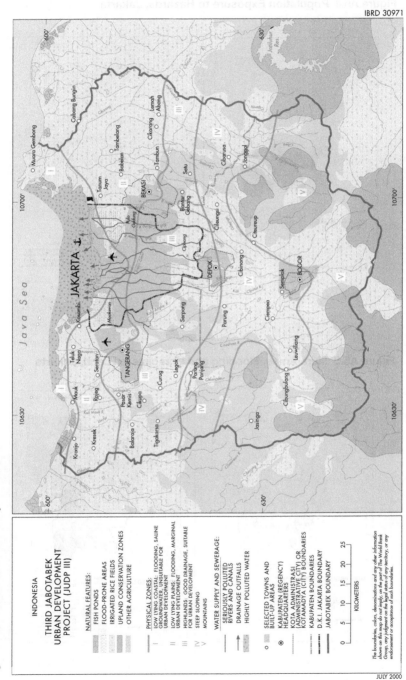

JULY 2000

Figure A5.4 Population Exposure to Hazards, Jakarta

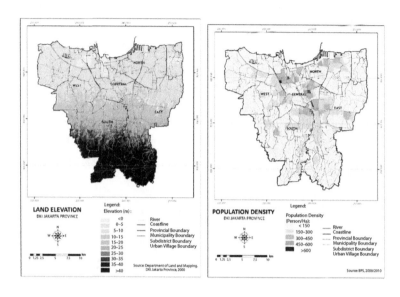

Figure A5.5 Slum Areas, Flooding and Unregistered Land, Jakarta

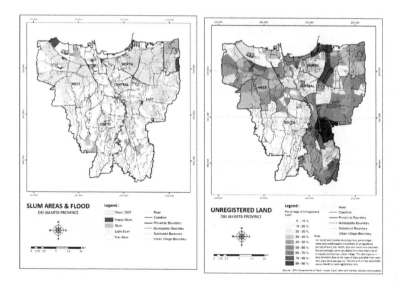

Figure A6.5 Vulnerable Areas in Terms of Population and Housing, Mexico City

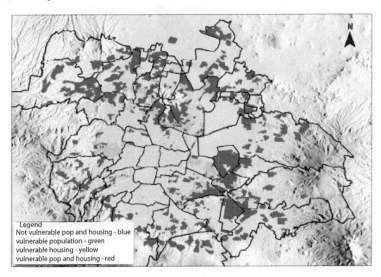

Figure A7.4 São Paulo´s Topography and Main Waterways

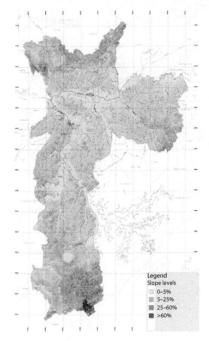

Source: PMSP—São Paulo Environmental Atlas.

Figure A7.9 Geotechnical Hazard Areas, São Paulo

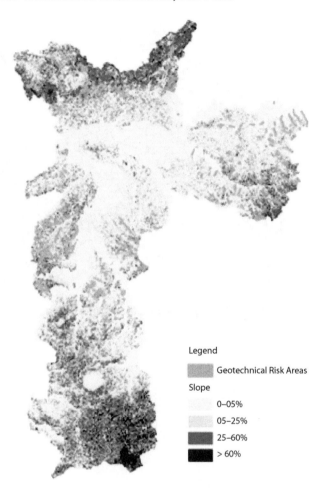

Legend

Geotechnical Risk Areas

Slope

0–05%

05–25%

25–60%

> 60%

Index

Boxes, figures, notes, and tables are indicated by b, f, n, and t following the page number.

Brazil. *See also* São Paulo
    Development Policy Loan for, 106
    flooding in, 8
    urban waste collection in, 46
Brigades of the Ministry of Social
    Development (Mexico City), 226
Buenos Aires (Argentina), flooding in, 159
building-back-better, good practices for,
    170–73
building codes, 71
building designs, climate projections and, 82
buildings expected to be heavily damaged
    (BEHD), 71
Bus Rapid Transit line (Mexico City), 222

C
Cairo (Egypt)
    "newtowns" in, 30
    public infrastructure in, 104
Caixa Econômica Federal (Federal Bank,
    Brazil), 263
California, water management in, 85
Ca Mau (Vietnam), urban upgrading in, 167
Cambodia, housing finance in, 120
Canadian Sustainable Environment
    Management Office, 73
Can Tho (Vietnam)
    Local Resilience Action Plan in, 155
    urban upgrading in, 167
capacity building, 89, 90*t*, 121, 153, 184,
    202, 204
Capacity Strengthening of Least Developing
    Countries for Adaptation to Climate
    Change (CLACC), 153
cap-and-trade programs, 117*b*
Cape Flats informal settlement
    (Cape Town), 40
Cape Town (South Africa), urban planning
    in, 70
Caracas (Venezuela), slums in, 38*b*
carbon credits, 265
Carbon Credits Auctions, 237
carbon footprints, 266–67
carbon markets, 110, 115
Carbon Partnership Facility, 115
carbon revenue, 165–66
Caribbean. *See also specific countries*
    cyclones in, 17
    earthquake exposure in, 144
    risk financing in, 170

Caribbean Catastrophe Risk Insurance
    Facility (CCRIF), 170
Casablanca (Morocco), action plans
    for, 102
Cash-for-Work program, 167
Cash for Work Temporary Employment
    Project (CfWTEP), 168
Catastrophe Risk Deferred Drawdown
    Option (CAT DDO), 170
Cayman Islands, risk financing in, 170
CBOs. *See* community-based organizations
CCRIF (Caribbean Catastrophe Risk
    Insurance Facility), 170
CDCF (Community Development Carbon
    Fund), 164–65, 166
CDHU. *See* Housing and Urban
    Development Agency
CDM. *See* Clean Development Mechanism
Central America. *See also specific countries*
    cyclones in, 17
    disaster-induced emergency
        funding in, 170
    volcanoes in, 20
Centre for Atmospheric Sciences, 218
Centre for Urban Studies (Bangladesh), 131
Centro de Previsão de Tempo e Estudos
    Climáticos (Eta-CPTEC) Model,
    249, 251
certified emission reductions (CERs),
    115, 116*b*
CET (Traffic Engineering Company), 255
C40 group, 237
CfWTEP (Cash for Work Temporary
    Employment Project), 168
CGE (Emergency Management Center, São
    Paulo), 244–45
Cheonggyecheon Restoration Project, 76
Chicago
    adaptation planning in, 84*b*
    emissions trading systems in, 117*b*
children
    health impacts of climate change
        on, 126
    public health and, 49
    self-insurance and, 168
    in slums, 257
    as vulnerable population, 86
Chile
    earthquakes in, 8, 173
    flood management in, 75

China, People's Republic of
cook stoves in, 47
cyclones in, 17
earthquakes in, 8, 19
floods in, 8
technical assistance programs in, 154
cholera, 48–49, 192
CIFs (Climate Investment Funds), 134
Cities Alliance, 161
Cities on the Move (World Bank), 130
City Assembly (São Paulo), 237
City Climate Law (São Paulo), 237
City Education Secretariat (SME,
    São Paulo), 263
City Emergency Management Agency
    (COMDEC, São Paulo), 244–45, 246
City Health Secretariat (São Paulo), 245
City Housing, Social Welfare and Social
    Development of Public Policies (São
    Paulo), 266
City Housing Secretariat (SEHAB,
    São Paulo), 245, 251, 254–55, 260,
    263, 264–65
City Public Safety Secretariat
    (São Paulo), 244
Ciudad Kenedy slum (Bogota), 30
CIUP (Community Infrastructure
    Upgrading Program), 161, 183–84
Civil Protection Agency (Mexico City),
    224, 226
CLACC (Capacity Strengthening of Least
    Developing Countries for Adaptation
    to Climate Change), 153
"clandestine" fields, 223
Clean Development Mechanism (CDM),
    110, 115, 116b, 165, 185, 237
Clean Technology Fund, 105, 106b, 107b
ClimAdapt, 73
climate change
    Dar es Salaam and, 181–97. *See also* Dar
        es Salaam
    disaster risk assessment and, 7–25.
        See also disasters and disaster risk
        assessment
    exposure in cities and, 141–47. *See also*
        exposure in cities
    finance opportunities and, 99–123. *See also*
        finance opportunities
    Jakarta and, 199–215. *See also* Jakarta
    literature review, 125–39. *See also* literature
        review

Mexico City and, 217–33. *See also* Mexico
    City
project and program experiences and,
    149–80. *See also* project and program
    experiences
São Paulo and, 235–68. *See also* São Paulo
urban poor, building resilience for, 63–97.
    See also urban poor, building
    resilience for
urban poor, vulnerability of, 27–62. *See also*
    urban poor, vulnerability of
Climate Change Adaptation Program
    (Mexico City), 69b, 223
Climate Change Economy Committee (São
    Paulo), 262
*Climate Change Risk Management Strategy
    for HRM* (Halifax Region
    Municipality), 73
Climate Committee (São Paulo), 263
Climate Investment Funds (CIFs), 134
Climate Resilient Cities (CRC) Primer, 154
Climate Resilient Communities
    Program, 153
*Climate Risks and Adaptation in Asian
    Coastal Megacities: A Synthesis Report*
    (World Bank), 100, 131, 133
climate sensitivity, 82–83, 83t
Climate SMART (Sustainable Mitigation
    and Adaptation Risk Toolkit), 73
Climate Summit for Mayors (2009), 9
coastal areas and cities, 17–18, 49, 144–45,
    189–90. *See also* port cities
coastal-defense projects, 82
CODELs (local emergency committees), 159
COHAB (Metropolitan Housing
    Company of São Paulo), 260, 265
cold waves, 135
Colombia
    public transport projects in, 133
    risk management in, 168–69
COMDEC (City Emergency Management
    Agency, São Paulo), 244–45, 246
communicable diseases, 48–49, 58–59n14, 92.
    See also specific diseases
community-based organizations (CBOs),
    86, 150–51, 162–63, 171–72
Community-based Settlements
    Rehabilitation and Reconstruction,
    171–72
Community Development Carbon Fund
    (CDCF), 164–65, 166

Dhaka (Bangladesh)
climate change vulnerability of, 144
drainage in, 44
security of tenure in, 52
slums in, 131
Dharavi slum (Mumbai), 32
diarrhea, 44–45, 48, 163, 192
Dinas Pekerjaan Umum (DPU, Indonesian
public works agency), 207
disaster-management plans, 50–51
disaster risk reduction (DRR), 106–7, 128–29,
130, 132, 134–35, 144
disasters and disaster risk assessment, 7–25.
See also specific disasters
(e.g., earthquakes)
background, analytical framework, and
approach, 9–12, 11–14t
decision making and, 64–65, 66–67b
early-warning systems. *See* early-warning
systems
emergency services and, 49–51
exposure, estimation of, 22–23, 22–23t
hazard risk and, 6f, 12–22, 15–16t, 18t
drought, 20
earthquakes, volcanoes, and landslides,
2f, 19–20
floods and cyclones, 2f, 12–19
heat waves, 20–22, 21b
key messages, 7
objectives of study, 7–9
service delivery and, 38–51, 64, 86–89
shelters and, 40
diseases. *See* communicable diseases;
noncommunicable diseases; *specific*
diseases
DKI. *See* Special Capital District
Dodman, David, 131
Dominica, risk financing in, 170
Dong Thap (Vietnam), urban upgrading
in, 167
Douglas, Ian, 129
DPLs (Development Policy Loans), 105–6
DPU (Dinas Pekerjaan Umum, Indonesian
public works agency), 207
drainage. *See also* sanitation
disaster risk and, 44–45, 189
job creation and, 167–68
partnerships to supply, 163–64
service delivery and, 129
solid-waste disposal and, 46
drawdown options, 170

droughts, 20
drowning, 18
dysentery, 192

E
early-warning systems, 51, 88, 93–94b, 102,
158–60, 225–26, 227
Earthquake Disaster Risk Index (EDRI), 145
Earthquake Master Plan for Istanbul, 71
earthquakes
disaster risk and, 19–20, 71–72, 145
exposure to, 2f, 144
shelters and, 40
slums and, 29, 38b
East Asia, earthquakes in, 19
Ebrard, Marcelo, 222
EcoEconomy Committee (São Paulo), 263
Ecofrota Program (São Paulo), 264
ecological services, green infrastructure
and, 74–76
EDRI (Earthquake Disaster Risk Index), 145
Egypt, public transport projects
in, 133
elderly
health impacts of climate change on, 126
heat waves and, 20
public health and, 49
as vulnerable population, 86
El Salvador
drawdown options in, 170
self-insurance in, 110, 168
Emergency Management Agency
(São Paulo), 87, 244, 245, 261
Emergency Management Center (CGE,
São Paulo), 244–45
emissions reduction (ER) units, 166
emissions trading systems (ETSs),
115, 117b
Empresa Paulista de Planejamento
Metropolitano (EMPLASA), 255
Enda-Tiers Monde, 163
energy services, 49–51, 133, 164–66
Environmental Agenda of Mexico City, 223
environmental health interventions, 92
environmentally sensitive lands, 52b
Environmental Public Fund (Mexico City),
219, 224
environmental traffic lights *(semaforos*
ambientales), 169
ER (emissions reduction) units, 166
Esteli (Nicaragua), social networks in, 54

SME (City Education Secretariat, São
Paulo), 263
SMS messages, 91, 94*b*, 208
Social Assistance Institute (Mexico City), 224
Social Development Agency (Mexico
City), 224
Social Dimensions of Climate Change
(Mearns & Norton), 127, 133
social networks, 51, 53–54
Social Partnership Program (São Paulo), 266
Social Vulnerability Index, 257
solar water systems, 264–65
solid-waste disposal, 33, 45–46. *See also*
sanitation
South Asia
cyclones in, 17
drowning in, 18
safe water in, 8
slums in, 37–38*b*
urban populations in, 12
volcanoes in, 20
Spain
building design in, 82
flood management in, 75
*Spatial Analysis of Natural Hazard and
Climate Change Risks in Periurban
Expansion Areas of Dakar, Senegal*
(Hoffman), 131
SPDMI (Strategic Plan for Disaster Mitigation
in Istanbul), 71–72
Special Capital District (DKI, Jakarta),
200–201, 204, 207, 210, 212, 214
Special Climate Change Fund, 134
Special Fund for the Environment and
Sustainable Development, 237
Special Interest Areas, 34*b*
Special Report on Emissions Scenarios
(SRES), 194
SP Trans (São Paulo), 264
squatter settlements. *See also* informal
settlements; slums
eviction and, 39
flooding of, 37*b*
public transportation and, 47
slums and, 29–30, 58*n*4
solid-waste disposal in, 37–38*b*
SRES (Special Report on Emissions
Scenarios), 194
stakeholders
action plans and, 68–69*b*
risk assessment and, 64, 65, 67*b*

Stanford University, 145
State of the World: Our Urban Future
(World Watch Institute), 9, 125–26,
127, 129, 131, 168
State of the World's Cities (UN-HABITAT), 131
Stern Report (2007), 134
Strategic Plan for Disaster Mitigation in
Istanbul (SPDMI), 71–72
Strategic Urban Development Plan
(SUDP), 188
Sub-Saharan Africa
drought in, 20
safe water in, 8
SUDP (Strategic Urban Development
Plan), 188
Summer Rainfall Operation (São Paulo),
87, 244, 245
Sustainable Building Project (São Paulo), 265
Sustainable Dar es Salaam Project, 188
SVMA. *See* Green and Environment
Secretariat
Swisscontact, 215

T
Tampa-St Petersburg (Florida), floods
in, 143
Tan Hoa-Lo Gom Canal (Vietnam), 167
Tanzania. *See also* Dar es Salaam
cholera in, 48–49
urban planning in, 160–61
Tanzania Marine Park authorities, 190
Tanzania Meteorological Agency (TMA),
182, 184, 188
taxes
government revenues through, 104
insurance and, 168–69
TCIP (Turkish Catastrophic Insurance
Pool), 169
technical assistance programs, 107, 108*t*,
121, 154
Technological Research Institute (IPT),
251, 252, 254–55
Temeke municipality (Dar es Salaam), 42
tenure, security of. *See* security of tenure
text messages. *See* SMS messages
Thailand
Asian Cities Climate Change Resilience
Network in, 154
housing finance in, 120
public transport in, 133
TMA. *See* Tanzania Meteorological Agency

health impacts of climate change
on, 126
heat waves and, 20
reconstruction projects and, 172
risk management and, 169
working groups for risk assessment, 67b
World Bank
carbon finance and, 115
Carbon Partnership Facility, 115
catastrophe bond programs from, 109, 109b
on climate change, 125, 126–28
Climate Resilient Cities Primer, 154
Community Development Carbon Fund
and, 166
cook stoves and, 58n10
Dar es Salaam case study and, 182
on finance instruments, 134
financing from, 103, 107, 107b, 108t,
121, 197
greenhouse emissions analysis
by, 106b
on "hotspot" cities, 131–32
on housing, 131
Jakarta case study and, 200, 212
job creation programs and, 168
local partnerships and, 92
methane gas capture projects and, 165
Mexico City case study and, 217
partial credit products from, 110
poverty ranking by, 259
poverty reduction and, 214
reconstruction projects, 171, 172
Resilient Cities program, 145
risk assessment and, 65, 66b
risk financing and, 169

sanitation and, 130, 164
São Paulo case study and, 235
on transportation sector, 130, 133
urban development and, 107
Urban Flood Prevention and Drainage
Project, 159
on urban poverty, 128–29
urban upgrading and, 161–62, 166
Volunteer Technology Communities and,
172–73
World Bank Climate Finance Options, 105
World Bank Group, 9, 105
World Business Council for Sustainable
Development, 130
World Development Report (World Bank)
*2004: Making Services Work for Poor
People,* 130
2009: Reshaping Economic Geography, 130
2010: Development and Climate Change,
9, 125, 126–27, 128
World Disasters Report: Focus on Urban Risk
(IFPC), 9
World Health Organization, 130
World Vision, 190
World Watch Institute, 9, 125–26,
127, 131, 168
World Wildlife Fund (WWF), 144, 190

Y
Yahoo, volunteer technology community
participation of, 173
Yusuf, A.A., 131

Z
zoning regulations, 81

CPSIA information can be obtained at www.ICGtesting.com
Printed in the USA
LVOW01s1946151013

357041LV00016B/940/P